I0787787

Woke
A Critique of Social Justice Ideology

Woke
A Critique of Social Justice Ideology

Jon Mills

Copyright © Jon Mills, 2026

All rights reserved. No part of this book may be reproduced in any form or by any means, electronic or mechanical, without permission in writing from the publisher except by scholars, researchers, journalists, and reviewers who may quote brief passages in their works.

Published by New English Review Press
a subsidiary of World Encounter Institute
PO Box 158397
Nashville, Tennessee 37215
&
27 Old Gloucester Street
London, England, WC1N 3AX

Cover art and design by Kendra Mallock

ISBN: 978-1-966833-07-9
Library of Congress Control Number: 2025949571

First Edition

NEW ENGLISH REVIEW PRESS
newenglishreview.org

CONTENTS

The New Culture Wars

Jon Mills

This project is intended as a scholarly cultural critique of the contemporary social justice movement, or what is generally referred to as wokeism. It is precisely because the term "woke" has become politicized, weaponized, and used pejoratively that it deserves a careful analysis. Given that the term is so widely used, researchers, academics, politicians, and policy makers, as well as the general public or lay audiences, will want to become acquainted with the arguments and criticisms offered in this book. To my knowledge, there is no other book that exists today that attempts a widespread critique of many of the topics that make up the contemporary culture wars.

The new culture wars are largely based in a schism of values driven by progressive or militant social justice activism on the political left and reactionary or corrective social justice criticism from the political right. But this simple binary does not neatly apply. Whatever one's personal politics may be, liberals are becoming increasingly critical of extreme forms of progressivism that serve to unravel the basic fabric of classical democratic liberalism, while conservatives are growing increasingly intolerant of the political, societal, and institutional impositions of woke ideology behind the Critical Social Justice (CSJ) activist movement often appearing as left-wing authoritarianism. This ontic division both between and within political parties and citizens at large naturally spills over into the cultural institutions that rule society including government, public authority, private industry, social policy, law and order, education, and capital. In today's climate of social divisions, we are increasingly told what is right and wrong, what we can and cannot say, what we should and should not do, and even what we are prohibited to say and do under the rubric of truth, moral certainty, and political legal intervention. Here we may observe how thought policing within the new culture wars has profound implications for the way we relate to one another based on a category of values, whether embraced or rebuffed, with their own brands of radical subjectivity, ethical relativism, moral absolutism, prescriptivism, indoctrination, censorship, deterrence, punishment, cancellation, and thought control. In other words, living in today's world requires us to engage the nature and question of social reality, morality, justice, fairness, and the philosophy of right. Regardless of what values one stands for or repudiates, we cannot elude the ideological forces that seek to persuade, intimidate, or coerce us to think and act in circumscribed parochial ways under the politics of experience and the rubric of power.

What is Wokeism?

Derived from American black slang, "woke" often refers to a societal awakening or having woken-up to social injustice, particularly when it comes to racism and oppressive forces of discrimination that are said to permeate the structural, systemic, and institutionalized fabric of contemporary culture and its social organizations and agencies. Notwithstanding that the term has now become a slur based on conservative criticism and reactionary politics in the US largely in response to progressive left-wing values and policies, wokeism deserves to be taken as a serious social phenomena creating polarization on each side of the political divide kindling mutually shared dysidentifcations and authoritarian tendencies directed toward alterity. For this reason alone, it needs to be properly studied, analyzed, and critiqued. Whether this is based on a fundamental clash of values or in the weaponization of *ad hominem* and *ad populum* attacks against political opponents, wokeism has many overdetermined meanings and motivations fueling both its affirmation and negation.[1]

Woke ideology has also acquired a broad general meaning in popular culture that is based on the negation of anything deemed "white," hence Western, European, and/or English, "heteronormative," and "male." If you happen to fall within any of these arbitrary categories as identity markers it has become fair game to vilify—if not demonize the token "whitey," particularly "old" white, heterosexual men of so-called "privilege" who symbolize the evil imperial oppressor who has enslaved and colonized the Other, namely, minority or disenfranchised groups of different races, ethnicity, gender, and sexual orientation who often claim to have no voice or power over their white dominants. Despite the notion that the conspiratorial fantasy of global white supremacy and Jewish control over capital has no basis in empirical reality, which is merely the projection of individual and group prejudice, as Freud reminds us, large-group social psychology is easily motivated by conformity to authority, fear, emotional contagion, need for inclusion based on identification, exclusion based on difference, and a lack of self-reflectivity or critical thinking that upholds simple binaries based in splitting, prejudice, and authoritarian attitudes. Whiteness has become the new symbolic emotional whipping boy, condoned—if not celebrated—by non-whites who seek a cathartic revenge, particularly in the global South.

----

1 Robinson, Ishena, "How Woke Went From 'Black' to 'Bad.'" *Legal Defense Fun*d, August 26, 2022, https://www.naacpldf.org/woke-black-bad/

The Infiltration of Critical Social Justice Ideology

Culture wars in Western society have entered the academy, public institutions, and private industry, hence affecting the integrity of the professions, business, trade, and geopolitics by introducing identity politics in government, education, workplace training, and public policy in the name of social justice. What seems like a noble ethical endeavor is in fact a harmful and destabilizing movement that aims to displace and overturn established structures, traditions, and democratic paradigms that regulate civil dialogue and social order. Antiracism, decolonialization, queer-feminism, intersectionality, transgenderism, postmodern discourse theory, and standpoint epistemology nurtures a distorted social narrative purportedly based in colonialization, victimization, and oppression caused by white supremacy, systemic racism, capitalism, and heteronormative patriarchy that are promulgated by critical social justice theory. Here wokeism becomes the new hysteria as political propaganda perpetrating antiwhite racism, antisemitism, left-wing progressive authoritarianism, and identitarianism that create more social divisions focused on aggrieved disparities and perceived inequities rather than building bridges in the name of peace, equality, and justice. Such political divisiveness introduces a real threat to humanitarian egalitarian principles that have traditionally informed civic praxis and social welfare initiatives based on apolitical commitments of concern for all peoples regardless of their personal and cultural identities or past collective suffering. A return to domestic, public, and professional civility, prudence, and ethical integrity requires an apolitical philosophy that stays focused on our universal humanistic obligations to society as a whole.

Since the global pandemic, much of the academic world has now fully embraced the culture wars where decolonial studies, identitarianism, critical race theory (CRT), the Trans movement, queer identities, gender-critical feminism (TERFs), intersectionality, ableism, and hatred for white people have all been fueled by CSJ activism. In cursory form, critical social justice theory views all forms of oppression to be the result of hegemonic power differentials, unfair advantage, and unearned privilege wielded by Western societies, capitalist exploitation, and heteronormative straight white men who have historically dominated, displaced, and traumatized indigenous, minority, and racialized groups, and who are *a fortiori* blamed as the direct cause of their suffering *today*. CSJ adopts a victimization mentality that renders anyone white, Jewish, conservative, elite, economically well-off, and normative to be a nemesis in the (idealized) pursuit of universal justice and equity for all people regardless of class, race, education, wealth, talent, skill, merit, or demography. In other words, CSJ broaches a neo-reformed Marxist philosophy that aims toward a contemporary standardization in enforcing egalitarian communist principles that equals-out all disparities in society and human nature, what we may call "equitarianism." Given that many successful national social democracies cannot even approach this level of ideality, we may anticipate that such a grand vision of humanity is bound to fail.

Calling for the reform of higher education, the Manhattan Institute, led by Christopher Rufo, recently issued a statement criticizing the woke ideology that governs academe dominated by the progressive left. Although there are valid criticisms of the statement, it is worth quoting in length:

> The universities have brazenly, deliberately, and repeatedly violated their compact with the American people. They have engaged in a long train of abuses, evasions, and usurpations which, with every turn of the ratchet, have moved our society toward a new kind of tyranny—one in which ideology determines truth, and the university functions as a political agent of the left.
>
> Let us enumerate the facts:
>
> - The universities have capitulated to the radical left's "long march through the institutions," which has con-

verted them into laboratories of ideology, rather than institutions oriented toward truth.

- The universities have violated their commitment to serve in a position above day-to-day politics and, instead, have adopted a narrow political agenda and engaged directly in partisan activism, with particularly disastrous results for the humanities and social sciences.

- The universities have built enormous "diversity, equity, and inclusion" bureaucracies that discriminate on the basis of race and violate the fundamental principle of equality—that high prize which was inscribed in the Declaration of Independence and codified into law with the Fourteenth Amendment and the Civil Rights Act.

- The universities have contributed to a new kind of tyranny, with publicly funded initiatives designed to advance the cause of digital censorship, public health lockdowns, child sex-trait modification, race-based redistribution, and other infringements on America's long-standing rights and liberties.

- The universities have corrupted faculty hiring practices with racial quotas, ideological filters, and diversity statements, which function as loyalty oaths to the left and have virtually eliminated conservative scholars from the prestige institutions.

- The universities have degraded the liberal arts with reductive ideologies that no longer aim to preserve and discover what is highest in man, but to unleash resentments against Western civilization, from the Greeks and Romans to the English and the Americans.

- The universities have ceased to represent the nation as a whole; rather, they have divided Americans into "oppressor" and "oppressed," and have, in effect, declared war on millions of Americans who simply want to live, work, worship, and raise families in peace.

Enough. The American people provide status, privileges, and more than $150 billion per year to the universities. In light of these transgressions, we have every right to renegotiate the terms of the compact with the universities and to demand that they return to their original mission: to pursue knowledge, to educate the citizen, and to uphold the law. In exchange for continued public support, these institutions must abide by the principles of the Constitution and honor their obligation to public good.

To that end, we call on the President of the United States to draft a new contract with the universities, which should be written into every grant, payment, loan, eligibility, and accreditation, and punishable by revocation of all public benefit.

- The universities must advance truth over ideology, with rigorous standards of academic conduct, controls for academic fraud, and merit-based decision-making throughout the enterprise.

- The universities must cease their direct participation in social and political activism; the proper vehicle for criticism is through the individual scholar and student, not the university as a corporate body.

- The universities must adhere to the principle of color-blind equality, by abolishing DEI bureaucracies, disbanding racially segregated programs, and terminating race-based discrimination in admissions, hiring, promotions, and contracting.

- The universities must adhere to the principle of freedom of speech, not only in theory, but in practice; they must provide a forum for a wider range of debate and protect faculty and students who dissent from the ruling consensus.

- The universities must uphold the highest standard of civil discourse, with swift and significant penalties, including suspension and expulsion, for anyone who would disrupt speakers, vandalize property, occupy buildings, call for violence, or interrupt the operations of the university.

- The universities must provide transparency about their operations and, at the end of each year, publish complete data on race, admissions, and class rank; employment and financial returns by major; and campus attitudes on ideology, free speech, and civil discourse.[2]

Here it becomes obvious, for reasons enumerated above, that the Manhattan Institute is declaring war on the culture wars. Whether this will lead to future reforms, foment fervor, or cement more derision and division, is yet to be seen.

But social justice progressivism is not merely confined to the academy, where it influences the next generation of students being indoctrinated in higher education; rather, it has infiltrated many domains of the general public. Woke ideology has slowly crept into mainstream society and popular culture largely through the news media, social media, and AI manipulation with an obsessional emphasis on identity, difference, and so-called oppressed communities that largely attribute their existence to injustices perpetrated by colonialism, white supremacy, systemic racism, capitalism, Western or Eurocentric normativity, and heterosexual men. The clarion call to decolonize the academy, re-envision education and training, reform policies and professional standards including ethical mandates, proselytize the so-called wisdom of antiracism advocacy, DEI propaganda, and vilify dead European males, straight white men, and Jews for supposedly having power, privilege, and economic advantage, and who have purportedly systematically enslaved, subjugated, and abused alterity, has all become a new-age neurosis.

---

2 "The Manhattan Institute Statement on Higher Education," *Manhattan Institute* (2025). July 15. https://manhattan.institute/article/the-manhattan-statement-on-higher-education.

Overview

In the summer of 2025 at the newly minted Centre for Heterodox Social Science at the University of Buckingham, UK, the theme of their inaugural conference was "Post-Progressivism? Toward a New Social Science." Here Professor of Politics and Director of the Centre, Eric Kaufmann, introduced The Buckingham Manifesto for a Post-Progressive Social Science that calls for academic scrutiny in the social sciences and humanities to identify and analyze the excesses of the progressive cultural left. He summarizes the phenomena that tersely captures the current culture wars:

> The left-wing movement that came to be known as progressivism played a vital role in rectifying th[e] exclusion [of marginalized women and racial, ethnic, and sexual minorities]. Yet as it began to achieve its goals, it shifted to new ones: from equality of opportunity to equality of outcomes, from greater inclusiveness to a hypersensitivity to ever-more-elusive forms of emotional harm, from the opening of new perspectives to the enforcement of rigid orthodoxies. These shifts became institutionalized in policies such as racial and sexual preferences, mandatory diversity training, speech codes, and editorial policies that privilege the avoidance of perceived harm over scholarly and scientific rigour. And they were accompanied by a change in the norms of academic discourse, from vigorous debate to censorship, deplatforming, mobbing, and moralistic denunciation. The unfortunate result of this progressivist overreach has been a decline of trust in cultural and academic institutions and growing political polarization, including a populist backlash.[3]

---

3 Kaufmann, Eric (2025). "The Buckingham Manifesto for a Post-Progressive Social Science." Spoke at "Heterodox Social Science Conference," Centre for Heterodox Social Science (https://www.heterodoxcentre.com), University of Buckingham, UK; June 05, 2025. Reproduced in *Unsafe Science*, August 03, 2025; https://unsafescience.substack.com/p/the-buckingham-manifesto-for-a-post.

Top of the list is to devise an intellectual, academic, and scholarly agenda that has two main thrusts:

> **Heterodox Social Science.** Progressive dogmas have increasingly constricted the social sciences, including an obsession with race, gender, sexual orientation and identity, and an insistence that bias and oppression are the only acceptable explanations (to the exclusion of culture, history, and demographics). At the same time, deeper questions about human nature, and explanations that are consilient with the natural sciences, have been marginalized. We call for a new social science to free up inquiry, fill in blind spots, and render a richer and more accurate account of our social world. This does not require that every conceivable question be researched, only that those that are researched be treated with scientific objectivity and openness to multiple hypotheses.
>
> **Critical Woke Studies.** In the second two decades of the 21st century, academic and cultural institutions were suddenly seized by a radical ideology known as Critical Social Justice, Intersectionality, the Identity Synthesis, the Successor Ideology, or most commonly, Wokeness. This takeover took many by surprise and remains unexplained. We hold that the wokeness revolution was not compelled by new discoveries or moral imperatives but is a contingent historical episode that needs to be studied, just as scholars have sought to explain the rise of nationalism, communism, neoliberalism, and populism.[4]

It is in the spirit of these forms of inquiry that this book was conceived.

Throughout this project we provide a comprehensive exploration and critique of the social, political, and philosophical principles underlying woke ideology and how they manifest in contemporary society. This volume attempts to cover the new culture wars broadly, with nuance and depth, and involves an array of disciplines in the humanities and social sciences including interdisciplinary scholar-

---

4 Ibid.

ship. Topics covered in the rise of CSJ dogma include an analysis of identity politics, Diversity, Equity, and Inclusion (DEI), white privilege and the myth of white supremacy, the racialization of culture, Critical Race Theory (CRT) and antiracism programing, Trans phenomena, biological sex and gender theory, intersectionality in identity, antisemitism and antizionism, decolonial movements, cancel culture and institutional capture, polarization of right- and left-wing politics as authoritarianism, free speech vs. hate speech, thought and language policing, postmodern epistemology and ethics, classism, religious, cultural, and ethnic identities, social media frenzy, biased journalism, fake news, conspiracy theories, and new feminism.

In chapter 1, Michael Shermer reviews the changing meaning of "woke" over time, considers the vision of human nature as a blank slate held by most people who identify as woke, argues that this worldview is contrary to the scientific evidence about human thought and behavior, and provides specific examples for how this erroneous vision has led to mistaken social policies related to race and gender, suppressed free speech in academia, cancel culture and general censoriousness for ideas contrary to the woke agenda, corrupted many sciences, and wasted billions of dollars and endless hours in academic and corporate training programs in Diversity, Equity, and Inclusion (DEI).

In the next chapter, David Pilgrim uses critical realism as a philosophical resource to explore the limitations of identity politics. He argues that identity politics have been present on the left and right of the polities of Western liberal democracies, though narrow claims of "wokery" have dominated discussions from social conservatives. Identity politics take two important aspects of reality, namely, (1) subjectively expressed identities and (2) interpersonal expectations of recognition, and privileges their importance. This excludes the need to see power in terms of two other planes of material reality: our relationships to nature and our embeddedness in a socio-economic context that fluxes across time and space. Examples are given to demonstrate this tendency toward psychological reductionism in relation to antiracism and the contestation about sex and gender. The conditions of possibility for the emergence of identity politics are explored throughout the chapter.

Whiteness studies is an active area of academic research that brings a fresh dimension to the study of racism and racial inequality. Focusing on the social construction of white privilege and white supremacy, it seeks to investigate, scrutinize, and decenter social norms, customs, beliefs, behaviors, and practices that purportedly uphold white supremacy. While this field of study yields valuable insight into the nature of whiteness as a means of social control, it also risks becoming so tenaciously committed to the critique of whiteness that it veers into dogmatism. In chapter 3, Jonathan Church examines the epistemic shortcomings of whiteness theory and the myth of white supremacy in contemporary culture. In its zeal to expose the sin of whiteness, it becomes vulnerable to apophenia and confirmation bias. It also overlooks three logical fallacies that threaten to undermine its enterprise: (1) the fallacy of begging the question, (2) the reification fallacy, and (3) the fallacy of ambiguity.

In the next chapter, I argue that antiracist political activism modelled after the teachings of critical race theory (CRT) and critical social justice theory (CSJ) more generally, is an unethical form of pedagogy and clinical praxis that will likely damage members of society by producing incompetent mental health professionals. If the premises and arguments put forward by antiracist frameworks are not allowed to be critiqued and debated within academe, let alone within clinical training and service delivery environments, then we will be fostering a learning milieu based on prejudice, dogma, and indoctrination that will predictably have a deleterious effect on professional education and its impact on society. Focusing on group identity based in essentialism determined by biology, race, gender, sex, or intersectional hybridity is to commit a reductive ontological fallacy that strips away a person's unique individuality, freedom, and subjective agency. In other words, categories of race or ethnicity do not determine individual personality. Antiracist propaganda in education fails to address (1) the axiological humanistic priorities that center on the distinct phenomenology of individual lives, and (2) inappropriately focuses on race essentialism and colonial blame rather than on (3) universal egalitarian principles mental health disciplines should prioritize in education, training, and public service. If the next generation of mental health professionals are trained to be social justice activists with the public, then we will predictably see (1) a decline in trust toward the helping professions, (2) an increase in ethics complaints to regulatory bodies, and (3) a spate of lawsuits for psychological damages to vulnerable patients who were emotionally abused by incompetent practitioners.

In his chapter, Bret Alderman traces the evolution of the concept "gender" and its changing relationship to the concept of "sex." In doing so, he focuses primarily on how this evolution was facilitated by the postmodern critique of linguistic reference and representation. Such critique owes a great deal to the structuralist linguistics of Ferdinand de Saussure, which, in turn, informed the post-structuralism of Jacques Derrida and Michele Foucault, both of whom offered a conceptual framework for the queer theory of Judith Butler. In tracing this genealogy, he highlights a progressive decoupling of the two concepts—sex and gender—that were previously understood to be synonymous and/or indissociable. This decoupling is portrayed as but one example of the broader conceptual dissociation of language from the objective world that it ostensibly describes. This portrayal extends itself to Butler's more recent misappropriation of philosopher J. L. Austin's idea of a *performative utterance* in the creation of her concept of "gender performativity" and contrasts her "queer" understanding of gender with that of gender critical feminists such as Holly Lawford-Smith.

In chapter 6, Jaco van Zyl critically examines critical social justice as a revolutionary socio-political ideology adapted from Marxian and postmodern philosophies. CSJ's central premise posits that all disparities in social demographics are due to persistent systemic injustices on victim groups by dominant oppressor groups. These injustices are normalized due to the ubiquity of racist, homophobic, sexistic, and ableist societal structures. CSJ proposes a solution to these social ills, namely, through revolutionary action, identity-based discrimination against oppressor groups, and dismantling of all structures maintaining this status quo. Drawing from concepts in psychoanalytic theory, he argues that utopian CSJ fantasies are evidence of the illusory yearning to restore what is psychoanalytically known as primary narcissism. He maintains that any ideological pursuit at restoring primary narcissism is futile and will have destructive repercussions for society. This is already evident in CSJ, which fosters victimhood culture and grievance-based narratives, which collectively resist reconciliation and perpetuate societal polarization. To this end, he uses three lenses to examine how CSJ ideology is a manifestation of illusion. First, from a Kleinian perspective, CSJ encourages the enactment of primitive defenses like schizoid-paranoid splitting, projective identification, and primitive envy to maintain a cynical position towards Western culture while sustaining an illusion of moral purity. Second, from an Oedipal perspective, CSJ disavows cultural, ethical, and empirical realities while indulging the gratification of victim groups. And third, CSJ acts as an entitlement ideology inducing the illusory state of narcissistic large-group regression risking societal deterioration and collapse. Through these psychoanalytic lenses, his analysis offers a nuanced critique of CSJ's ideological and psychological underpinnings, contributing to broader discussions on ideology and societal transformation.

In recent years, biological sex has become a controversial topic in academia, science, anthropology, and the broader culture. Some have argued that the notion of a sex binary or two biological sexes invalidates the transgender experience and that it can cause "harm." This trend has seen the promotion of the view by transgender activists that sex is non-binary and that it exists on a spectrum. Individuals who oppose this view have been cancelled and have had their careers ruined. In this chapter, Gary Clark looks specifically at the cancellation of a group of "gender critical" anthropological researchers by the American Anthropological Association (AAA) and the Canadian Anthropology Society (CASCA). He then goes on to discuss the evidence for evolved biological sex differences from a Jungian perspective and then uses that evidence to analyze sex-based social roles and cultural and religious symbolism in a number of hunter-gatherer cultures. While biological sex is binary and human cultures are structured around this binary, identification with the social roles and behaviours of the opposite sex seems to be a natural part of human psychobiological variation. Consequently, acknowledgment that sex is binary does not necessarily entail the invalidation of transgenderism. He concludes by offering a middle ground that can accommodate the views of gender critical feminists while also validating the transgender experience.

In chapter 8, Nathan Honeycutt and Lee Jussim explore the connection between bias and academic censorship. After defining terms, they review recent scholarship on varieties of censorship and bias in contemporary life. These are then applied to political processes of power and suppression during peer review, drawing heavily on recent work identifying the ways in which such biases often manifest in academia. They further highlight a series of psychological and social prejudices by which biases can lead to academic censorship articulated by several concrete examples.

In our final chapter, Cary Nelsen analyzes the phenomena of antisemitic antizionism on college campus. From October 7, 2023, through the end of 2024, much of the Western world suffered an extraordinary upsurge in antisemitism. It fed on deep reserves of hostility to Jews and Judaism channeled through a woke consensus that cultural and political understanding must be organized by an opposition between so-called oppressed and oppressor nation states. Stigmatized for a generation as the worst of all oppressor states, Israel after 10/7 became the target of a new consensus that it was beyond reform. As a consequence, the Jewish state had to be erased from the face of the earth. Colleges and universities were at the forefront of this newly expanded and consolidated movement, displayed in hundreds of demonstrations and tented encampments worldwide. Antizionist faculty encouraged those developments by celebrating Hamas's 10/7 assault. This chapter analyzes this phenomenon.

Taken as a whole, this book advances our understanding of the deep divisions, animosity, and grievances in social and political thought in contemporary culture emphasizing radically different perspectives on truth and social reality, consciousness, moral discourse, distributive justice, and the objective conditions for a fair and equitable society. We hope the contributions assembled here in this collection will spur further research, understanding, and critique into critical woke studies and social justice movements that serve to undermine classical liberalism, academic freedom, democratic principles of fairness, equality, and liberty devoid of discrimination and identity politics, and further advance our knowledge of the underlying philosophical, psychological, political, and social forces driving this new iteration of the culture wars.

1

ON THE WOKE PHENOMENON

MICHAEL SHERMER

Before the transmogrification of the word *woke* into the pejorative slur against far-left politics it represents today, I would have called myself woke—and even a social justice warrior—inasmuch as I believe in civil liberties, civil rights, women's rights, LGBTQ rights, animal rights, and the continued expansion of the moral sphere to include all sentient beings. As the author of a book-length defense of the principles behind these social justice movements for which previous generations were woke to—*The Moral Arc*[1]—I think I have earned the moniker, and yet because of how the word and concept has devolved along with the ever-leftward shift into lunacy of woke social justice activists—I must distance myself from the label.

What is Woke, Anyway?

Although the descriptor "woke" is today hurled by those on the political right as an invective against various leftist and progressive

---

1 Shermer, Michael. 2015. *The Moral Arc: How Science and Reason Lead Humanity to Truth, Justice, and Freedom.* New York: Henry Holt.

social activists and the movements they represent,[2] its etymological origin was an African-American synonym for being awake to the numerous social, economic, and political injustices primarily experienced by that community throughout much of the twentieth century and before.[3] By mid-twentieth century and the rise of the civil rights movement, the phrase "stay woke"[4] denoted one's awareness of such inequities, along with a commitment to collective consciousness raising through political activism.

By the third decade of the twenty-first century, however, a major linguistic transformation of the word led the linguist John McWhorter to replace "the woke" with "the elect," because "They do think of themselves as bearers of a wisdom, granted them for any number of reasons—empathic leaning, life experience, maybe even intelligence. But they see themselves as having been chosen, as it were, by one or some of these factors, as understanding something most do not. 'The Elect' is also good in implying a certain smugness, which, sadly, is an accurate depiction."[5] "Woke," McWhorter explains, "migrated from Black vernacular to mainstream use," and that the expression "stay woke . . . went from being insider progressive-speak to a term of derision for a progressive agenda." At its worst, McWhorter concludes, the word "allowed many progressives, supposedly attuned to injustice, to signal their commitment to combating it without actually demonstrating an understanding of its causes or remedies." (This is likely what the social theorist Thomas Sowell had in mind with his descriptor "the anointed" in *The Vision*

---

2   Marsden, Harriet. 2019. "Whither 'Woke': What Does the Future Hold for a Word That Became a Weapon?" *The New European*. November 25.

3   Zimmer, Ben. 2017. "'Woke', From a Sleepy Verb to a Badge of Awareness—Word on the Street," *The Wall Street Journal*. April 14.

4   "'Stay Woke: The New Sense of "Woke" is Gaining Popularity'—Words We're Watching," *Merriam-Webster. n.d.*

5   McWhorter, John. 2021. *Woke Racism: How a New Religion Has Betrayed Black America*. New York: Portfolio.

of the Anointed: Self-Congratulation as a Basis for Social Policy).[6]

The Woke Vision of Human Nature

The transformation of "woke" from awareness of societal inequalities of opportunities and the concomitant discriminations based on prejudices against members of certain cohorts to a virtue signal that one is committed to the equality of outcomes, however achieved, was accompanied by another shift: from equal opportunities to equal outcomes. The metamorphosis was elevated to national prominence during the 2024 Presidential election campaign when Kamala Harris released a video story of two alpinists ascending a mountain in which one of them had a head-start over the other:

> Not everybody's starting out from the same place. So if we're all getting the same amount, but you started out back there and I started out over here, we could get the same amount, but you're still going to be that far back behind me. . . . So there's a big difference between equality and equity. *Equitable treatment means we all end up in the same place.*[7]

Underlying the political policy of equal outcomes is the blank slate model of human nature, which holds that since people are inherently equal, any inequalities in education, health, wealth, income, housing, home ownership, employment, and the like, can only be the result of societal, political, and economic discrimination, rather than inequalities in cognitive intelligence, emotional intelligence, creativity, drive and ambition, personal responsibility and volitional choices, and of course, luck, good and bad. Once such discriminatory policies are eliminated, woke blank slaters believe, then such outcome inequalities should disappear.

---

6 Sowell, Thomas. 1995. *The Vision of the Anointed: Self-Congratulations as a Basis for Social Policy.* New York: Basic Books.

7 https://x.com/KamalaHarris/status/1322963321994289154?s=20.

So, the deepest problem with wokeness is that it is based on a flawed theory of human nature, a point made by Thomas Sowell in *A Conflict of Visions*, in which he argued that the vision one holds about human nature—either as *constrained* (conservative) or *unconstrained* (liberal)—determines if one emphasizes equal opportunities or equal outcomes. "If human options are not inherently constrained, then the presence of such repugnant and disastrous phenomena virtually cries out for explanation—and for solutions. But if the limitations and passions of man himself are at the heart of these painful phenomena, then what requires explanation are the ways in which they have been avoided or minimized." Which of these natures you believe is true will largely shape which solutions to social ills will be most effective. "In the unconstrained vision, there are no intractable reasons for social evils and therefore no reason why they cannot be solved, with sufficient moral commitment. But in the constrained vision, whatever artifices or strategies restrain or ameliorate inherent human evils will themselves have costs, some in the form of other social ills created by these civilizing institutions, so that all that is possible is a prudent trade-off."[8]

In his magisterial analysis of human nature, *The Blank Slate*, Steven Pinker re-labels Sowell's *constrained* and *unconstrained* visions of human nature as the *Tragic Vision* and the *Utopian Vision*, and re-configures them slightly.[9] The distinct Left-Right divide consistently cleaves the (respectively) Utopian Vision and Tragic Vision along numerous specific contests, such as the size of the government (big versus small), the amount of taxation (high versus low), trade (fair versus free), healthcare (universal versus individual), environment (protect it versus leave it alone), crime (caused by social injustice versus caused by criminal minds), the constitution (judicial activism

---

8 Sowell, Thomas. 1987. *A Conflict of Visions: Ideological Origins of Political Struggles*. New York: Basic Books, 24-25.

9 Pinker, Steven. 2002. *The Blank Slate: The Modern Denial of Human Nature*. New York: Viking, 290-291.

for social justice versus strict constructionism for original intent), and many others. Pinker's "utopian" descriptor for Sowell's "unconstrained" vision is apt, since in the original Greek *utopia* literally means "no place." An unconstrained utopian vision of human nature holds that custom, law, and traditional institutions are sources of inequality and injustice and should therefore be heavily regulated and constantly modified from the top down; it holds that society can be engineered through government programs to release the natural unselfishness and altruism within people; it deems physical and intellectual differences largely to be the result of unjust and unfair social systems that can be re-engineered through social planning, and therefore people can be shuffled across socioeconomic classes that were artificially created through unfair and unjust political, economic, and social systems inherited from history. Such a vision exists in literally *No Place*.

Although some liberals embrace just such an unconstrained vision of human nature, most understand that human behavior is at least partially constrained—especially those educated in the biological and evolutionary sciences who are aware of the research in behavior genetics—so the debate between more centrist liberals and conservatives turns on degrees of constraint. By contrast, *woke illiberals*—as I shall call liberals who moved so far to the authoritarian left that they are nearly indistinguishable from the authoritarian right—are full-on blank slaters, unconstrained visionaries, and utopian dreamers with no purchase on the reality of human nature, or what I call a *Realistic Vision*. If you believe that human nature is partly constrained in all respects—morally, physically, and intellectually—then you hold a *Realistic Vision* of our nature. In keeping with the research from behavioral genetics and evolutionary psychology, let's put a number on that constraint at 40 to 50 percent. In the *Realistic Vision*, human nature is relatively constrained by our biology and evolutionary history, and therefore social and political systems must be structured around these realities, accentuating the positive and attenuating the negative aspects of our natures—our better angels and our inner demons, in Pinker's description.[10]

A *Realistic Vision* rejects the blank slate model that people are so malleable and responsive to social programs that governments can engineer their lives into a great society of its design, and instead believes that family, custom, law, and traditional institutions are the best sources for social harmony. A *Realistic Vision* recognizes the need for strict moral education through parents, family, friends, and community because people have a dual nature of being selfish and selfless, competitive and cooperative, greedy and generous, and so we need rules and guidelines and encouragement to do the right thing. A *Realistic Vision* acknowledges that people vary widely both physically and intellectually—in good part because of natural inherited differences—and therefore will rise (or fall) to their natural levels. Therefore, governmental redistribution programs are not only unfair to those from whom the wealth is confiscated, but the redistribution of the wealth to those who did not earn it cannot and will not work to equalize these natural inequalities. As Friedrich Hayek articulated the problem in 1945: "There is all the difference in the world between treating people equally and attempting to make them equal. While the first is the condition of a free society, the second means, as De Tocqueville described it, 'a new form of servitude'."[11] A *Realistic Vision* of human nature is what James Madison was thinking of when he penned (literally) his oft-quoted dictum in the *Federalist Paper Number 51*:

> If men were angels, no government would be necessary. If angels were to govern men, neither external nor internal controls on government would be necessary. In framing a

---

10 Pinker, Steven. 2011. *The Better Angels of Our Nature: Why Violence Has Declined*. New York: Viking.

11 Hayek, Friedrich. 1945. In: *Finlay Lecture, delivered at University College, Dublin, on December 17, 1945*. Published by Hodges, Figgis & Co., Ltd., Dublin, and B. H. Blackwell, Ltd., Oxford, 1946.

government which is to be administered by men over men,
the great difficulty lies in this: you must first enable the
government to control the governed; and in the next place
oblige it to control itself.[12]

The resulting structure of the United States government and its
nearly 250-years of successful governance is a tribute to Madison's
(and the other founders') realistic vision of human nature. If you
have a flawed theory of human nature, however, much follows that
will also be flawed, including disastrous social policies and movements that have taken hold in recent years.

Woke Racism

When Dr. Martin Luther King Jr. delivered what, in the fullness
of time, would become his most memorable vision from his 1963
majestic "I Have a Dream" speech, he could not have known how
much progress in civil rights would ensue over the coming half century, in no small measure because of his work. As documented in
numerous books, databases, and surveys,[13] there has never been another time in history when it has been better to be alive than today,
including and especially for people of color, women, and minorities
of any kind. Six decades on we should be celebrating the instantiation of Dr. King's dream that . . . "one day this nation will rise up,

---

12   Madison, James. 1788. "The Federalist No. 51: The Structure of the
Government Must Furnish the Proper Checks and Balances Between the
Different Departments," *Independent Journal*, Wednesday, February 6,
https://www.coursesidekick.com/political-science/3077848.

13   See, for example: Pinker, Steven. 2011. *The Better Angels of Our Nature:
Why Violence Has Declined.* New York: Viking; Shermer, Michael. 2015; *The
Moral Arc: How Science and Reason Lead Humanity to Truth, Justice, and
Freedom.* New York: Henry Holt; Rosling, Hans. 2018; *Factfulness.* New
York: Flatiron Books; Easterbrook, Greg. 2018; *It's Better Than it Looks.*
New York: PublicAffairs; Norberg, Johan. 2017; *Progress.* New York:
OneWorld; Marian Tupey's HumanProgress.org and Max Roser's OurWorld-
inData.org.

live out the true meaning of its creed: 'We hold these truths to be self-evident, that all men are created equal.' I have a dream that one day on the red hills of Georgia sons of former slaves and the sons of former slave-owners will be able to sit down together at the table of brotherhood."

Lamentably, the past decade has witnessed what appears to be a reversal of Dr. King's dream in the form of woke identity politics, or the collectivization of individuals into groups competing for status and power and perceived persecution by privileged identities. In Dr. King's time, race was the primary political power dimension. Since then, identity politics has expanded to include not only race but gender identity, sexual orientation, class, religion, ethnicity, language, dialect, education, generation, occupation, political party, disability, marital status, veteran status, and more, all competing for political power in the public sphere.

Added to this new instantiation of ancient tribalism is intersectionality theory, in which membership in multiple intersecting identity groups brings more or less power, more or less persecution. Thus, for example, the historical subjugation of blacks by whites is measured along a single axis of race, while the oppression of women by men is assessed along a single axis of gender; that black women have different experiences than black men or white women can be traced along two intersecting axes of race and gender; a non-white transgender lower-class disabled Muslim woman faces a world different from that of a white cisgender upper-class able-bodied Christian man along these multiple intersecting axes, of which there are more than a dozen, including:

> White—Non-White
>
> Male—Female
>
> Light—Dark
>
> Cisgender—Transgender
>
> Heterosexual—Homosexual

Gender-typical—Deviant

Young—Old

European—Non-European

Anglophone—English as Second Language

Gentile—Jews

Rich—Poor

Fertile—Infertile

Able-bodied—Disabled

Credentialed—Non-Literate

As philosopher Kathryn Pauly Morgan explained intersectionality, each of us may be identified and judged on where we fall "on each of these axes (at a minimum) and that this point is simultaneously a locus of our agency, power, disempowerment, oppression, and resistance." The Chicana feminist activist Elizabeth Martinez worried what such hierarchical assessments might lead to: "There are various forms of working together. A coalition is one, a network is another, an alliance is yet another. But the general idea is no competition of hierarchies should prevail. No Oppression Olympics."[14]

Unfortunately, as detailed in numerous books,[15] the Oppression Olympics are well past their opening ceremonies in colleges, corporations, and Congress, tearing institutions asunder as conflicting cohorts vie for who has suffered the most historical inequities. My lament is echoed by the African-American jazz poet Langston Hughes in his 1951 poem *Harlem*, when he asked, "What happens to a dream deferred?," which he answered in a series of rhetorical questions, most famously: "Does it dry up / like a raisin in the sun?" Let us not allow Dr. King's noble dream of judging others by the

---

14 https://en.wikipedia.org/wiki/Intersectionality.

15 Goldberg, Jonah. 2018. *Suicide of the West.* New York: Crown; Mac Donald, Heather. 2018. *The Diversity Delusion.* New York: St. Martin's Press; Lukianoff, Greg and Jonathan Haidt. 2018. *The Coddling of the American Mind.* New York: Penguin.

content of their character alone to wither on the vine under the collectivist drought brought on by these politically intersecting tribal identities, which we must shed if we are to return to the moral path leading to a unifying humanity.

Woke Academia

The French political journalist and supporter of the Royalist cause in the French Revolution, Jacques Mallet du Pan, poignantly summarized what often happens to extremists: "The Revolution devours its children."[16] I was thinking about this idiom while giving public lectures at colleges and universities as they were undergoing the woke revolution in the 2010s that were erupting in protester paroxysms under the guise of protecting students from allegedly offensive speech and disagreeable ideas, with demands for everything from trigger warnings and safe spaces to microaggressions and speaker disinvitations.

Trigger warnings are supposed to be issued to students before readings, classroom lectures, film screenings, or public speeches on such topics as sex, addiction, bullying, suicide, eating disorders, and the like, involving such supposed prejudices as ableism, homophobia, sizeism, slut shaming, transphobia, victim-blaming, and who-knows-what-else, thereby infantilizing students instead of preparing them for the real world where they most assuredly will not be so shielded. At Oberlin College,[17] for example, students leveled accusations against the administration of imperialism, white supremacy, capitalism, and the *ne plus ultra* in gender politics, cissexist heteropatriarchy, or the enforcement of "gender binary and gender

---

16   Sir Bernard Mallet. 1902. *Mallet du Pan and the French Revolution.* Longmans, Green, p. 164; Jacques Mallet du Pan. 1793; *Considerations sur la Nature de la Revolution de France*, p. 80.

17   Neff, Blake. 2015. "Oberlin Students Release Gargantuan 14-Page List of Demands," *Daily Caller*, Dec. 17. https://dailycaller.com/2015/12/17/oberlin-students-release-gargantuan-14-page-list-of-demands/.

essentialism" against those who are "gender variant (non-binary) and trans identities." The number of such categories has expanded into an alphabet string, LGBTQIA, or lesbian, gay, bisexual, trans, queer/questioning, intersex, asexual and any other underrepresented sexual, gender, and/or romantic identities.[18] This is not your parents' protest against Victorian sexual mores.

As often happens in moral movements, a reasonable idea with some evidentiary backing gets carried to extremes by engaged moralists eager for attention, sympathy, and the social standing that being a victim or victim sympathizer can bring. Soldiers suffering from PTSD, for example, may be "triggered" by the backfire of a nearby automobile, but no one has proposed that automobile manufacturers put "trigger warnings" on cars to accommodate soldiers. As well, the Harvard psychologist Richard McNally points out that trigger warnings may have the opposite effect for which they are intended, because "systematic exposure to triggers and the memories they provoke is the most effective means of overcoming the disorder." McNally sites an analysis by the Institute of Medicine, which found that "exposure therapy is the most efficacious treatment for PTSD, especially in civilians who have suffered trauma such as sexual assault."[19] In other words, face your problems head-on and deal with them. An additional problem with trigger warnings is that the number of triggers has expanded to the point where nearly every conversation, speech, or lecture could contain triggering words, turning communication into a moral hazard.

Then there are *safe spaces*, or places "where anyone can relax and be fully self-expressed, without fear of being made to feel un-

---

18   This list comes from a memo sent to all faculty at Chapman University in the context of a workshop we were all invited to attend on safe spaces related to students who fall into one of these categories.

19   McNally, Richard J. 2014. "Hazards Ahead: The Problem with Trigger Warnings, According to the Research," *Pacific Standard*, May 20. https://psmag.com/education/hazards-ahead-problem-trigger-warnings-according-research-81946/.

comfortable, unwelcome or challenged on account of biological sex, race/ethnicity, sexual orientation, gender identity or expression, cultural background, age, or physical or mental ability; a place where the rules guard each person's self-respect, dignity and feelings and strongly encourage everyone to respect others."[20] That sounds reasonable enough, but in addition to infantilizing adults, extreme versions of the practice often means protecting students from opinions that they don't happen to agree with, or shielding them from ideas that challenge their beliefs, which has always been one of the most venerable hallmarks of a college education.

Microaggressions are comments or questions that slight, snub, or insult someone, intentionally or unintentionally, in anything from casual conversation to formal discourse. According to the University of California publication Tool: Recognizing Microaggressions and the Messages They Send,[21] examples include (see full table of microaggressions below):

- Asking "Where are you from or where were you born?" or "What are you?" This implies someone is not a true American.

- Inquiring "How did you become so good in math?" (to people of color) or suggesting "You must be good in math" (to an Asian), which is stereotyping.

- Proclaiming "There is only one race, the human race" or "I don't believe in race." This denies the significance of a person of color's racial/ethnic experience and history.

- Opining "I believe the most qualified person should get the job" or "America is the land of opportunity."

---

20   Crockett, Emily. 2016. "Safe Spaces, Explained," *Vox*. August 25.

21   "Tool: Recognizing Microaggressions and the Messages They Send." Adapted from: Sue, Derald Wing. 2010. *Microaggressions in Everyday Life: Race, Gender, and Sexual Orientation*. New York: Wiley and Sons. https://www.scribd.com/document/268516319/Tool-Recognizing-Microaggressions-and-the-Messages-They-Send.

This suggests that the playing field is level, so if women or people of color do not fill all jobs and careers in precise proportion to their population percentages, it must mean that the problem is with them, an accusation purportedly offensive.

Tool: Recognizing Microaggressions and the Messages They Send

Microaggressions are the everyday verbal, nonverbal, and environmental slights, snubs, or insults, whether intentional or unintentional, that communicate hostile, derogatory, or negative messages to target persons based solely upon their marginalized group membership *(from Diversity in the Classroom, UCLA Diversity & Faculty Development, 2014).* **The first step in addressing microaggressions is to recognize when a microaggression has occurred and what message it may be sending. The context of the relationship and situation is critical.** Below are common themes to which microaggressions attach.

THEMES	MICROAGGRESSION EXAMPLES	MESSAGE
Alien in One's Own Land When Asian Americans, Latino Americans and others who look different or are named differently from the dominant culture are assumed to be foreign-born	• *"Where are you from or where were you born?"* • *"You speak English very well."* • *"What are you? You're so interesting looking!"* • A person asking an Asian American or Latino American to teach them words in their native language. • Continuing to mispronounce the names of students after students have corrected the person time and time again. Not willing to listen closely and learn the pronunciation of a non-English based name.	You are not a true American. You are a perpetual foreigner in your own country. Your ethnic/racial identity makes you exotic.
Ascription of Intelligence Assigning intelligence to a person of color or a woman based on his/her race/gender	• *"You are a credit to your race."* • *"Wow! How did you become so good in math?"* • To an Asian person, *"You must be good in math, can you help me with this problem?"* • To a woman of color: *"I would have never guessed that you were a scientist."*	People of color are generally not as intelligent as Whites. All Asians are intelligent and good in math/science. It is unusual for a woman to have strong mathematical skills.
Color Blindness Statements that indicate that a White person does not want to or need to acknowledge race.	• *"When I look at you, I don't see color."* • *"There is only one race, the human race."* • *"America is a melting pot."* • *"I don't believe in race."* • Denying the experiences of students by questioning the credibility /validity of their stories.	Assimilate to the dominant culture. Denying the significance of a person of color's racial/ethnic experience and history. Denying the individual as a racial/cultural being.
Criminality/Assumption of Criminal Status A person of color is presumed to be dangerous, criminal, or deviant based on his/her race.	• A White man or woman clutches his/her purse or checks wallet as a Black or Latino person approaches. • A store owner following a customer of color around the store. • Someone crosses to the other side of the street to avoid a person of color. • While walking through the halls of the Chemistry building, a professor approaches a post-doctoral student of color to ask if she/he is lost, making the	You are a criminal. You are going to steal/you are poor, you do not belong. You are dangerous.

Again, it sounds reasonable enough to acknowledge that some comments people make are cringe- worthy, but do we really need a list of DOs and DON'Ts handed out to students and reviewed like they were five-year olds being taught how to play nice with the other kids? Can't adults work out these issues themselves without administrators stepping in as surrogate parents? And as with the problem of trigger words, the list of microaggressions grows, turning normal conversation into a cauldron of potential violations that further restricts speech, encourages divisiveness rather than inclusiveness, and forces people to censor themselves, dissemble, withhold opinion, or outright lie about what they believe.

Speaker disinvitations are the natural outcome of obsessive concerns over trigger warnings, safe spaces, and microaggressions, in which invited speakers are cancelled or deplatformed after student protesters express their displeasure at the very presence on campus of someone with whom they disagree.[22] According to the Foundation for Individual Rights and Expression (FIRE), between 2000 and December, 2024, 1,564 deplatforming attempts have been recorded by the organization, with a success rate of 663 speakers prevented from giving their talks. One of the prominent speakers to be disinvited was the women's rights scholar and activist Ayaan Hirsi Ali in 2014, when her scheduled commencement address was canceled after student protests over her criticism of Islam for its mistreatment of women.[23] The effects of such protests are often the opposite of what the protesters sought. Ayaan Hirsi Ali's speech, for example, was published in the Wall Street Journal under the header "Here's What I Would Have Said at Brandeis,"[24] where it was seen by that paper's 2.5 million readers—orders of magnitude more than would have heard it on campus.

---

22   Stevens, Sean. 2017. "Campus Speaker Disinvitations: Recent Trends," *Heterodox Academy*. Jan. 24. https://heterodoxacademy.org/blog/campus-speaker-disinvitations-recent-trends-part-1-of-2/.

23   Perez-Pena, Richard and Tanzina Vega. 2014. "Brandeis Cancels Plan to Give Honorary Degree to Ayaan Hirsi Ali, a Critic of Islam," *The New York Times,* April. 8. https://www.nytimes.com/2014/04/09/us/brandeis-cancels-plan-to-give-honorary-degree-to-ayaan-hirsi-ali-a-critic-of-islam.html.

24   Ali, Ayaan Hirsi. 2014. "Here's What I Would Have Said at Brandeis," *The Wall Street Journal*, April 10. https://www.wsj.com/articles/SB10001424052702304512504579493410287663906 B.

THE WALL STREET JOURNAL.

Home   World   U.S.   Politics   Economy   Business   Tech   Markets   Opinion   Arts   Life   Real Estate

REVIEW & OUTLOOK
Clinton's False Email
Equivalence

REVIEW & OUTLOOK
Rumors of Recession

REVIEW & OUTLOOK
Warren's Criminal
Complaint

Marco Rubio's New
Hampshire Crucible

COMMENTARY

Here's What I Would Have Said at Brandeis

We need to make our universities temples not of dogmatic orthodoxy, but of truly critical thinking.

By AYAAN HIRSI ALI
April 10, 2014 6:38 p.m. ET

On Tuesday, after protests by students, faculty and outside groups, Brandeis University revoked its invitation to Ayaan Hirsi Ali to receive an honorary degree at its commencement ceremonies in May. The protesters accused Ms. Hirsi Ali, an advocate for the rights of women and girls, of being "Islamophobic." Here is an abridged version of the remarks she planned to deliver.

One year ago, the city and suburbs of Boston were still in mourning. Families who only weeks earlier had children and siblings to hug were left with only photographs and memories. Still others were hovering over bedsides, watching as young men, women, and children endured painful surgeries and permanent disfiguration. All because two brothers, radicalized by jihadist websites, decided to place homemade bombs in backpacks near the finish line of one of the most prominent events in American sports,

Most Popu

The H
Maste
Selfie

Buildi
After I
Rocks

Earth,
Found
White

Super
Snicke

Aerial

What may have started out as well-intentioned actions at curbing prejudices and attenuating bigotry with the goal of making people more tolerant, these woke policies when put into practice metamorphosed into thought police attempting to impose totalitarian measures that resulted in silencing dissent of any kind. In this case the solution is as simple as it is obvious: *viewpoint diversity.* Invite speakers from a wide range of perspectives—political, economic, and ideological—even (or especially) if they are offensive to faculty and students. *And no more disinvitations!* If you invite someone to speak, honor your word, own your decision, and stand up to the protesters.

Woke Science

The infiltration of wokeness into the sciences is now well documented, from academic science departments hiring practices based on a bingo-card of intersectioning identities (race, gender, sexual orientation, ethnicity, etc.) to granting agencies demanding statements explaining how the research project will be supportive of or sensitive to oppressed minorities, even those that have nothing to do with politics, economics, or social policies, such as astrophysics. Case in point: the German physicist Sabine Hössenfelder went out to her Twitter/X followers in 2022 to inquire what woke formulaic language she should plug into her grant proposal for studying black holes:

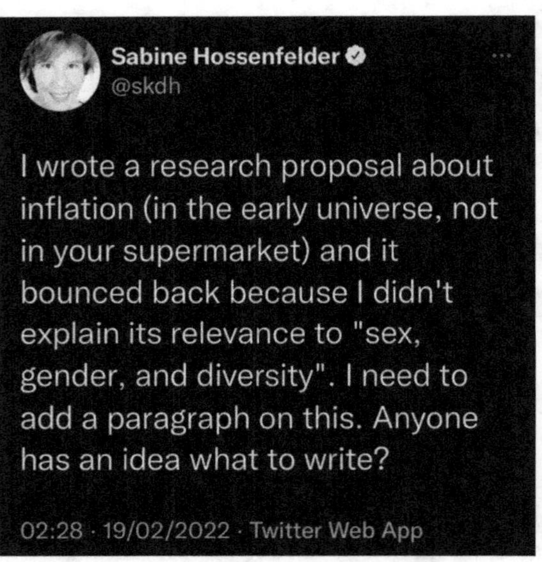

The pushback she experienced in the comments section of the post led her to delete it, as apparently even asking the question challenged the woke agenda, which must never be done.[25] Another physicist and cosmologist, Lawrence Krauss, has carefully documented the extensive politicization of the sciences, for example a *Physical Review Physics Education Research* paper titled "Observing Whiteness in Introductory Physics: A Case Study," that included an objection to the use of "whiteboards" in classrooms because:

> Though whiteboards have been shown to have a number
> of affordances when they are used as a collaborative tool

---

25   Remix News Staff. 2022. "How Woke Gatekeepers Control Western Education," *RemixNews*, Feb. 25. https://shorturl.at/FNqDk.

that all members have access to, in this episode, they also play a role in reconstituting whiteness as social organization. In particular, whiteboards display written information for public consumption; they draw attention to themselves and in this case support the centering of an abstract representation and the person standing next to it, presenting. They collaborate with white organizational culture, where ideas and experiences gain value (become more central) when written down.[26]

PHYSICAL REVIEW PHYSICS EDUCATION RESEARCH **18**, 010119 (2022)

Observing whiteness in introductory physics: A case study

Amy D. Robertson[1](she/her) and W. Tali Hairston[2](he/him)
[1]*Department of Physics, Seattle Pacific University, Seattle, Washington 98119-1997, USA*
[2]*Equitable Development, LLC, Seattle, Washington 98178, USA*

(Received 13 June 2021; accepted 7 December 2021; published 11 March 2022)

Within whiteness, the organization of social life is in terms of a center and margins that are based on dominance, control, and a transcendent figure that is consistently and structurally ascribed value over and above other figures. In this paper, we synthesize literature from Critical Whiteness Studies and Critical Race Theory to articulate analytic markers for whiteness, and use the markers to identify and analyze whiteness as it shows up in an introductory physics classroom interaction. We name mechanisms that facilitate the reproduction of whiteness in this local context, including a particular representation of energy, physics values, whiteboards, gendered social norms, and the structure of schooling. In naming whiteness and offering a set of analytic markers, our aim is to provide instructors and researchers with a tool for identifying whiteness in their own contexts. Alongside our discussion, which imagines new possibilities for physics teaching and learning, we hope our work contributes to Critical Whiteness Studies' goal of dismantling whiteness.

DOI: 10.1103/PhysRevPhysEducRes.18.010119

America's largest funder of science, the Energy Department's Office of Science, now requires all grant proposals to include a PIER (Promoting Inclusive and Equitable Research) plan to "describe the activities and strategies of the applicant to promote equity and inclusion as an intrinsic element to advancing scientific excellence." Upon reading this new requirement, Krauss wondered what his last grant proposal involving the exploration of gravitational waves, the early universe, neutrino cosmology, dark-matter detection, and black-hole physics has to do with diversity and inclusion, concluding

---

26 Krauss, Lawrence. 2022. "Physics Education: The Hordes Are at the Gates," *Critical Mass*, April 11. https://shorturl.at/bbRbT.

"nothing."[27]

Examples of such woke corruption of science are now legion. The Russian-born chemist Anna Krylov, the USC Associates Chair in Natural Sciences and Professor of Chemistry at the University of Southern California in the field of theoretical and computational quantum chemistry, explained the problem in a keynote address—"Merit-Based Science is Effect and Fair: How Such a Banal Idea Has Become Controversial" —at a retreat of her department in November of 2024.[28] Critical Social Justice, she summarizes, insists that

> everything (including science) is racist, sexist, colonial. Existing social inequalities and unequal representation are due to systemic racism and sexism. Everything (including academia) is about power struggle between the oppressors and oppressed. Everything (including science and education) needs to be dismantled and rebuilt to ensure Diversity, Equity, and Inclusion. "Those who are not with us are against us" and must be punished.

Examples could be ripped from the headlines of *The Onion* or *Babylon Bee*:

- A collection of 67 papers published in the *Journal of Chemical Education* include "Decolonizing the Undergraduate Chemistry Curriculum." "Chemistry and Racism." "Integrating Antiracism, Social Justice and Equity Themes in a Biochemistry Class."

- A module in a chemistry class at East Carolina University explores "the development and interrelationship between quantum mechanics, Marxist materialism, Afro-futurism/pessimism, and postcolonial nationalism."

---

27 Krauss, Lawrence. 2022. "Now Even Science Grants Must Bow to 'Equity and Inclusion'," *The Wall Street Journal*, Oct. 12. https://shorturl.at/dabv6.

28 Krylov, Anna. 2024. "Merit-Based Science is Effective and Fair: How Such a Banal Idea Has Become Controversial," *YouTube*, https://tinyurl.com/3rk8skz9.

- An American Chemical Society Inclusivity Style Guide advises scientists to replace phrases such as "obesity is a public health crisis" with "antifat bias and discrimination are public health crises", replace "cast a dark cloud over the meeting" with "created a tense atmosphere at the meeting," replace "boring and lame" with "boring and uninteresting," and so forth.

- Rice University now offers a course on "Afrochemistry: The Study of Black-Life Matter."

As Krylov joked amidst this litany of examples of the woke corruption of science, "if you fall into a black hole we know what will happen to you, regardless of your pronouns."

The biologists Jerry Coyne and Luana Maroja co-authored a stunning revelatory article on "The Ideological Subversion of Biology" in which they warned:

> Biology faces a grave threat from "progressive" politics that are changing the way our work is done, delimiting areas of biology that are taboo and will not be funded by the government or published in scientific journals, stipulating what words biologists must avoid in their writing, and decreeing how biology is taught to students and communicated to other scientists and the public through the technical and popular press.[29]

Coyne and Maroja documented six cases of misrepresentation of facts in evolutionary and organismal biology, including:

1. Sex in humans is not a discrete and binary distribution of males and females but a spectrum.

2. All behavioral and psychological differences between human males and females are due to socialization.

3. Evolutionary psychology, the study of the evolutionary roots

---

29 Coyne, Jerry A. and Luana S. Maroja. 2023. "The Ideological Subversion of Biology," *Skeptical Inquirer*, July/August. https://shorturl.at/9nvRA.

     of human behavior, is a bogus field based on false assumptions.

4. We should avoid studying genetic differences in behavior between individuals.

5. "Race and ethnicity are social constructs, without scientific or biological meaning."

6. Indigenous "ways of knowing" are equivalent to modern science and should be respected and taught as such.

The final recommendation comes straight out of the new anthropology wars over science and indigenous peoples, most notably in New Zealand, Australia, and North America. The experiences of the San Jose State University (SJSU) archaeologist Elizabeth Weiss are emblematic of the problem when she was defamed as a "racist" and locked out of her fossil collection for simply opposing the teaching as science of Native American creationism myths (that there was no migration from Asia to the Americas—they were always here), and the repatriation movement that argues Paleo-Indian fossil remains from many thousands of years ago, with little to no genealogical linkage to current Native American tribes, be reburied and lost to science forever.[30]

On the former, for example, in 2021 Weiss delivered a talk for the Society for American Archaeology (SAA) conference titled "Has Creationism Crept Back into Archaeology?," in which she "compared creation myths of Native Americans to other creation myths while pointing out that the SAA has previously taken a stand against the teaching and use of biblical interpretations, such as intelligent design, to understand the past." Many of the 7,000 members of the SAA objected to the talk even being delivered, and after it was "the comment box quickly filled up with name-calling and accusations of racism," and the talk was promptly removed from the SAA website.

30　Weiss, Elizabeth. 2024. "The New Archaeology Wars: How Cancel Culture and Identity Politics Have Corrupted Science," *Skeptic*, Vol. 29, No. 2. https://shorturl.at/XmUlS.

On the latter, Weiss was told by SJSU Provost Vincent Del Casino that a photograph of her holding the skull of an ancient Native American with the caption "so happy to be back with some old friends" (after the Covid-19 shut down of her campus) "has evoked shock and disgust from our Native and Indigenous community on campus and from many people within and outside of SJSU." This was followed by SJSU President Mary Papazian ordering that she be locked out of the collection (*"They literally changed the locks!"*). Papazian "also stated that no photos were allowed of the Native American collection or even of the boxes that held the bones (a key aspect to understanding past diseases in sharing and comparing images). One cultural anthropologist asked whether I had written permission from these individuals to take the photos, knowing full well that they had been dead for centuries!"

On the left, the image that Provost Del Casino said did "not align with the values of SJSU" and "evoked shock and disgust from our Native and Indigenous community on campus and from many people within and outside of SJSU." On the right, the image that the University used for multiple websites and promotional material. This image was removed from the University website in July 2023.

If all this madness were not enough to convince people to forego joining a Fair Play for Archeological Wokeness committee, Weiss presented a protocol draft that would determine access to archaeological collections that "included a menstruation taboo" for which the authors "couldn't bring themselves to state that women who are menstruating are not allowed in the curation facility or to handle remains and artifacts; thus, they used the term "menstruating personnel," to avoid the implication that only females menstruate! Seriously?" Yes, seriously, as Weiss concluded:

> How did we get to a situation in which opposing the re-burial of human remains is automatically deemed racist and can derail an anthropologist's career? It's about turning anthropology into an ideological battleground weighted in favor of victimhood and (often disproven by evidence) tribal identity—both political and social—rather than a scientific endeavor aimed at better understanding the past for the benefit of all humankind. It doesn't matter who is correct, it matters who gets to tell the story, with Native American narratives now considered expert testimony that cannot and must not be questioned.

Unquestioned narratives were on full display in my final stretch at *Scientific American,* where I was a monthly columnist for nearly 18 years. I have documented elsewhere how political ideology crept into the magazine,[31] culminating in the departure of the deeply-woke Editor-in-Chief, Laura Helmuth, shortly after the 2024 Presidential election when she went on a rant in which she apologized "to younger voters that my Gen X is so full of fucking fascists," upbraided high-school classmates for celebrating Trump's win— "fuck them to the moon and back" —and described her home state of Indiana as "racist and sexist." Shortly after, she resigned "to take some time to think about what comes next (and go birdwatching)." The president of *Scientific American,* Kimberly Lau, released a statement thanking Helmuth for her leadership and wishing "her well for the future."[32] In my final analysis of this sad state of affairs documenting the decline of a once storied institution,[33] I proposed

---

31 Shermer, Michael. 2021. "Scientific American Goes Woke," *Skeptic,* Nov. 17. https://shorturl.at/DEsI5.

32 https://shorturl.at/dNILN.

33 Shermer, Michael. 2024. "An Unscientific American," *Quillette,* Nov. 21. https://shorturl.at/jMFLK.

a counterfactual test that this corruption of the magazine really is due to wokeness:

> Imagine what would have happened if the editor-in-chief of *Scientific American* had spoken about or published articles on the average difference in IQ test scores between white and black Americans and argued that the gap might be partially due to genetics—or, alternatively, if she had correctly stated that, on average, women score higher than men in trait Neuroticism on the Big 5 personality scale and suggested that that is why there are fewer female than male Fortune 500 CEOs. She would surely have been summarily fired and publicly denounced and we would have been told that such comments or articles "do not reflect the positions or policies of *Scientific American* or its governing board or staff; we apologise to all who have been harmed by them." She would almost certainly *not* have been thanked for her years of loyal service and offered good wishes for her future.

Actual examples from the pages of *Scientific American* make my point:

- There was Allison Hopper's July 2021 "Denial of Evolution is a Form of White Supremacy"[34] that denied creationists their religious motivation for their beliefs and instead labeled them with the "racist" calumny.

- An August 2021 article, "Modern Mathematics Confronts its White Patriarchal Past,"[35] contrary to all available evidence, accused an entire profession of both misogyny and racism while simultaneously ignoring all the other fields in which women outnumber men in graduate degrees, such as health and medical sciences (71%), social and behavioral sciences (61%),

---

34 https://shorturl.at/oFClP.

35 https://shorturl.at/ER8nb.

and biological sciences (51.4%).[36] Do patriarchy and misogyny exist only in fields in which men outnumber women?

- A December 2021 article, "The Complicated Legacy of E. O. Wilson"[37] accused the renowned evolutionary biologist of racism, a charge so incendiary that it caused a cavalcade of Wilson's colleagues, post-docs, students, friends, and supporters to come to his defense.[38]

- Peak wokeness was reached in the September 2021 issue when it was explained "Why the Term 'JEDI' is Problematic for Describing Programs that Promote Justice, Equity, Diversity and Inclusion,"[39] examples of which included Star Wars characters who were too white, toxically masculine, cultish, religious, ableist, eugenicist, and worst of all resolved their conflicts through "duels with phallic lightsabers." Phallic lightsabers?

- Then there was the November 2023 article "The Theory That Men Evolved to Hunt and Women Evolved to Gather is Wrong,"[40] concluded from this (mis)reading of the scientific literature that "inequity between male and female athletes is a result not of inherent biological differences between the sexes but of biases in how they are treated in sports." This is pure blank slate pablum that if true would mean an end to all women's sports.

- As if all this were not problematic enough for a magazine with the word "scientific" in its title—the editors threw their weight behind the youth gender med-

---

36 Perry, Mark J. 2020. "Women Earned Majority of Doctoral Degrees in 2019 for 11th Straight Year and Outnumber Men in Grad School 141 to 100," *AEI*, Oct. 15. https://t.ly/ed_J5.

37 https://shorturl.at/Rf9k7.

38 Shermer, Michael. 2022. "Was the Great Scientist E. O. Wilson a Racist? No!" *Skeptic*, April 27. https://tinyurl.com/yc3b72x7.

39 https://tinyurl.com/bd943ctn.

40 https://tinyurl.com/37445a7h.

icine and trans lobby, claiming that gender-affirming care for trans kids is good health care.[41] It isn't: that "rapid onset gender dysphoria" is not a thing[42] (it most certainly is), and that biological sex is on a spectrum[43] (it is binary). Numerous scientists published rebuttals of these dubious claims, including evolutionary theorist Richard Dawkins[44] and biologist Colin Wright.[45]

Does anyone actually believe such claptrap? Obviously, some do, and the fervour of their woke faith only makes them all the more able to convince themselves (and others of parallel ideological stripes) of the truth of claims that nearly everyone else can see have little-to-no contact with reality. It is also possible that the majority of people do not believe any of this woke ideology, but out of fear of cancel culture and being accused of bigotry keep their mouths shut, leading to *pluralistic ignorance*, in which each individual is under the illusion that *everyone else* believes it, even though most people do not.

Transcending Wokeness

At the core of woke ideology is DEI—Diversity Equity Inclusion—which when put into practice translates into Uniformity Inequality Exclusion. Every year DEI training programs consume the time of millions of students, faculty, and employees both government and private, and cost upwards of $8 billion a year to implement. Not only do they not work to reduce the purported epidemic of racism, misogyny, homophobia, and bigotry, a new study shows that

---

41 https://tinyurl.com/y4awwbdh.

42 https://tinyurl.com/39asdt53.

43 https://tinyurl.com/bdf2t9zt.

44 Dawkins, Richard. 2024. "Race is a Spectrum. Sex is Pretty Damn Binary," *Quillette*, Sept. 6. https://tinyurl.com/mvn8p73w.

45 Wright, Colin. 2024. "Understanding the Sex Binary," *Reality's Last Stand*, Aug. 4. https://tinyurl.com/yepcua4f.

they actually make matters worse. According to Rutgers University psychologist Lee Jessim, co-author of a study conducted by the Network Contagion Research Institute (NCRI) in conjunction with Rutgers University Social Perception Lab testing the effects of DEI pedagogy and rhetoric, found:

1. *Anti-Oppressive Intervention*: DEI training rooted in anti-oppressive rhetoric introduces narratives that lead people to assume that certain groups are inherent oppressors and others as inherent victims.

2. *Increased Racial Suspicion*: Exposure leads to hostile attribution bias, causing participants to see discrimination when there is no evidence that discrimination has occurred, driving racial prejudice, intergroup hostility, suspicion and division.

3. *Authoritarian Policing*: This heightened suspicion triggers authoritarian policing tendencies, leading people to endorse surveillance and purity testing, strict social controls, and escalating responses from corrective to coercive.

4. *Punitive Retribution*: Participants show greater support for extreme punitive measures against perceived oppressors as well as those seen as ideologically impure.

5. *Calls for More Interventions*: The heightened punitive atmosphere feeds back into demands for more anti-oppressive DEI training, creating a self-reinforcing cycle of suspicion and intolerance.

"These findings suggest that exposure to anti-oppressive narratives can increase the endorsement of the type of demonization and scapegoating characteristic of authoritarianism," the authors report, adding that "Educational materials from some of the most well-published and well-known DEI scholars not only failed to positively enhance interracial attitudes, they provoked baseless suspicion and encouraged punitive attitudes."[46] Unsurprisingly, these findings that DEI programs not only do not work to reduce discriminatory

---

46 Jessim, Lee, et al. 2024. "Instructing Animosity: How DEI Pedagogy Produces the Hostile Attribution Bias," https://networkcontagion.us/wp-content/uploads/Instructing-Animosity_11.13.24.pdf.

attitudes but make them worse, were suppressed by the *New York Times* and Bloomberg.[47]

Beyond the failings of DEI policies, the deeper problem, as we've seen, is that wokeness leads to treating people as members of identity groups rather than as *individuals*. It is when individuals are subsumed into and sacrificed for the good of the group that abuses of freedom have been most widespread and body counts have been driven highest. It is when people are judged not by the content of their character but by the color of their skin—or by their gender chromosomal constitution, or by whom they prefer to share a bed with, or by what accent they speak with, or by which political or religious affiliation they identify with—that freedom falls and liberty is lost.

---

47 Wright, Colin. 2024. "Why Was this Groundbreaking Study on DEI Silenced?" *Reality's Last Stand*. Nov. 25. https://www.realityslaststand. com/p/why-was-this-groundbreaking-study.

2

Critical Realism and Identity Politics

David Pilgrim

Introduction

It has been obvious that since the 1970s in Western liberal democracies, left wing campaigning has been captured increasingly by appeals to identity politics (IP) aimed at delivering social justice. This has created an open goal for those on the right. The recent success of Donald Trump in part at least can be accounted for by the virtue signalling of the Democrats about transgenderism. Some feminists of all political hues have made this point in despair, and many have found themselves in the strange position of supporting the early executive orders of a man not known for his sensitivities about women's rights.

For the left, identity politics certainly have a seductive surface appeal; what might be called 'face validity' in psychology textbooks. Who with any modicum of progressive impulse or ordinary compassion would be against granting respect and full citizenship to anyone, whatever their skin color, religious belief, or sexual orientation? And within that progressive desire for inclusivity in relation to citizenship surely the experience of those previously excluded should be prioritised or privileged. And surely those who have enjoyed the legacy of uneven power relationships should now be held in deep suspicion (white, straight 'cis' men are candidates for unending derision and contempt). And this logic goes on, with spiralling threads of indignation driving the sanctimony of identity politics.

I want to argue in this chapter that this logic has a hollow ring, which is the inevitable outcome of a false premise, which is that social justice can be attained by responding comprehensively to all the claims of oppression that rest upon subjective assertions. The fetish of 'lived experience' (can experience be anything other than lived?) has created a warm glow. Be kind! We welcome our trans sisters! The self-satisfied slogans of today resonate with the ancient injunction to 'love thy neighbour as thy self'. So far so good: hence the face validity I noted. However, the consequences have already proved to be a disaster for the left. Not only have there been advantages given freely to the right (I noted Trump as a beneficiary recently), but the left has lost its way about distributive justice. The politics of recognition have created a form of amnesia about the latter.

With these introductory comments in mind, I now offer a critical realist appraisal of the faux radicalism of IP on the left, while noting that they have also been present on the right as well. The right, without acknowledging it have been throwing stones in a glass house. The arguments below are elaborated in my book *Identity Politics: Where Did It All Go Wrong?* (Pilgrim 2020).

Critical Realism as a Resource to Appraise Identity Politics

The current use of the term IP predominantly refers to their emergence, partly in tandem with New Social Movements (NSMs), since the 1960s in Western societies (Habermas, 1981; Touraine, 1981). Whilst a definition of IP risks a reified and positivistic notion of permanence, we can say reasonably that in recent decades they have certain recurring or semi-stable characteristics.

First, IP are the discursive or ideological manifestation of some but not all NSMs. For example, sub-populations such as women, gay people, or ethnic minorities offer their versions of IP. However, some NSMs are not about sub-groups but refer to other species, such as animal rights activism, or the avoidance of environmental catastrophe, such as the green and nuclear disarmament movements.

Second, they entail special pleading for such sub-groups, which implies outgroup members are actually or potentially antagonistic. Thus, whilst power is a central aspect of IP, it is understood in personal and interpersonal terms, rather than impersonal or supra-personal ones. Extra-discursive forms of power, such as biological or economic determinants tend to be backgrounded, taken for granted with little considered attention, or used selectively for ideological purposes.

Third, that antagonism at the group level becomes manifest then in individual oppression. This creates a focus upon the politically oppressive potential, not just of groups of people (say white people), but the qualities of individuals within those outgroups. The 'whiteness' of individuals brings with it immediate political advantage, 'privilege' to them. The same logic could link patriarchy as a social process to the privilege of this particular man.

Fourth, claims about these feared outcomes create a focus on moralisation, especially about the suspect motives of outgroup members or their assumed privileges at the expense of in-group members. This legitimises the role of virtue signalling and 'moral grandstanding' in daily life. IP then is a form of direct and immediate politics, which pervades daily routines in the here and now: hence 'everyday sexism' or 'casual racism'.

Fifth, although IP have been linked to a transformation of the left, with its traditional emphasis upon class struggle and the oppressive features of economic inequalities, forms exist across the political spectrum.

Sixth, in their more recent incarnation, IP have also invoked forms of counter-hegemony in relation to a normative shift about the tolerance of diversity and expanded citizenship for all. These forms reflect a range of criticisms. IP have been accused of being anti-realist at times and of being incompatible with cherished post-Enlightenment values, especially the unconditional defence of freedom of expression and the role of rationality and evidence-based approaches to political analysis and strategy.

These points are now elaborated using examples. If IP have been criticised on a number of grounds, then how have they survived for so long and why are they so appealing to so many? Why have they become a form of doxa in policy formation, in so many Western societies? In order to answer these questions, the meta-theoretical resource of critical realism is utilised. In preparation for that utilisation, critical realism is outlined for any reader new to it, and the particular aspects relevant to making sense of the emergence and survival of IP will be explained.

1. Aspects of Critical Realism Relevant to Understanding IP

The philosophy of critical realism is both post-Popperian and it is critical of the postmodern turn. It is traceable to Heraclitus, the pre-Socratic philosopher, who emphasised that reality is in constant flux. This can be contrasted with his contemporary, Parmenides, who saw the world as fixed and permanent at the hands of the gods (a metaphysical precursor to positivism in modernity). The Heraclitean emphasis was then re-worked after the 1960s by a group of predominantly post-Marxian writers, especially the Oxford philosopher Roy Bhaskar, though others have contributed significantly to the canon (e.g., Bhaskar, 2016; Porpora, 2015; Archer, 2000; Norrie, 2009).

The focus of critical realism is on emergence. If we are studying any topic or process in the natural or social world, how did it come into being? What must have the world been like for us to witness what we do today? We can try to answer these questions rationally and cautiously (a process of 'judgmental rationality') by considering the evidence available to us in good faith. This will help to clarify provisional truth claims under the caution of epistemic humility, faced with the challenges of a complex fluxing world. This sceptical caution avoids the error of positivism (seeking to verify permanent laws and assuming their manifestation in empirical invariance) on one side, but also the risks of the nihilism and irrealism of postmodernism on the other. Following Nietzsche, the latter emphasises that there are 'no facts; there are only interpretations.'

Critical realism is concerned with the process of becoming, afforded by antecedent generative mechanisms, actualised or not actualised, and (tentatively) with possible futures in open systems in degrees of flux. The limits to the overlap of critical realism with some aspects of more recent critical theory relate to the latter's inflection at times by French poststructuralism. By contrast, radical or strong social constructivism is dismissed by critical realists.

Critical realism assumes that humans have moral agency (Archer, 2000; Vogler, 2022), but they are also largely unaware of real forces, without and within, and so their decision making is constrained by processes beyond their immediate consciousness; hence the interest of some critical realists in psychoanalysis (e.g., Collier, 1981). Accordingly, critical realism can be thought of as a form of critical hermeneutics. As partially aware moral agents we might challenge or reproduce current political arrangements, and those individual and collective trends are of interest to critical realists.

In addition to judgmental rationality, critical realism has two other axioms: ontological realism (the world exists in a mind-independent way); and epistemological relativism (as a language-using, meaning-seeking species we construe, re-construe and debate what the world is and how it is best understood).

The world is construed: note, not merely socially constructed, the fetish of postmodernists (Craib, 1997; Callinicos, 1991). However, social constructions are themselves part of reality to be traced and understood and ideas have causal powers (Bhaskar, 1997; Elder-Vass, 2012). Because critical realism considers epistemological relativism to be important *but not all important*, it might be considered a weak rather than strong version of constructivism, though that self-appraisal remains unresolved within critical realism as a community of scholars (Sayer, 1999).

Critical realism has a focus on laminated reality, conceptualised as four main concomitant planes by Bhaskar: the natural world; our relationship to one another; the socio-economic structures we are embedded within; and our unique personalities. This 'four planar social being' is used below to make sense of the emergence and maintenance of IP. Let us proceed now by considering why IP are appealing despite their shortcomings, offering two short case studies of antiracism and the sex/gender debates, and then elaborating a critical realist appraisal of the survival of IP.

2. Doubts From Left and Right About IP

IP may be normative for now on the left, but they have had their critics for many decades. An early expression of dissent, about the socially progressive aspirations of IP and their inherent divisiveness, came from the Marxist historian Eric Hobsbawm in the 1990s:

> The political project of the Left is universalist: it is for all human beings. However we interpret the words, it isn't liberty for shareholders or blacks, but for everybody. It isn't equality for all members of the Garrick Club or the handicapped, but for everybody. It is not fraternity only for old Etonians or gays, but for everybody. And identity politics is essentially not for everybody but for the members of a specific group only. (Hobsbawm, 1996, the Barry Amiel and Norman Melburn Trust Lecture, Institute of Education, London, May 2, emphasis added).

Subsequent leftist critiques could be found for example in Mark Fisher's attack on what he called the 'Vampire Castle' containing the 'liberal-bourgeois perversion' of identity politics. For him they have been a diversion from dealing fully with the social context of their own origins. Moreover, they fail to reflect on their tactical incompetence at ensuring the social justice, which they claim bogusly in their self-righteous rhetoric (Fisher, 2013). More recently, a veteran of both feminism and antiracist struggles from the 1970s, Pragna Patel, who was the founder of the Southall Black Sisters in London made this point, echoing Hobsbawm and Fisher:

> Identity politics is a considerable challenge for us, not just in feminist circles but actually within all social justice movements. Identity politics have taken root in a way that I feel is profoundly regressive. It is a focus on individual experiences of victimhood. It is a focus on difference rather than unity. . . . I fear that all social movements are now tainted by a narrow form of identity politics…it has fragmented our struggles. . . . It is leading us down a political blind alley. (Interview on BBC, Radio 4's Woman's Hour January 5th, 2022.)

Together these critics from the left are pointing up three features of relevance to the weaknesses of IP, when interpreted as a form of politics with claims of progressive potential or impact. First, their special pleading for sub-groups is inherently divisive and antithetical to universal political solidarity. Second, they are psychologically reductionist and so individualistic. They fail to address seriously, or in the required depth, either social context or the powers of the material natural world. Third, they begin with legitimate insights about power. However, they then get stuck, as it were on first base; IP are a good place to start but not to finish.

As for critics of the right of IP, their focus is on depicting them as a form of 'cultural Marxism,' which is intent upon undermining the integrity of the family, Christian values, and those of the free world. The 'cultural Marxism' attribution is conflated at times with critical theory. The latter is seen as the central intellectual justification underpinning IP ideology from conservative critics, ironically inviting an interest in critical theory for the previously uninformed (Jamin, 2014). Right wing Christians, such as the Canadian clinical psychologist Jordan Peterson, have popularised this cultural Marxism notion, to explain identity politics and its shortcomings. Critical theory (used interchangeably at times with the Frankfurt School) became the named intellectual source of the intention to wreck American civilisation via 'political correctness' and the encouragement of identity politics. This conspiracy theory, with critical theory at its centre, espoused by the 'alt-right' during the rise of Donald Trump, became a dominant trope to encourage populist resistance.

Ironically, the insights from critical theory could account for such populism and faith in a new form of demagoguery to 'Make America Great Again.' So many of those in support of Trump were acting against their own objective interests; it was their emotionally-driven sense of ontological insecurity that determined the deference to an amoral and narcissistic father-figure, promising simple solutions to complex problems (Hochschild, 2016). Identity politics of the right followed a similar pattern for older nostalgic voters for Brexit in the UK, many of whom were well educated, suggesting that emotionality not rationality drives nationalisms at times (Sobolewska & Ford, 2020). Modern representative democracy has always had within it the risk of capture by the authoritarian right, and this trend has remerged strongly in the last decade (Stahl & Popp-Madsen, 2022). Ethnocentric identity politics have been central to that capture.

Here then we encounter IP being attacked from right and left but with differing emphases and assumptions. Those differences in turn reflect the variegated social ontology of IP and possibly a shared denial of that variability on each side. IP reflect a very wide range of forms of special pleading. They can be found in theocratic movements, nationalist movements, paedophile groups, BDSM advocates and incels (e.g., Rubin, 1992; Hansen, 2021; Sen, 2006;

O'Carroll, 1980; Fekete, 2016). If only the safer targets of race, gender, and homosexuality are reserved for the scorn of critics from the right, then this is a selective engagement. IP are embraced for their instrumental advantage, at times, across the political spectrum (Pilgrim, 2022a).

However, critics of right and left of IP can agree on some shared concerns, for the very reason that their recent social ontology cannot be gainsaid by observers from any political stable. They are inflected heavily with authoritarianism. They casually cast aside a central gain of the Enlightenment (freedom of expression); cancellation, trolling on social media, and ruined careers are part of this wreckage. They invert a traditional scholarly dismissal of ad hominem reasoning with claims of epistemological privilege. With any query of that personalistic authority, follow up claims of bigotry are made about critics.

The suffix of 'phobia' is common in these retorts, which are assertions requiring no rationale. If those within an oppressed group ever challenge the collective line of reasoning expected of them, they are deemed to have internalised such a phobia. Many in the academy have not challenged this shift of norms about freedom of expression, but have simply complied with it at times, using forms of deferential self-censorship to evade career damage.

Until, in their expanding diversity, IP began to displace economic inequities as the focus of the left, the matter of freedom of speech was a given, in its own interests. Indeed, the free speech movement in the USA came from the left, by and large, during the 1960s and there remain some insistent defenders of that tradition today, such as the veteran anarchist Noam Chomsky.

However, the rise of IP has afforded the opportunity for right wing libertarians to claim the defence of freedom of expression as their own; see for example, most of the writers in the highly polished magazine *The Critic*. Other similar expressions in *Sp!ked* reflect a radical switch of former members of the tiny Revolutionary

Communist Party, to now adopt a form of right-wing libertarianism in their attack on IP. That shift was becoming evident in the 1990s, with their short-lived magazine *Living Marxism.* That switch was even rewarded by one in the group now being made a peer of the realm for services to Brexit.

The bottom line is that today distinguishing right from left is increasingly difficult, whether it is in relation to either supporting or scorning IP. IP, right or left, are obsessed by moralisations and a manifest a loss of irony (and humour) about the complexities and uncertainties of life. In an earlier context considering the totalising grip of mass culture in the West, Adorno had spotted that a loss of irony was a tell-tale sign of mindless conformity. IP can be framed as one recent form of the mass culture that he warned of. This new form of self-righteous certainty, with its special feature of 'moral grandstanding' (Tosi & Warmke, 2020), is an elephant in the room that is now difficult to ignore by any honest observer.

When only the politics of protest, since the 1960s, are the focus of critical attention from the right, then IP are dismissed as 'wokery' or 'political correctness.' However, for other reasons, they have also been held in suspicion by many on the left, as was noted above. For this reason, it is an inaccurate empirical binary to conflate IP with the left alone, and their critics with the right alone. To appreciate that ambiguity, it is necessary to trace the antecedents of IP in their wider social context.

3. The Conditions of Possibility for the Emergence of IP

If we consider the social ontology of IP, we see that it is itself empirically complex. If we seek to trace the antecedents of IP, then we find the following:

First, as with critical theory itself, we can identify a confluence of European thought and US cultural sensibilities about personal experience and individual autonomy, but they cannot be conflated, despite efforts to do so by conservative critics of IP. If French post-structuralism began the process, then it was then developed in the USA by critical race theorists and Queer Theorists. The alt-right claims are bogus that the source of recent forms of IP on the left was in Frankfurt in the 1930s.

Second, during the 1960s, the emergence of civil rights resistance in a particular racialized, post-slavery US society, was an important condition of possibility for the rise of forms of IP there. Quick on the heels of antiracism came second wave feminism and gay liberation, which became politically vibrant by the mid-1970s. We see here then the adaptation of French notions (themselves rooted in 19th century German idealism) to the liberal individualism of post-war USA. Autobiographical assertion, with its starting sovereignty (now fetishized as 'lived experience' or 'epistemological privilege') could soon be the basis of small group solidarity, creating the conditions for suspicion and blame in relation to outgroup members.

Third, given the tensions within the feminisms of the 1970s (especially between radical, liberal, and socialist versions) were already signalling the divisive potential of IP, more fragmentation was to come, with the impact of poststructuralism: third wave feminism and Queer Theory (Watkins, 2016). An inherent characteristic of IP is that identities are numerous: at their most absurd they could be unending, meaning that even shared group characteristics could be displaced by individual self-descriptions. There would now be as many identities as there are people and those individuals could even keep changing their notions of self-identity over time.

Fourth, IP in their liberal form are aligned with unfettered voluntarism ('I can be anything I want to be' or 'I am who I am and this must be recognised by others'.) In the sentiment of popular funeral songs we find, 'I did it my way' and 'I am myself and no one else'. These narcissistic self-attributions fit hand in glove with consumerism in late capitalism, with its focus on choice and immediate expressed needs. Moreover, identities themselves can be commodified and marketized. Personal experience is then a source of these processes (what the customer wants) and a potential form of commodity. We now buy not just material products but also preferred subjective 'experiences' and the superrich acquire their expensive tailored authenticity, with a surcharge that can be readily afforded (Frank, 2007).

Fifth, the retreat of the left from the old labour movement and the diminution of the scale and power of trade unions, contributed to the shift of political demands and activity from the workplace to civil society. In the US context, this reflected the muting of class antagonisms and a generic cultural acceptance that system change was not feasible. With the 'end of history' came the assumption that there was the end of ideology. However, postmodern perspectivism itself is a form of ideology (Schwarzmantel, 2008). Ideology did not end, it merely broke up into a range of forms, with IP being one of these.

If society could not be changed, then instead individuals might make their personal direct demands about citizenship (possibly via shared group activity). This was articulated by Herbert Marcuse in his *One Dimensional Man*, which ended then with the prospect of those outside the labour market being a new driver of liberation, including what Marxists had previously dismissed ambivalently as the 'lumpenproletariat'. At the very end of the book, Marcuse cited Walter Benjamin with the rise of the Nazis, with the loose translation: "it is only for those without hope that hope is given to us" (Marcuse, 1964).

Antiracism and the Contestation About Sex and Gender

Two central campaigns arising from variegated NSMs in the past few decades are now examined to elaborate and illustrate the points just made. Antiracism arguably kick-started recent IP trends, initially as a pacifistic movement of black and white activists, seeking racial equality for all US citizens. The Jim Crow laws and segregation practices in education and transport had provoked this resistance, though its key leader Martin Luther King Jr. argued that racism had pervaded US culture even before the slave trade:

> Our nation was born in genocide, when it embraced the doctrine that the original American, the Indian, was an inferior race. Even before there were large numbers of Negroes on our shore, the scar of racial hatred had already disfigured colonial society. From the sixteenth century forward, blood flowed in battles over racial supremacy. We are perhaps the only nation which tried as a matter of national policy to wipe out its indigenous population (King, 1964).

If the emergence of this movement was linked to the particular 20th century context of the USA, this created the tendency, thereafter, to focus on the meaning and salience of race under specific historical conditions and referring to those with dark skins. Recently this has stimulated a critique of race reductionism from the left. For example, Reed argues that:

> In the antiracist political project white supremacy/racism is—like 'terrorism' —an amorphous, ideological abstraction, whose specific content exists largely in the eyes of the beholder. Therefore, like antiterrorism, antiracism's targets can be porous and entirely arbitrary; this means that, also like antiterrorism, the struggle can never be won (Reed, 2018).

That point about an unwinnable struggle recurs in IP and will be picked up again below. Reed (as a black intellectual) considers that race reductionism deflects our attention from supra-personal aspects of capitalism and class-based inequalities in their wake. Once race displaces class as a determinant, then this allows the black middle class in the US to game an advantage over their white peers, leaving poorer people (of any colour) ignored. Reed goes on elsewhere:

> Race should be treated as an historical phenomenon comparable to others—a category I call 'ideologies of ascriptive differentiation' —that comes into existence at a certain point in relation to specific patterns of social relations and institutions. 'Race' is more often taught in universities in a way much closer to how Victorian era racists used it (Reed, 2020, https://daily.jstor.org/adolph-reed-jr-the-perils-of-race-reductionism/).

This point about historicising race rather than leaving it in its doxic form, to mean being black in America today, is also a concern of Wacquant (2022). He insists that race is a reification in that context and is best conceptualised as a variant of ethnicity, to be specified in time and space. He suggests that:

> To assert that race is a subtype of ethnicity, logically as well as historically, is not to deny the brute and brutal reality of racial domination, as feared by activists and scholars who cling to the distinction between race and ethnicity, as if their life depended on it. On the contrary: it is to give ourselves the analytic means to discover under what conditions and due to what forces and mechanisms ordinary ethnicity gets turned into racialized (denigrated) ethnicity, and the difference that naturalization makes in different arenas of social action—say, friendship, marriage, schooling, the labour market, or civic membership (Wacquant, 2022).

These 'arenas of social action' are points in a fluxing open social system that can be studied case by case. That elaboration would displace blanket de-contextualised explanatory accounts, such as 'whiteness' or 'white privilege', applicable *a priori* to whole social groups (cf. DiAngelo, 2018; Kendi, 2019).

Wacquant's doubts about race reductionism in the US cultural context led to him offering a framework of analysis which involves: historicising race; expanding its discussion beyond the 'sin of the West', dislodging the United States of America from its 'Archimedean position'; avoiding the 'logic of the trial' to pre-emptively judge rather than explore; and finally suspending common sense in order to expand our appreciation of ethnic complexity and uncertainty. This is why he favours placing ethnicity, not race, centre stage in what he calls the current 'doxic duet'.

Dislodging the USA from its 'Archimedean position' reinforces Reed's point about historicisation. Moreover, his point about 'the logic of the trial' is pertinent to understanding the confidence of protests within IP and the moralistic certainties, which have become normative. His point about uncertainty encourages epistemic humility as an alternative to the rhetorical binary within IP ('you are either for us or against us'). The simplifications of such binaries became immediately apparent within the NSM of antiracism, which prompted factionalism.

The liberal, pacifistic, racially plural and Christian version predominating at first, soon gave way to a different one: masculinist, Islamic and secessionist. By the 1970s 'race' was coming to mean race as understood in the USA. When the racial focus was on being white then another version of IP arose: the white supremacist movement. This was violent and pitched against the US state in the wake of the ignominy of the victory of the Vietcong (Belew, 2020); it was pro-Aryan but not pro-USA.

When the focus was on being black, the Christian pacifist and the Islamic militant versions diverged. With the latter came accusations of anti-Semitism and of an instrumental collaboration with the white far-right, inviting comparisons with South African apartheid and white-hating 'reverse racism' (Stone, 1976; Allen, 1996). The preference for a religious formation with the black secessionists made sense historically given that in the USA, slaves were subordinated to Christianity, while at the same time their basic humanity was denied (Gerbner, 2018). But historical intelligibility was no guarantee of protection from another version of IP: feminism. The patriarchal character of the masculinist secession movement soon drew criticisms from black feminists (Collins, 2006).

The doubts from the left about antiracism (exemplified by those from Reed and Wacquant) focus then on the problem in IP of the reductionism that is required to sustain special pleading for *this* rather than *that* social group (echoing Hobsbawm). They also raise another question, worthy of exploration, about the relationship between biological and social ontology. Within the human species there is no biological basis for race as a fixed characteristic. What exist are phenotypical differences, which have arisen during the evolution of the species as a result of people moving between climes.

The typical Scandinavian and the typical West African are distinct in appearance but are both humans (defined by the capacity to reproduce together). The false premises of white supremacy (traceable to the doxic European assumption, even of worthies such as Hume and Kant) are now obvious to biologists (Sussman, 2019). A caution here is that there are some tendencies between regional human groups, across the globe, about susceptibility to disease (Dyson et al., 2014; Bickel et al., 1981). However, tendencies and categorical differences are different types of epistemic claim. For example, fair skinned people are more prone to melanoma, but it is a risk for all people.

It is the social ontology of race that has fired the political imagination of both antiracists and racists. As James Baldwin said, 'to be black in America is to be a constant state of rage'. This required that he saw himself and others saw him in a particular way. The Nazi or the KKK member see the white Aryan in a particular way. In the UK, the Generation Identity movement consider that white British people are hard wired to be different and superior.[1]

The term 'identitarian' is used sometimes as a synonym for IP, but it is also used to describe the pan-European racist movement, traceable to Enoch Powell in England and Renaud Camus in France. They shaped the 'great replacement theory', that European 'stock' is being diluted deliberately by dubious ('cosmopolitan') elites by encouraging migration from Africa and Asia. As with the US right, the European right racialize their ethnocentricity with claims of the threat to white Christian values. The 'great replacement theory' is a variation on the older anti-Semitic trope, about the 'Protocols of the Elders of Zion' favoured after the Russian pogroms by fascists in the early 20th century.

This uneven attention to biological and social ontology, in relation to racial IP, is even more obvious in the fractious debates about sex and gender. This is the arena of IP, which is arguably the most contentious and divisive, arising from the claim that all human characteristics are socially constructed, including sex. The radical constructivism adopted in the USA in Third Wave feminism and Queer Theory reworked the French roots of postmodern thought to promote and celebrate variations in both sexuality, note including paedophilia (Rubin, 1992), and gender identity (Butler, 1990).

The implications of these developments have been more divisive than in other arenas of IP probably because of the abrupt stand-off it has created within feminism. The second wave (including both radical and socialist feminists) retained a biological focus. Being born a girl, with XX chromosomes, created a typical trajectory of social and political disadvantage, when thrown into a patriarchal world. For some radical feminists, biology also played a role in male aggression, traceable to differences in testosterone levels between the sexes.

---

1 See: https://www.freep.com/story/opinion/columnists/stephen-henderson/2017/08/14/white-supremecy/564082001/; and https://www.penguin.co.uk/discover/articles/best-james-baldwin-quotes-still-true-relevant-today

For this second wave, sex is described as not 'assigned' at birth, as a woman is an adult female. One is an ontological claim, whereas to 'assign' implies it is an epistemic matter of opinion by adults in the room at the time of birth or an obstetrician viewing an ante-natal scan. The third wave and its partner Queer Theory, riding the very strong incoming tide of postmodernism at the end of the 20th century, claimed that a transwoman is a woman and that both sex and gender are social constructs. The second wave feminists were predominantly gender abolitionists, whereas the third wave emphasised personal choice about gender expression and it tended to retain pre-existing stereotypes of femininity and masculinity.

These opposing groups, note within leftist IP, cannot both be correct about the transitivity or otherwise of biological sex. Sex is either immutable (based on our chromosomes) or it is merely a linguistic matter. That difference of view about epistemology and ontology has underpinned considerable rancour in 'progressive politics' in recent years. Indeed, if one were to invent a divisive topic, implicating a tiny fraction of people, as a diversion from the wider political challenges facing humanity, the transgender debate would fit the bill well.

Transgender activism has created resistance from both second wave feminists, who dismiss it as a version of a conservative men's movement (Brunskell-Evans, 2020) and from scientific realists and ethical objectors within the healthcare professions. The latter have pushed back against the iatrogenic medicalisation of physically healthy children, many of whom are gay, come from abusive family systems, or have autistic challenges (Pilgrim, 2022b).

Biological ontology then is weaponised within IP by either denying its relevance or selectively attending to its features, when it is instrumentally convenient. An example here is the incel movement, with special pleads for young men who cannot find sexual partners. Incels invoke evolutionary biology and psychology to argue that women, not men, control the world. They use the notion of 'strategic pluralism' to defend this view: women are the gatekeepers of sexual activity who look for 'bad boys' to impregnate them (for their strong genes) and 'good boys' to share child rearing within stable pair bonds. As with some radical feminists, they emphasise the role of testosterone to explain why males are determined to impregnate females, if needs be forcefully. Incel ideology thus defends male domination, including rape and violence against women (or even men who have amicable relationships with them).

A Critical Realist Discussion of the Survival of IP

The examples outlined above about race and sex/gender began to introduce some notions from critical realism about ontology and epistemology. That discussion will now be extended by focusing on the uneven consideration of our four planar social being within IP. Whilst the totality of reality is always beyond the grasp of human inquiry, working towards a fuller understanding will fail, for sure on a priori grounds, if all four planes are not respected in principle as sources of causality. If doing our best, in an interdisciplinary context, to keep all four balls in the air is difficult, IP simplifies the task by dropping two of them (consciously or unconsciously).

The recurrent error of reasoning within the ideologies contained within IP is that two planes are differentially emphasised and two are ignored, backgrounded, or used selectively. The two planes emphasised are relationality and unique personal experience (our concrete singularity as personalities or 'souls'). The other two planes are played down to various degrees.

To be clear, the two planes in focus for IP *are* important: partiality does not imply irrelevance. This is why they are an appealing starting point to understand power. Black people really do encounter 'micro-aggressions', such as when a security guard follows them watchfully in a supermarket. Everyday sexism is obvious in the way that women are treated at times in social settings. However, they may be a good starting point, but they are not the alpha and omega of power (as Pragna Patel pointed out above).

As Fraser (1999) noted, if we are to work towards 'parity of participation' then we also must develop a sensibility about the conditions of possibility for existing disparities of power and wealth. Those conditions reside in the supra-personal and the extra-discursive. These are the other two planes (our relationship to the natural world and embedding socio-economic processes and structures, contingent to our lives). Biology does matter then, as do the extra-discursive powers operating in the past and present in society, such as unemployment, poverty and exploitative work practices. It is misleading to reduce power to the personal and the interpersonal, as do all forms of IP, albeit on the basis of widely different value-led claims about human sub-groups. And because these forms of psychological reductionism dominate IP, their weaknesses and contradictions are exposed for critical scrutiny in the following ways:

1. Special pleading for *this* rather than *that* sub-group of humanity will reveal only one aspect of power discrepancies in society. Moreover, it will, and does, then unleash disagreements about priorities, with no clear criteria of adjudication. The phrase Reed uses about antiracism ('the struggle can never be won') applies more generally in IP.

2. The perspectivism germane to special pleading reflects a form of idealism, which is open to legitimate doubt. For Nietzsche to argue that there are 'no facts there are only interpretations' is interestingly wrong. Not only are some factual truths reasonably claimed (e.g., John Doe is a person and is an animal but is not a tiger, or six million Jews were murdered deliberately by the Nazi state), some other forms of truth are there, whatever we do or do not think or say. For example, at the end of the Anthropocene the world will still revolve around the sun and the force of gravity and speed of light will remain the same. Sexual dimorphism (problematized by transgender activism) is true in the mammalian world in 99.99% of

cases.[2] This fact would hold true if our species disappeared tomorrow, but dogs did not.

3. To date there is some evidence that some reforms have been achieved to protect some groups to some degree via the demands of IP. For example, protected characteristics in law can prevent direct discrimination against individuals. However, unless there is overall system change this will always be limited. For example, the alteration of hierarchical positions by enlarging access may do little but achieve the success of some individuals at the expense of others (the point made by Reed about race reductionism and gaming by middle class black people in the USA).

4. The form of direct power expressed in IP is characterised by authoritarianism, moral absolutism, and personalised attacks. Whatever legitimate doubts are expressed about the Enlightenment, it did challenge the arbitrary authority, to be obeyed, of religious clerical elites. The religiosity of IP is clear, and it creates dogmatic certainties warranting the disparagement of a new iteration of 'sinners' (outgroup members deemed on an a priori basis to be morally inferior and hostile, because of their transgressions of word or deed). In the case of some forms of IP, the religiosity point reflects homology not just analogy, such as theocratic identities and organisations, like the Nation of Islam. At times, offence against those religious identities has triggered claims of warranted extra-judicial violent vengeance, which have been acted out 'heroically'. The Charlie Hebdo attacks and the stabbing of Salman Rushdie are examples here of violent religious fervour, as are social media memes of 'Kill A Terf!' typically issued anonymously.

---

2 Sax, L. (2002), "How common is intersex?" *Journal of Sex Research*, 39, 3, pp. 174-8.

More on the Conditions of Possibility for IP

Earlier, the conditions of possibility for the emergence of IP were discussed. These will now be elaborated more, in light of the two illustrative case studies offered, highlighting the biopsychosocial complexity associated with our four planar social being and necessitating interdisciplinary forms of understanding.

1. A trans-historical consideration is that of ontological security in the human species. Our attachment to those we identify with (family, locale, language group, religious affiliation, tribe, etc.) serves that sense of security. People with a shared predicament, task, or worldview tend to converge and attach themselves to one another (homophily). This reflects the second plane of our four planar social being: relationality. The proneness to attachments also reflects plane one and has an evolutionary character. We share the tendency towards homophily with other species ('birds of a feather flock together'). Attachment ensures survival of the species not just individuals within it. These species-specific features from evolution were then over-lain with recorded religious affiliations in the last three thousand years. National loyalties emerged in the past few centuries only, as regional and linguistic groupings were subsumed within the political boundaries of nationhood defined by those in power and in conflict with one another for dominance. The European nations themselves, like France, Germany, and Italy, were not unified even at the very point they indulged in colonial adventurism abroad (see e.g., Weber, 1976). As language users, we can now symbolise our loyalties beyond proximate ties with our fellows in a locale or nation, especially aided by new social media (see below). IP are one, but not the only, version of these 'imagined communities' (Steger, 2008; Anderson, 1983).

2. As individuals we are prone to cognitive and emotional habits that protect our ego and ward off internal and external threats to it. In psychoanalysis the defence mechanisms of splitting and

projection describe these processes. We split off threats to the ego and project them outwards onto outgroup members. This both creates in-group loyalty and it protects the security of the individual. Cognitive psychology offers another version of this process of ego protection: fast and slow thinking, which is considered to have evolved in our species during the fight-flight mode of personal defence (against enemies or predators) (Kanhneman, 2011). We are then 'wired' to defend ourselves intuitively and rapidly, when faced with threat (or when identifying prey). As with point 1 just noted, we see the relevance of the personal (plane 4) to roots in our biological past (plane 1). However, with our enlarged cerebrum, that fast thinking was overlain by slow deliberation, which was the basis of sustainable and transmissible forms of knowledge, including reflective wisdom (phronesis), academic knowledge (episteme) and practical know-how (techne). Today we are capable of both fast and slow thinking, but some social contexts will encourage one more than the other. IP reflects a clear imbalance based upon rapid thinking, which triggers rigid binary, or black and white, reasoning. By contrast, slow thinking entails permitted doubts or changes of mind (epistemic humility), option appraisal, and careful and respectful exploration in the presence of others (Dutton, 2020). The norms of IP tend to undermine this scenario of exploring nuance and complexity, intelligently and maturely.

3. Biology is also relevant to our capacity for meaning seeking, which is both an individual pursuit and a social activity. The impulse to seek freedom begins in the unconscious (the instinctual need to discharge desire and aggression, despite the constraints imposed by others in the world and reality more generally). As we mature, social transaction and compromise then emerge through adaptive argumentation. The latter is the source of both knowledge production and deliberative democracy (Arendt, 2005; von Heiseler, 2020; Mercier & Sperber, 2011). Once we negotiate with others, then we have to create norms of pragmatic engagement, and freedom of expres-

sion is a necessary condition for that engagement (Nossel, 2020). However, IP are selectively attentive to this point (or at times treat it with seeming indifference). Authoritarian and repressive norms might emerge along with a hierarchy of authority and entitlement. These might be structured by religion, patriarchy, wealth, property ownership, social status, sex, ethnicity, or age. In turn, such hierarchies will be destabilised by resistance from the less powerful or those excluded from power. Conflicts then ensue inevitably between those sustaining regimes of power and those challenging them.

4. As Erich Fromm noted in his views on the rise of both Stalinism and Nazism, our socialisation in the family and the securities that this brings (see point 1 above) can make us prone to masochistic obedience. This psychodynamic theme of accounting for authoritarianism was explored subsequently by Theodor Adorno, and earlier by Wilhelm Reich. The authoritarianism now pervading IP on the left reflect a re-emergence of a version of that sado-masochistic tendency, but now inflected by modern norms of individualism. Under Stalinism strict conformity was to the vanguard party and its apparatchiks. However, under the IP of the left today, conformity is to an in-group defined by a shared identity or the masochistic obeisance of outgroup members, who crave an 'ally' status, when virtue signalling, while lacking the necessary 'lived experience' to ever warrant full respect. (Other benign emotions of pity and compassion may be at play as well here, and so must be conceded case by case when demonstrable.)

The postmodern turn created a paradox. On the one hand, the 'I can be anything I want to be' emphasis reflected a form of asserted libertarianism or 'anything goes'. On the other hand, to sustain that assertion others have to comply with the demand, thereby curtailing their freedom of expression. The emergence of newer forms non-conformity to be punished include being identified as a 'TERF', 'white silence is violence', 'misgendering', 'dead naming' and existing in a state of unconfessed or 'unchecked' personal privilege. That non-conformity also includes saying the 'wrong' thing; hence IP encouraging an anxious norm of watching our 'Ps and Qs' in everyday life, as well as self-censorship in the academy.

5. The cultural norms of the USA at the end of the 20th century are another important condition of possibility to consider. Mention was made above about the rise of the civil rights movement and the point made by Marcuse about the blocking of class-based struggles to create a mollified and neutered form of social conformity. With macro-system change now pre-empted, this limited the left in the USA to contingent culturally acceptable alternatives, which had to endorse individualism and the assumption of freedom of choice in the market place. Choosing to be anything one wanted to be was thus normative within that cultural setting. Increasingly, the left began to love diversity and ignore socio-economic inequality (Michaels, 2006). However, empirically this was complicated by the initial endorsement of one version of intersectionality, with a sensitivity to embedding socio-economic conditions. After the postmodern turn, this residue of reasoning, which gave due respect to the third plane of our four planar social being was displaced by a different emphasis: the valorisation of a kaleidoscope of subjectivities. Plane 3 was backgrounded and plane 4 kicked in strongly with its emphasis on lived experience and epistemological privilege. The material ontological underpinnings of power were thereby backgrounded, more and more, within the discourse of intersectionality and its newer forms of individualism and victimhood (Bell, 1973; Crenshaw, 1991; Flatschart, 2017).

6. In the past decade the above conditions have been added to by a newly emergent technological one: social media and their rapid responding norms and safe anonymity for protagonists (or antagonists). The new norms of social media encouraged fast, not slow, thinking. The emphasis was on speed and brevity, not considered elaboration (slow thinking and attempts at deliberative democracy). Moreover, another emergent norm was that the alias, previously a

characteristic of crooks and scoundrels, became socially acceptable and routine. Interactions on social media are now often between people with pseudonyms and so authorial responsibility for content cannot be traced and the ethical responsibility of named participants cannot be expected. This is a formula for disrespectful spite and casual bullying.

This then is the new technological context for IP and its encouragement of 'clictivism'. With no deliberation, in less than a second a respondent can endorse or dismiss the views of others in the world. Communities of 'clickers' shape positive or negative emotions of those, who they often do not know personally and may never meet. The technology severs the link between conduct and its consequences, routinizing forms of disrespect, which would be unacceptable in the older norms of faces to face contact. Celebrity provocateurs encourage controversy for narcissistic and financial gain using 'clickbait' (Charles, 2020) in a normative narcissistic context in which to be offensive is preferable to being ignored.

7. A functional aspect of IP relates to their alignment ideologically and commercially with neoliberalism. Identities can be commodified and turned into marketing targets (Yewande et al. 2020; Goulding, 1999; Matthews & Besemer, 2015). The moralistic character of IP also makes them a safe source of pieties and virtue-signalling. For example, cable sports channels promote Black Lives Matter. When the players take the knee at the start of the game the commentator can say sternly, with no threat to his employer's interests, 'we must root out racism wherever it occurs on or off the field'. This ethical attention does not extend to examining the money laundering of Russian kleptocrats or the promotion of the international gambling industry, which can ruin the lives of ordinary fans. Recently in Britain some black players have begun to refuse the ritual of 'taking the knee' for being an empty gesture. To use another recent example of cost-free commercial virtue signalling, British supermarkets swiftly changed the labelling of packets of 'Chicken

Kiev' to 'Chicken Kyiv'. They were in tune with their customers, many of whom had replaced their house Union Jack, post-Brexit proud, with the Ukrainian flag.

8. A final condition of possibility to consider is long term depression on the left. One plausible reading of the 20th century is that it was largely a pattern of defeat: the betrayal of the Russian revolution and its culmination in Stalinism; the failure of the British general strike; the failure of the German left to stop the rise of Nazism; the brutal turning of Marxist-Leninist elites on their own people in China, Cambodia, and North Korea; the weakening of social democratic gains in Europe (e.g., the success of Blairism and the failure of Corbynism the UK); and the seemingly unending adaptability of capitalism, culminating most recently in a culture of narcissism, superficial materialism, and the fetish of consumption under the regime of neoliberalism.

Faced with that pattern, the promise of instant success, via daily moralisations and legalistic efforts to end racism or offer 'protected characteristics', like gender, age, or disability, afforded a new optimism about social justice. IP then is, in part, a collective manic defence against the grim complexity of the world. With the emergence of new social media, those prospective victories for social justice might even be achieved on a laptop, without even leaving one's seat, let alone home. Charles (2020) describes 'clictivism' in the British vernacular as 'it wants to be activism but it can't be arsed'.

The long struggle to find a stable form of humanistic socialism untainted by sado-masochistic forms of authoritarianism (for example aspired to by Fromm) has now given way, in large part, to the preference for IP. However, authoritarianism has been sustained within the left version of the latter, while the theocratic and xenophobic right continue with their own version of indignant and often violent IP. Despite the claimed values of progressive IP of respect and recognition (Sennett, 2000; Honneth, 1995), many on the left have been preoccupied in practice with the very opposite in relation to any non-conformist or those failing the test of prescribed moral purity.

'Calling out', 'the cancel culture', censorship and self-censorship resonate still with the dynamics of the KGB or Stasi, and their citizen-collaborator informants, described so well in the evergreen literature of George Orwell. The end game of this new regime of 'progressive authoritarianism' remains unclear, given Reed's observation that the 'struggle can never be won'. Daily moral recriminations are debilitating and any evidence of social progress they achieve is not always easy to discern. After the manic defence of IP fails, the left may need to come down with a bump about the seriousness of its long-term challenges.

Conclusion

An explanatory critique of IP has been offered, which identifies the failure, to date, of respectful deliberative democracy, favoured by anti-authoritarian theorists like Hannah Arendt, as an alternative to representative democracy and its perennial risk of capture by violent ethnocentricity. The authoritarianism and binary reasoning common to IP in practice subvert, they do not enhance, deliberative democracy and universalism. The role of new social media has encouraged 'clictivism' at the expense of genuine activism and solidarity. Slow reflection and full debate, in a tolerant spirit of mutuality with our fellows, including those we do not agree with, have been displaced by an angry suspicion of outgroup members. Consequently, subgroups of humanity have been divided against one another. Dogmatism has displaced epistemic humility. Moreover, to use Wacquant's apposite phrasing, 'the logic of the trial' has displaced the cautious appraisal of the ontological complexity of fluxing 'arenas of social action' in open human systems.

The emergence of IP in their modern form since the 1960s can, on the one hand invite, or even demand, obedience to progressive values, newly defined and articulated. On the other hand, they can invite slow and sceptical curiosity about the very form itself. The above discussion has used the resource of critical realism for that task. The doubts expressed by leftist critics of IP have been expanded in the chapter to explain why, despite their clear limitations, for now they have survived and have been incorporated readily into both public policy and mass culture.

The synergistic conditions of possibility for the emergence of IP have been elaborated. Their focus on planes 2 and 4 of our four planar social being are a legitimate starting point of understanding power. However, without an equal respect for planes 1 and 3, IP will produce partial and reductionist forms of political understanding. They will also confuse persistent moralisations with a plausible political strategy. These moralisations induce guilt, shame, and anxiety in the daily lives of us all, while creating self-reinforcing but unreflective pride for in-group members. Whether this emotional climate encourages human emancipation is open to debate. Such moralisations, with their personal and interpersonal character, will pose no serious threat to the current political and economic interests of our global elites.

As Fisher, Reed, and Charles noted, IP do not challenge neoliberalism, and so structural inequalities of wealth and power remain unscathed. That lack of threat for now aids and abets the survival of IP. As with the NSMs, with which they partially articulate, IP are an ongoing presence in civil society. A consequence of this presence has been that a cause once so strongly defended by the left, freedom of expression, has now been abandoned instrumentally, thereby undermining an important gain of the Enlightenment.

References

Allen, E. (1996) "Religious heterodoxy and nationalist tradition: the continuing evolution of the Nation of Islam," *The Black Scholar*. 26 (3–4): 2–34.

Anderson, B. (1983) *Imagined Communities: Reflections on the Origin and Spread of Nationalism*. London: Version.

Archer, M. (2000) *Being Human: The Problem of Agency*. Cambridge: Cambridge University Press.

Arendt, H. (2005) *The Promise of Politics*. New York: Schocken.

Belew, S. (2020) *Bringing the War Home: The White Power Movement and Paramilitary America*. Harvard: Harvard University Press.

Bell, D. (1973) *Race, Racism and American*. Law New York: Little Brown.

Bhaskar, R. (2016) *Enlightened Common Sense: The Philosophy of Critical Realism*. London: Routledge.

Bhaskar, R. (1997) "On the Ontological Status of Ideas," *Journal for the Theory of Social Behaviour*. 27, 2/3, 135-7.

Bickel, H.; Bachmann, C.; Beckers, R. et al. (1981) "Neonatal mass screening for metabolic disorders," *European Journal of Pediatrics*. 137, 137, 133–139.

Brunskell-Evans, H. (2020) *Transgender Body Politics*. North Geelong: Spinifex.

Butler, J. (1990) *Gender Trouble: Feminism and the Subversion of Identity*. New York: Routeldge.

Callinicos, A. (1991) *Against Postmodernism: A Marxist Critique*. Bristol: Polity.

Charles, A.D. (2020) *Outraged: Why Everyone is Shouting and No One Is Talking*. London: Bloomsbury.

Collier, A. (1981) "Scientific realism and the human world: The case of psychoanalysis," *Radical Philosophy* 0-29, Autumn.

Collins, P.H. (2006) *From Black Power to Hip Hop: Racism, Nationalism, and Feminism*. Philadelphia: Temple University Press.

Craib, I. (1997) "Social constructionism as a social psychosis," *Sociology* 31, 1, 1-15.

Crenshaw, K. (1991) "Mapping the margins: intersectionality, identity politics, and violence against women of color," *Stanford Law Review*. 43, 6, 1241–1299.

DiAngelo, R. (2018) *White Fragility: Why It's So Hard for White People to Talk about Racism*. New York: Beacon Press.

Dutton, K. (2020) *Black and White Thinking: The Burden of a Binary Brain in a Complex World*. London: Bantam.

Dyson, S., Atkin, K. and Culley, L. (2014) "Critical realism, agency and sickle cell: case studies of young people with sickle cell disorder at school," *Ethnic and Racial Studies* 2379-2398.

Elder-Vass, D. (2012) *The Reality of Social Construction*. Cambridge: Cambridge University Press.

Fekete, L. (2016) "Hungary: Power, punishment and the 'Christian-national ideal'," *Race and Class,* 57(4), 39–53.

Fisher, M. (2013) "Exiting the Vampire Castle," *The North Star,* 29 November.

Flatschart, E. (2017) "Feminist standpoints and critical realism: the contested materiality of difference in intersectionality and the new materialism," *Journal of Critical Realism* 16, 3, 284-302.

Frank, R. (2007) *Richistan: A Journey Through the 21st Century Wealth Boom and the Lives of the New Rich*. New York: Random House.

Fraser, N. (1999) "Social justice in an age of identity politics: redistribution, recognition and participation," In Ray, L. and Sayer, A. (eds.), *Culture and Economy after the Cultural Turn* (pp. 25-52) London: Sage.

Gerbner, K. (2018) *Christian Slavery: Conversion and Race in the Protestant Atlantic World.* Philadelphia: University of Pennsylvania Press.

Goulding, C. (1999) "Heritage, nostalgia, and the 'grey' consumer," *Journal of Marketing Practice: Applied Marketing Science*, 5(6), 177–199.

Habermas, J. (1981) "New Social Movements," *Telos* 49: 33-37.

Hansen, T.B. (2021) *The Law of Force: The Violent Heart of Indian Politics.* New Delhi: Aleph Books.

Hochschild, A.R. (2016) *Strangers in their Own Land: Anger and Mourning on the American Right.* New York: New Press.

Honneth, A. (1995) *The Struggle for Recognition: The Moral Grammar of Social Conflicts.* Cambridge: Polity Press.

Jamin J. (2014). *Cultural Marxism and the Radical Right. The Post-War Anglo-American Far Right: A Special Relationship of Hate.* Palgrave Macmillan UK. pp. 84–103.

Kahneman, D. (2011) *Thinking Fast and Slow.* New York: Macmillan.

Kendi, I.X. (2019) *How To Be An Anti-Racist.* New York: Bodley Head.

King, M.L. (1964) *Why We Can't Wait.* New York: Harper and Row.

Marcuse, H. (1964) *One Dimensional Man.* New York: Beacon Press.

Matthews, P. and Besemer, K. (2015) "The 'Pink Pound' in the 'Gaybourhood?' Neighbourhood Deprivation and Sexual Orientation in Scotland," *Housing, Theory and Society*, 32 (1), pp. 94-111.

Mercier, H. and Sperber, D. (2011) "Why do humans reason? Arguments for an argumentative theory," *Behavioral and Brain Sciences*, 34, 2, 57-74.

Michaels, W.B. (2006) *The Trouble With Diversity: How We Learned to Love Identity and Ignore Inequality*. New York: Macmillan.

Norrie, A. (2009) *Dialectic and Difference: Dialectical Critical Realism and the Grounds of Justice*. London: Routledge.

Nossel, S. (2020) *Dare To Speak: Defending Free Speech for All*. New York: HarperCollins.

O'Carroll, T. (1980) *Paedophilia: The Radical Cause*. London: Owen.

Pilgrim, D. (2022a) *Identity Politics: Where Did It All Go Wrong?* Bicester: Phoenix Books.

Pilgrim, D. (2022b) "Transgender debates and healthcare: a critical realist account," *Health*. 26, 5, 535-553.

Porpora, D.V. (2015) *Reconstructing Sociology: The Critical Realist Approach*. Cambridge: Cambridge University Press.

Reed, A. (2018) "Antiracism: a neoliberal alternative to a left," *Dialectical Anthropology* 42, 105-115.

Rubin, G. (1992) "Thinking sex: notes for a radical theory of the politics of sexuality," In C.S. Vance (ed.), *Pleasure and Danger: Exploring Female Sexuality*. London: Pandora.

Sayer, A. (2000) *Realism and Social Science*. London: Sage.

Schwarzmantel, J. (2008) *Ideology and Politics*. London: Sage.

Sen, A. (2006) *Identity and Violence: The Illusion of Destiny*. New York: Norton.

Sennett, R. (2000) *Respect In A World of Inequality*. London: Penguin.

Sobolewska, M. and Ford, R. (2020) *BrexitLand*. Cambridge: Cambridge University Press.

Stahl, R. M., & Popp-Madsen, B. A. (2022). "Defending democracy: Militant and popular models of democratic self-defense," *Constellations*, 00, 1– 19. https://doi.org/10.1111/1467-8675.12639.

Steger, M. B. (2008) *The Rise of the Global Imaginary; Political Ideologies from the French Revolution to the Global War on Terror.* Oxford: Oxford University Press.

Stone, J. (1976) "Black nationalism and apartheid: Two variations on a separatist theme," *Social Dynamics.* 2 (1): 19–31.

Sussman, R.W. (2019) *The Myth of Race: The Troubling Persistence of an Unscientific Idea.* Cambridge: Harvard University Press.

Tosi, J. and Warmke, B. (2020) *Grandstanding: The Use of Moral Talk.* Oxford: Oxford University Press Online.

Touraine, A. (1981). *The Voice and the Eye: An Analysis of Social Movements.* Cambridge: Cambridge University Press.

Vogler, G (2022). "A critical realist contribution to debates on complicity in systemic injustice and violence," *Constellations.*22; 29: 107– 120.

von Heiseler T.N. (2020) "The social origin of the concept of truth - how statements are built on disagreements," *Frontiers in Psychology* Apr 28;11:733.

Wacquant, L. (2022) "Resolving the trouble with 'race'," *New Left Review* 133/4.

Watkins, S. (2018) "Which feminisms?" *New Left Review* 109, 5-76.

Weber, E. (1976) *Peasants into Frenchmen: The Modernization of Rural France, 1870-1914.* Stanford: Stanford University Press.

Yewande O. A., Ball, B. and Adams, K-A. (2020) "For us, by them?: A study on black consumer identity congruence and brand preference," *Howard Journal of Communications*, 31:4, 351-371.

3

WHAT'S WRONG WITH WHITENESS THEORY

JONATHAN CHURCH

Introduction

"Whiteness Studies" is an active area of academic research and popular writing in the ongoing attempt to grapple with race relations in America. The critique of Whiteness, a core objective of (critical) Whiteness Studies, is not designed as a malign attack on white people. Rather, it seeks to investigate, scrutinize, and decenter social norms, customs, beliefs, behaviors, and practices that purportedly uphold white supremacy. Whiteness is conceived as an ideological and discursive apparatus—ways of thinking, talking, and behaving in our routine interpersonal relationships—that sustains unequal social relations between white and nonwhite people. This apparatus consists of purportedly "white" beliefs in individualism, universalism, rationality, objectivity, and other ideas rooted in Enlightenment epistemology and values.[1] The

---

1 The supposedly Enlightenment values of universalism, individualism, rationality, and objectivity refer to the idea that individuals should be regarded as partaking in a common universal humanity, or universal human

underlying thesis is that the centering of Whiteness in American culture is a significant contributing factor to persistent racial inequality.

Like Critical Race Theory and the sociological study of racism, Whiteness Studies defines racism not simply as the expression of prejudice and discriminatory intent, but as a system of structural inequality in which a racialized prevailing group (e.g., white people) dominates and oppresses a racialized marginalized group (e.g., non-white people). The engine of this system of domination is a set of norms and beliefs that elevate the social status of white people at the expense of non-white people. These norms and beliefs mutate and evolve in response to circumstances, but they invariably support, preserve, and enforce exclusionary social practices that uphold white supremacy.

Race is not an immutable biological characteristic. It is a feature ascribed to people based on historically derived beliefs that constitute the ideological scaffold of a racist system. Society "racializes" people as white or black when people habitually define racial identity in terms of traits such as skin pigmentation that are arbitrary rather than fundamental to who they are as human beings. In other words, race is "socially constructed." It may be that government policies have engendered these racist ideas,[2] or that racist ideas have engendered racist policies, or both,[3] but in either case, "white

----

nature, that transcends their social and historical circumstances, and that this universal standard of human nature entails a faculty for rational thinking that is able to assess the world objectively and from a standpoint of neutrality. Race scholars and activists tend to believe that these Enlightenment values reflect a "white" commitment to color-blind ideology that ignores the difficulty, if not the impossibility, of assuming the neutral perspective of a non-racialized self, i.e., an identity independent of the historical circumstances in which one becomes a self. For discussion, see Gary Peller, "Race Consciousness," 1990, *Duke Law Journal,* pp. 758-847 (1990).

2 Ibram X. Kendi, *Stamped from the Beginning,* (New York: Bold Type Books, 2016).

3 Jonathan Church, "Ibram Kendi's Thesis Could Use a Lot More Rigor," Part 1, *Merion West,* November 7, 2020, https://merionwest.com/2020/11/07/ibram-kendis-thesis-could-use-a-lot-more-rigor/. Jonathan Church, "Ibram

privilege" —the benefits that white people derive from exclusionary social practices—is the result of a historical process in which social norms and institutions that stem from specific ideas and policies have racialized some people as white and other people as nonwhite.

Whiteness Studies seeks to reveal how "white" social practices continue to center and empower people racialized as white, while marginalizing and disempowering people racialized as nonwhite. The objective is to expose and decenter Whiteness as a prevailing system of social norms that institutionalize structural inequality between whites and nonwhites. In so doing, however, the examination of Whiteness can exhibit a tendency to perceive Whiteness as a kind of "virus" that permanently, pervasively infects and endangers the whole of society. "Whiteness," in other words, "is a public health crisis…[that] shortens life expectancies . . . pollutes air . . . constricts equilibrium . . . devastates forests . . . melts ice caps . . . sparks (and funds) wars . . . lattens dialects . . . infests consciousnesses, and . . . kills people—white people and people who are not white."[4]

This singular, all-encompassing mindset deploys an analytical framework in which racism is conceived as a system of ubiquitous, rigid, exploitative social relations between white and nonwhite people. Omowale Akintunde, an African American scholar and filmmaker, once stated that "[r]acism is a systemic, societal, institutional, omnipresent, and epistemologically embedded phenomenon that pervades every vestige of our reality."[5] Similarly, in seeking to ex-

Kendi's Thesis Could Use a Lot More Rigor," Part 2, *Merion West*, November 12, 2020, https://merionwest.com/2020/11/12/ibram-kendis-thesis-could-use-a-lot-more-rigor-part-ii/.

4   Damon Young, "Whiteness Is a Pandemic," *The Root*, March 17, 2021, https://www.theroot.com/whiteness-is-a-pandemic-1846494770.

5   Robin DiAngelo, *White Fragility: Why It's So Hard for White People to Talk about Racism,* (Boston, MA: Beacon Press, 2018), p. 72. Omowale Akintunde, "White Racism, White Supremacy, White Privilege, and the Social Construction of Race: Moving from Modernist to Postmodernist Multiculturalism," *Multicultural Education*, Winter 1999, Vol. 7, No. 2, pp. 2-8.

pose Whiteness as a core pillar of racial inequality, scholars and activists of Whiteness acquire the habit of perceiving Whiteness as a systemic, societal, institutional, omnipresent, and epistemologically embedded phenomena that pervades every vestige of American society. White people, even "good white people,"[6] cannot help but be infected by the insidious virus of "Whiteness."

In her seminal paper on "white fragility" theory, Robin DiAngelo writes that "Whiteness Studies begin with the premise that racism and white privilege exist in both traditional and modern forms, and rather than work to prove its existence, work to reveal it."[7] In one sentence, DiAngelo illustrates both the central contribution and the central shortcoming of Whiteness Studies. The meritorious aim of exposing racism and white privilege is clear enough, though in keeping with a theme we will explore later in this chapter, "racism" and "white privilege" are not without ambiguity. In practice, however, the project of Whiteness Studies can become unmoored when, in its zeal to expose racism and white privilege, it risks succumbing to cognitive errors like apophenia and confirmation bias.

Apophenia is the tendency to believe that unrelated things or occurrences have meaningful connections. Confirmation bias is the tendency to consider only evidence that supports a belief and to ignore evidence that does not support a belief. Apophenia and confirmation bias both weaken the epistemic discipline of Whiteness Studies by fueling a "hermeneutics of suspicion"[8] that strives heroically to perceive the shadow of Whiteness in every thought and action of white (and nonwhite) people. As Robin DiAngelo insists,

---

6 Shannon Sullivan, *Good White People: The Problem with Middle-Class White Anti-Racism,* (Albany, New York: State University of New York Press, 2014).

7 Robin DiAngelo, "White Fragility," *International Journal of Critical Pedagogy,* Vol 3 (3) (2011), p. 56.

8 Joseph Heath, "When does Critical Theory Become Conspiracy Theory?" *Department of Philosophy, University of Toronto,* https://utoronto.academia. edu/JosephHeath.

"the question is not, is this racist, but how is racism manifesting in this situation?"[9] As regards Whiteness, the labor historian Eric Arsenen has observed, "whiteness has become a blank screen onto which those who claim to analyze it can project their own meanings."[10]

This tenacious commitment has the virtue of a rousing, dogged, and noble effort to unwind the ideological and discursive apparatus of white supremacy. There is no doubt that racism has blighted American history, and that a deeply embedded culture of "white" expectations about the social roles of white and nonwhite people has established white supremacy as an enduring force in the development of American history. It is also true, however, that American history is not exclusively a story about racism and white supremacy, and that there has been a great deal of progress in the effort to dissolve and dismantle the culture of white supremacy.

Whiteness scholars and activists seem not to agree. When Robin DiAngelo insists that "the question is not, is this racist, but how is racism manifesting in this situation,"[11] she gives voice to an obsession afflicting Whiteness scholars and activists that not only tends to overlook or downplay the progress that has been made in racial relations, but also positions Whiteness as an indelible and incorrigible foundation of American society. As a result, Whiteness Studies can fall into a dogmatic slumber that, as this chapter explains, overlooks three logical fallacies that threaten to undermine its enterprise: (1) fallacy of begging the question, (2) fallacy of reification, and (3) fallacy of ambiguity.

---

9   Robin DiAngelo, "Anti-Racism Handout," https://robindiangelo.com/wp-content/uploads/2016/06/Anti-racism-handout-1-page-2016.pdf.

10   Eric Arsenen, "Whiteness and Historians' Imagination," *International Labor and Working-Class History Society*, Vol. 60, October 2001, pp. 3-32.

11   Robin DiAngelo, "Anti-Racism Handout," https://robindiangelo.com/wp-content/uploads/2016/06/Anti-racism-handout-1-page-2016.pdf.

Whiteness as a Means of Social Control

In *The Invention of the White Race*, Theodore W. Allen argues that Whiteness emerged in American history as a tool used by the ruling class to control the working class.[12] For example, Allen provides a detailed account of centuries of British oppression in Ireland, only to show that this history of oppression did not, as might be expected, inspire solidarity with African Americans among Irish American immigrants who came to identify as "white" upon their settlement in New York City. Cultivation of the Irish vote by Tammany Hall, which supported the antebellum regime of slavery and white supremacy, aligned the interests of Irish immigrants with the interests of the Southern plantation class. This political alignment cut off any potential that Irish immigrants might join forces with African Americans to challenge the rule of "white" capital.

Given that "white" European immigrants vastly outnumbered African Americans in the competition for jobs in New York City, working class Irish immigrants did not support the Tammany Hall machine, and its opposition to abolitionism, because they feared job competition from African Americans. Instead, Irish immigrants in New York City supported the Tammany Hall machine because they received "white skin" privileges such as rights to immigration, naturalization, and suffrage. Tammany Hall political patronage then helped Irish immigrants in New York City to assimilate into "white" American politics, culture, and industry. Despite their ancestral history of racial oppression in Ireland, working class Irishmen adopted the political interests of the American ruling racial class because Whiteness elevated their political and social status, and leverage, relative to African Americans.

This story is familiar to other scholars of Whiteness, such as Ian Haney Lopez, David Roediger, and Joe Feagin. In *White by Law*,

---

12 Theodore W. Allen, *The Invention of the White Race: The Origin of Racial Oppression*, (London, New York: Verso, 1994, 1997, 2012, 2021).

Lopez traces the "legal construction of race" by examining the history of legislative action and court rulings by which people came to be regarded as "white." In 1790, for example, the U.S. Congress enacted legislation that restricted naturalized citizenship to "white" immigrants. As Lopez writes, "[f]rom the earliest years of this country until just a generation ago, being a 'white person' was a condition for acquiring citizenship." He cautions, however, that determining who was white "was often no easy question."[13] In the case of *Ozawa v. United States,* Takao Ozawa applied to become an American citizen in 1914. He supported his case by listing several aspects of his life that supposedly proved that "at heart I am a true American."[14]

Ozawa informed the court that he had been educated in American schools, that he sent his children to an American church and an American school, that he spoke English at home in part to prevent his children from learning Japanese, and that he had lived in the United States for more than 28 years. Nevertheless, as Lopez writes, "[t]he U.S. District Attorney for the District of Hawaii opposed Ozawa's application on the ground that he was of the 'Japanese race' and therefore not a 'white person'."[15]

Ozawa pursued his case for citizenship in the courts for eight years, but he was consistently denied citizenship. When his case reached the U.S. Supreme Court, he "acknowledged that he was of Japanese descent, but nonetheless asserted that his skin made him 'white'."[16] The Court was not convinced, arguing that race and skin color are not necessarily synonymous—e.g., one can have light skin and still be non-white.[17] At the time, scientists had not reached a consensus on what "race" encompasses, but "the vast majority of

---

13 Ian Haney Lopez, *White by Law: The Legal Construction of Race,* (New York and London: New York University Press, 2006), p. 1.

14 Ibid., p. 56.

15 Ibid., p. 56.

16 Ibid., p. 57.

17 Ibid., p. 58.

experts consistently placed the Japanese wholly outside of the Caucasian race." The Court thus denied Ozawa's application by defining "white" as "Caucasian," or alternatively, associating "non-Caucasian" with "non-white."[18]

The development of Whiteness in American history, then, has not been a simple matter of distinguishing between people of different skin color. Whiteness is malleable and multifaceted. Three months after the *Ozawa* case, the U.S. Supreme Court rejected the application for citizenship of Asian Indian immigrant Bhagat Singh Thind, who had argued that he was Caucasian based on anthropological classifications that included Asian Indians as Caucasian.[19] The Supreme Court conceded that he had Caucasian ancestors, but then wrote that, "It may be true that the blond Scandinavian and the brown Hindu have a common ancestor in the dim reaches of antiquity, but the average man knows perfectly well that there are unmistakable and profound differences between them today."[20] In other words, a brown Hindu was not "white" because the "average man" thought so.

The meaning of Whiteness evolved not only in a legal context, but also in social, linguistic, cultural, and other contexts. In *Working towards Whiteness*, Roediger examines how generations of Northern and Southern European immigrants gradually came to be regarded as "white" after initial resistance. He notes that writers rarely drew a distinction between race and ethnicity before 1930, so various groups of European immigrants usually encountered prejudice not in ethnic but in racial terms.[21]

For example, after Italians were lynched in Louisiana in 1891, Roediger writes, "the press justified the atrocity by pointing to south-

---

18   Ibid., p. 60.

19   Ibid., p. 61.

20   Ibid., p. 63.

21   David Roediger, *Working Toward Whiteness,* (New York: Basic Books, 2005), p. 23.

ern Italian biology and habits" —e.g., their "low, receding foreheads, repulsive countenances, and slovenly attire." At the turn of the 20th century, the concept of race in American society encompassed "[d]ifferences in language, the arts, social organization, and aspiration." Theodore Roosevelt and others, for example, often employed the term "English-speaking races."[22]

These investigations are only a sample of many that illustrate how the history of white supremacy in American society depends on the meaning of Whiteness, and how this meaning has included different ethnic groups over time. Defining Whiteness, and distinguishing between white and nonwhite, have been no easy matter. But the institutionalization of white supremacy is foundationally grounded on this ongoing construction of Whiteness as a racialized identity for purposes of social control.

Understanding this development, and subjecting it to critique, are essential to undoing the legacy of white supremacy. This effort is undoubtedly a worthy and requisite project if we are to act upon the words of Martin Luther King, Jr. that "the arc of (America's) moral universe is long but bends toward justice."[23] Unfortunately, movement along the arc is a slow, grinding, and haphazard process in the face of inertia built into the racial status quo after centuries of institutionalized white supremacy.

A central pillar of this racial hierarchy is what sociologist Joe Feagin calls the "white racial frame." This frame refers to how our perceptions of white and non-white people entail deep-rooted assumptions and expectations that reflect, and stem from, perceptions of white people as superior to nonwhite people, effectively elevating the social status of white people above, and at the expense of,

---

22 Ibid., p. 52.

23 Deborah Ellis, "The Arc of the Moral Universe is Long, But it Bends Toward Justice," October 21, 2011, https://obamawhitehouse.archives.gov/blog/2011/10/21/arc-moral-universe-long-it-bends-toward-justice.

nonwhite people.[24] Centuries of white supremacy have given rise to a slew of routine everyday expectations about social roles and practices ascribed to people of different races. For example, human resource managers may associate "black names" with lower job performance, and thus call back fewer black applicants than white applicants after reviewing their resumes.[25]

This "white racial frame" entails expectations that continually reinforce the biases that undergird racial hierarchy. To topple white supremacy, we must change the expectations that reinforce this "white" racial frame in which white people are perceived as superior to nonwhite people. It is necessary to decenter Whiteness by, for example, questioning the assumptions we make about "black names" or the subliminal messages we receive when we watch movies in which white and black actors assume conventional racialized roles within the storyline (e.g., Scarlett O'Hara and Mammy in *Gone with the Wind*). These are only two of innumerable examples one can invoke to illustrate the operation of racial expectations that underlie the "white racial frame" of white supremacy.

This is an important insight into the nature of racial equality. However, the study of the "white racial frame" must be conducted with care if it is not to undermine its own effort with a zeal so overwhelming that it weakens the epistemic discipline that must be brought to bear on any scholarly enterprise, especially one aiming for insight into the regime of white supremacy. The "white racial frame" can become as much of an epistemic frame as it is a racial frame. The study of Whiteness may become so keen on finding

---

24   Joe R. Feagin, *The White Racial Frame: Centuries of Racial Framing and Counter-Framing,* (New York, NY: Taylor & Francis, 2013).

25   Joe Hernandez, "White-sounding names get called back for jobs more than Black ones, a new study finds," *NPR*, April 11, 2024, https://www.npr.org/2024/04/11/1243713272/resume-bias-study-white-names-black-names. Patrick M. Kline, Evan K. Rose, Christopher R. Walters, "A Discrimination Report Card - Working Paper 32313," *National Bureau of Economic Research,* https://www.nber.org/system/files/working_papers/w32313/w32313.pdf.

evidence of a "white" way of looking at reality that it succumbs to apophenia and confirmation bias. It may perceive connections between Whiteness and social phenomena that are illusory, and it may only consider evidence that appears to support a contention that some social phenomenon reinforces white supremacy. It may also ignore or downplay findings that run counter to its bedrock assumptions. For example, it may not take seriously research that suggests that "black names" do not have a significant influence on life outcomes.[26]

This concern is important because Whiteness Studies has become a kind of "normal science," a governing paradigm tethered to its own bevy of methodological assumptions and procedures that dictate what makes for acceptable scholarly inquiry and judgment.[27] As Thomas Kuhn famously argued, the history of scientific knowledge is not a story of steady, continuous accumulation of knowledge, but a series of revolutions in which one paradigm replaces another. A paradigm refers to foundational principles of scientific inquiry that determine a common understanding of what kinds of questions are acceptable to ask, and what are acceptable methodological approaches to answering these questions.

During the reign of a governing paradigm, a new paradigm may emerge, in a stage of immaturity, as new problems arise that the reigning paradigm cannot solve. As the new paradigm proves its ability to solve the puzzles and answer the questions that plague the old paradigm, it enters a period of normal science. For example, when racial inequality did not end after the Civil Rights revolution of the 1960s, the fields of Critical Race Theory and Whiteness Studies emerged to study unexplored dimensions of racism that could help explain the persistence of racial inequality.

---

26 Roland G. Fryer and Steven D. Levitt, "The Causes and Consequences of Distinctively Black Names," *The Quarterly Journal of Economics*, Vol. CXIX, Issue 3, August 2004, pp. 767-805.

27 Thomas Kuhn, *The Structure of Scientific Revolutions,* (Chicago: University of Chicago Press, 1962).

Whiteness Studies has a history that goes back at least as far as writers and social commentators W.E.B. DuBois and James Baldwin, but it began to mature in the 1990s, not long after the inception of Critical Race Theory, as numerous scholars examined how Whiteness is a crucial contributor to systemic racism and white supremacy. However, it has also encountered resistance from social critics who question whether the field has overreached, has shown a tendency to ask the wrong questions, or has failed to address doubts about its findings and its methodological merits. For example, despite a common claim that Whiteness is invisible to white people, one empirical study finds that many white Americans are consciously aware of their racial identity as white and do not subscribe to color-blind ideology.[28]

In the Kuhnian analysis, crises have the potential to produce a revolution in thought that leads to the development of a new paradigm that resolves the unanswered questions of critics. It is too early to declare a crisis in Whiteness Studies. But we have arrived at a point where critics have posed serious objections. This chapter raises the concern not only that Whiteness Studies risks succumbing to apophenia and confirmation bias, but also that in the rush to advance the field, scholars and activists have overlooked three logical fallacies seemingly inherent to its intellectual enterprise.

Three Logical Fallacies

1. The Fallacy of Begging the Question

The overriding objective of Whiteness Studies is to study, scrutinize, and ultimately sever the centripetal grip of "white" norms, be-

---

28 Douglas Hartmann, Joseph Gerteis and Paul R. Croll, "An Empirical Assessment of Whiteness Theory: Hidden from How Many?" *Social Problems*, Vol. 56, No. 3 (August 2009).

liefs, customs, habits, and behaviors to which white (and nonwhite) people, willfully or unwittingly, adhere in their daily lives. While this pursuit can yield useful insights on how people "perform" their racial roles as white or nonwhite people based on deeply rooted social expectations, it also risks becoming a crusade that insists everything white people think and do centers Whiteness and must be met self-righteously with reprimand and rehabilitation, if not retribution.

This fanatical concern with decentering and deconstructing the supposedly ossified ideological and discursive apparatus of "Whiteness" easily morphs into a quasi-conspiratorial "hermeneutics of suspicion"[29] whereby all situational intricacies of lived experience are perceived, or measured, through the lens of Whiteness. The quest to "decenter Whiteness" assumes the reification of "racist" social relations between white and nonwhite people, and then seeks to reveal (prove) it.

As an argumentative matter, Whiteness Studies effectively begs the question. To "beg the question" is a logical fallacy in which the conclusion of an argument is embedded in the premise of the argument—in other words, the premise of an argument does not support the conclusion but instead assumes that the conclusion is true. On the one hand, as DiAngelo writes, "Whiteness Studies begin with the premise that racism and white privilege exist in traditional and modern forms." On the other hand, it seeks to reveal it, rather than to prove it.[30] Aside from the dubious distinction between "revealing" and "proving" racism, the examination of Whiteness becomes an exercise in circular reasoning—it seeks to reveal, if not prove, what it already assumes from the beginning.

To be fair, this approach is not unlike the German philoso-

<hr>

29 Joseph Heath, "When does Critical Theory Become Conspiracy Theory?" *Department of Philosophy, University of Toronto*, https://utoronto.academia.edu/JosephHeath.

30 Robin DiAngelo, "White Fragility," *International Journal of Critical Pedagogy*, Vol 3 (3) (2011), p. 56.

pher Martin Heidegger's famous hermeneutic circle, according to which one is unable to interpret a whole without reference to its parts, and vice versa. In *Being and Time*, Heidegger claimed that one is unable to investigate the meaning of Being without first laying bare our pre-existing understanding of the meaning of Being. Part of Heidegger's project, then, is to disentangle fundamental aspects of this pre-existing understanding as an essential step on the way to explaining the holistic meaning of Being.[31] Similarly, we might say that one is unable to investigate the meaning of (the Being of) Whiteness without first laying bare our pre-existing entanglement in the culture of Whiteness. To assume the existence of racism and white privilege is to acknowledge that we are already "thrown" into a world anchored on Whiteness. To reveal racism and white privilege is to discover how Whiteness undergirds white supremacy.

The study of Whiteness, then, should not be regarded as a purely deductive enterprise that begins with premises and ends with an analytic conclusion. The study of Whiteness involves an ongoing interplay—a circular process—between trying to grasp the whole of Whiteness in relation to its parts, and vice versa, while already being entangled in a pre-existing apprehension of this whole and its parts. The study of the meaning of Being, or the meaning (culture) of Whiteness, is a process of unraveling what one already is vaguely familiar with, to grasp it more explicitly and clearly.

Of course, one must start somewhere. The key is to start in the right place. Heidegger's *Being and Time* endeavors to explain how we may approach the study of what it means to be as a human being. It is a monumental effort that illustrates the difficult, disciplined, and delicate nature of an expansive hermeneutic exercise focused on one of the most fundamental metaphysical questions in Western philosophy. If one chooses the wrong starting point, one can easily lose the plot and go astray. It is not unlike choosing an ambiguous

---

31 Martin Heidegger, *Being and Time,* (New York: State University of New York Press, 1996).

premise in a faulty deductive argument.

This risk of ambiguity sheds light on why we cannot escape entirely the treatment of Whiteness as an argumentative matter. We will explore the fallacy of ambiguity below, but for now we can observe that the hermeneutic circle can fail in its interpretative expedition if it does not exert sufficient care and discipline in the attempt to discern the essential aspects of Whiteness that illuminate the nature of white supremacy. Similarly, as an analytic undertaking, begging the question means that Whiteness Studies can often become an exercise in filtering the situational intricacies of lived experience through the narrow lens of its analytic prior. As noted, Robin DiAngelo insists, "the question is not, is this racist, but how is racism manifesting in this situation?"[32] If so, Whiteness Studies serves not strictly to illuminate the presumed reification of "racist" social relations based on the norms of "Whiteness," but to assume this reification and then attempt to reveal (prove) it even if the situational intricacies of lived experiences suggest contrary inferences. The concept of white privilege, which we examine in detail below, is a case in point.

2. The Reification Fallacy

The circular affirmation of reified domination embodied in "white" social relations also brings to light how Whiteness Studies can succumb to the reification fallacy, alternatively known as the fallacy of misplaced concreteness. This is the belief that an abstraction can assume a concrete form—i.e., to make an idea into a thing. For example, Whiteness is conceived as a "virus" infecting the DNA of society,[33] embodied in things like ethnic food aisles, books in a li-

---

32   Robin DiAngelo, "Anti-Racism Handout," https://robindiangelo.com/wp-content/uploads/2016/06/Anti-racism-handout-1-page-2016.pdf.

33   "The Racism Virus," May 11, 2022, https://www.nbcnews.com/now/video/the-racism-virus-139820613958. Viola Davis post on X: "Racism is

brary, or public monuments.[34]

The notion of reification does make a compelling metaphorical point that people come to perceive social relations as fixed and ahistorical, not subject to critique leading to historical change. For example, people may champion a "white" liberal commitment to the ideal of color-blind neutrality in professional environments as the manifestation of classic Enlightenment values of universalism, individualism, rationality, and objectivity.[35] In so doing, they can overlook the possibility that the principle of color-blind neutrality may obscure the historical legacy of racist social, political, and economic developments that underlie the persistence of racial inequality.

For example, a belief in "colorblind" meritocracy, rooted in the

---

built into the DNA of America. And as long as we turn a blind eye to the pain of those suffering under its oppression, we will never escape those origins." ~Annalise Keating; https://x.com/violadavis/status/1527013655778410496?lang=en.

34   Priya Krishna, "Why Do American Grocery Stores Still Have an Ethnic Aisle?" *The New York Times*, August 10, 2021, https://www.nytimes.com/2021/08/10/dining/american-grocery-stores-ethnic-aisle.html; "Equity & Social Justice Advisory Group Resources: Whiteness and Librarianship," *University of Buffalo*, November 13, 2024, https://research.lib.buffalo.edu/esjag-reading/whiteness; Andrea Jameson, *Decentering Whiteness in Libraries: A Framework for Inclusive Collection Management Practices*, (Lanham, Boulder, New York, London: Rowman & Littlefield Publishers, 2024), https://www.bloomsbury.com/us/decentering-whiteness-in-libraries-9781538162910/; Nicholas Mirzoeff, *White Sight: Visual Politics and Practices of Whiteness*, (MIT Press, 2023).

35   The supposedly Enlightenment values of universalism, individualism, rationality, and objectivity refer to the idea that individuals should be regarded as partaking in a common universal humanity, or universal human nature, that transcends their social and historical circumstances, and that this universal standard of human nature entails a faculty for rational thinking that is able to assess the world objectively and from a standpoint of neutrality. Race scholars and activists tend to believe that these Enlightenment values reflect a "white" commitment to color-blind ideology that ignores the difficulty, if not the impossibility, of assuming the neutral perspective of a non-racialized self, i.e., an identity independent of the historical circumstances in which one becomes a self. For discussion, see Gary Peller, "Race Consciousness," 1990, *Duke Law Journal*, pp,. 758-847 (1990).

idea that a fair and equal society is one in which no one is formally excluded from job opportunities based on racial identity, promotes an ideal of nondiscrimination that can effectively disempower nonwhites by ignoring the differential impact of informal networks on the job prospects of white and nonwhite people.[36] If standards of success are shaped at least in part by "white" social norms that characterize these social networks—perhaps an occasional proclivity in nonwhite people to use racially tinged dialect or slang in their speech is heard by white people as a signal that the nonwhite person does not know how to communicate in a "professional" manner— then any consistent expectation of neutrality may be implausible if a nonwhite person "slipping up" in conversation makes an unfavorable impression on a white person who is in a position to make an introduction that might lead to a job offer, or to a club membership, or to some other prospect for social advancement.

These ideas become "reified" —i.e., they come to be regarded as a fixed and "natural" feature of social relations—when they give rise to rigid beliefs about the inherent qualities of people that then dictate how people should relate to each other in society. Whiteness, in the words of law professor Cheryl Harris, becomes a form of property that entitles white people to a different set of expectations in social interactions than the expectations under which nonwhite people live their lives. Whiteness, she writes, is "constituted through the reification of expectations in the continued right of white-dominated institutions to control the legal meaning of group identity."[37]

"Whiteness as property," Harris continues, "is derived from the deep historical roots of systematic white supremacy that has given rise to definitions of group identity predicated on the racial subordination of the 'other,' and that has reified expectations of

---

36   Eduardo Bonilla-Silva, *Racism without Racists,* (Lanham, MD: Rowman & Littlefield, 2010), p. 33.

37   Cheryl Harris, "Whiteness as Property," *Harvard Law Review,* Volume 106, Number 8, June 1993, p. 1761.

continued white privilege."[38] This "property interest in whiteness has proven to be resilient and adaptive to new conditions:"[39]

> Over time it has changed in form, but it has retained its essential *exclusionary* character and continued to distort outcomes of legal disputes by favoring and protecting settled expectations of white privilege. The law expresses the dominant conception of "rights," "equality," "property," "neutrality," and "power": rights mean shields from interference; equality means formal equality; *property means the settled expectations* that are to be protected; neutrality means the existing distribution, which is natural; and, power is the mechanism for guarding all of this [emphasis added].[40]

This reification of Whiteness as property gives rise to what Ruth Frankenberg describes as (1) "a location of structural advantage, of race privilege"; (2) a standpoint, a place from which white people look at themselves, at others, and at society; and (3) "a set of cultural practices that are usually unmarked and unnamed."[41] According to DiAngelo:

> Whiteness is thus conceptualized as a constellation of processes and practices rather than as a discrete entity (i.e., skin color). Whiteness is dynamic, relational, and operating at all times and on myriad levels. These processes and practices include basic rights, values, beliefs, perspectives and experiences purported to be commonly shared by all but which are actually only consistently afforded to white people.[42]

---

38 Ibid., p. 1785.

39 Ibid., p. 1778.

40 Ibid., p. 1778.

41 Ruth Frankenberg, *White Women, Race Matters: The Social Construction of Whiteness,* (The University of Minnesota Press, 1993), p. 1.

42 Robin DiAngelo, "White Fragility," *International Journal of Critical Pedagogy,* Vol 3 (3) (2011) p. 56.

In other words, Whiteness is a set of *reified* expectations in society that, in centering Whiteness, give rise to an "invisible package of unearned assets" that Peggy MacIntosh has famously described as "white privilege."[43]

As noted, to "reify" is to take an abstract idea and make it into a real thing. In *History and Class Consciousness,* the Hungarian Marxist philosopher Geörg Lukács identifies the commodity as constituting the reification of social relations between capital and labor.[44] As is often the case with the reification of concepts, the commodity is used as a metaphor to describe how social relations between capital and labor come to be expressed in the "natural" form of commodity exchange despite developing from, and being immersed in, the historical evolution from feudalism to capitalism. But this is a fallacy because a commodity is not itself a social relation. It is not itself an abstract idea.

Whiteness reifies "white" cultural practices as if they are natural rather than historical. In the same vein, however, Whiteness Studies often sees Whiteness as a "thing" (a "virus") in societies with a history of white supremacy. It is manifest in the books we read (e.g., racist social relations allegedly express themselves in Othello),[45] in ethnic food aisles,[46] in the laws that are written,[47] and in the

43 Peggy McIntosh, "White Privilege and Male Privilege: A Personal Account of Coming to See Correspondences through Work in Women's Studies - Working Paper 189," *Wellesley Centers for Women*, Wellesley, MA, 1988, p. 2, https://www.wcwonline.org/images/pdf/White_Privilege_and_Male_Privilege_Personal_Account-Peggy_McIntosh.pdf.

44 *Georg Lukacs, History and Class Consciousness,* (Merlin Press, 1967), https://www.marxists.org/archive/lukacs/works/history/hcc05.htm.

45 Jonathan Church, "Shakespeare and Social Justice Ideology: 'Othello' Is Not About Racism," *Voegelin View,* April 29, 2022, https://voegelinview.com/shakespeare-and-social-justice-ideology-othello-is-not-about-racism/.

46 Priya Krishna, "Why Do American Grocery Stores Still Have an Ethnic Aisle?" *The New York Times*, August 10, 2021, https://www.nytimes.com/2021/08/10/dining/american-grocery-stores-ethnic-aisle.html.

47 Ian Haney Lopez, *White by Law: The Legal Construction of Race,* (New York and London: New York University Press, 2006).

cultural activities in which we participate, all of which are inextricably tied to the legacy of past racist practices. It is, in a sense, to conflate the legacy of racism with racism itself, by seeing "white" ideas as embodied in people and the cultural institutions that express and dictate the way they live.

3. The Fallacy of Ambiguity

Given the broad scope of what is supposed to be encompassed by Whiteness, especially if the study of Whiteness becomes so keen on finding evidence of a "white" way of looking at the world that it succumbs to apophenia and confirmation bias, the fallacy of reification risks turning into the fallacy of ambiguity. We have noted labor historian Eric Arsenen's observation that "whiteness has become a blank screen onto which those who claim to analyze it can project their own meanings."[48] When these meanings conflict or are otherwise confused, imprecise, or obscure, the argument that society is anchored on reified Whiteness succumbs to the fallacy of ambiguity.

There is perhaps no greater example of the risk of ambiguity in Whiteness Studies than the central concept of white privilege.

The Case of White Privilege

Peggy McIntosh famously defined white privilege "as an invisible package of unearned assets that I can count on cashing in each day, but about which I was 'meant' to remain oblivious." This "invisible weightless knapsack" consists "of special provisions, assurances, tools, maps, guides, codebooks, passports, visas, clothes, compass, emergency gear, and blank checks" that open the doors of opportunity and advantage for white people in society, but not for nonwhite

---

48 Eric Arsenen, "Whiteness and Historians' Imagination," *International Labor and Working-Class History Society*, Vol. 60, October 2001, pp. 3-32.

people. It is precisely because this invisible weightless knapsack provides social and economic advantages exclusively to white people that they collectively constitute "white" privilege.[49]

For McIntosh, the importance of this concept is that it "makes one newly accountable." [50] McIntosh begins her essay discussing how her discovery of male privilege led to her discovery of white privilege, and that one of the main discoveries she made about male privilege is that men "may say they will work to improve women's status, in the society, the university, or the curriculum, but they can't or won't support the idea of lessening men's."[51] These "[d]enials which amount to taboos surround the subject of advantages which men gain from women's disadvantages. These denials protect male privilege from being fully acknowledged, lessened or ended."[52]

Three points are made or implied. One, white people have systemic advantages in society by virtue of being racialized as white people. Second, their advantages are taken for granted. Privilege is not immediately apparent to white people. As a result, they continue to act and think as if their norms, beliefs, customs, attitudes, and habits are not "white" norms, beliefs, customs, attitudes, and habits that center Whiteness and thus undergird advantages otherwise seen as normal and neutral aspects of society. Third, if privilege is made visible to white people, they refuse to give it up.

The implication is that undoing racial inequality requires a robust effort to interrogate and unwind white privilege. McIntosh gets straight to it, deciding "to try to work on myself at least by identify-

---

49   Peggy McIntosh, "White Privilege and Male Privilege: A Personal Account of Coming to See Correspondences through Work in Women's Studies - Working Paper 189," *Wellesley Centers for Women*, Wellesley, MA, 1988, p. 2, https://www.wcwonline.org/images/pdf/White_Privilege_and_Male_Privilege_Personal_Account-Peggy_McIntosh.pdf.

50   Ibid., p. 3.

51   Ibid., p. 3.

52   Ibid., p. 2.

ing some of the daily effects of white privilege in my life."[53] These examples include seemingly straightforward and self-evident cases like being able to "take a job with an affirmative action employer without having co-workers on the job suspect that I got it because of race,"[54] or the ease with which one can "arrange to be in the company of people of my race most of the time."[55]

But a little inspection and reflection also reveal that many of her examples are less clearcut. How much of an advantage is it to be able to "be in the company of people of my race most of the time?" For most people, it probably is, as evidenced by the discomfort many white people would feel being in a crowd of mostly nonwhite people. But it does not take much effort or imagination to discover that there are also a nonnegligible number of white people who are perfectly at ease in a crowd of mostly nonwhite people. Moreover, in the "woke" age of social justice activism, there are surely many white progressives who are so eager to exhibit their social justice credentials that, conversely, they purposely disrupt social occasions, if not with insufferable proselytization, then with performances of irreverence in the interest of interrogating "polite" white society.

Similar thought experiments reveal ambiguities that arise in many of McIntosh's examples. It is hard to see, for example, how the greater availability of white skin-colored Band-Aids reflects more than the fact that white people have historically constituted a majority of the American population. The point, however, is not to deny the existence of white privilege. I have written several essays on the intricacies of white privilege and how we can understand the term more precisely and incisively.

For example, I have written about how the law of large numbers and Bayes theorem can help us understand white privilege in terms of the lower likelihood white people face, for example, of

---

53 Ibid., p. 4.

54 Ibid., p. 7

55 Ibid., p. 4.

being abused by the police.[56] But I have also argued that the search for examples of "white privilege is vulnerable to confirmation bias, which is the tendency to take into account only information that supports one's preconception, while discounting or ignoring information that does not support one's preconception."[57] For example, Peggy McIntosh invokes the example that "[w]hen I am told about our national heritage or about 'civilization,' I am shown that people of my color made it what it is."[58] As I wrote:

> Putting aside thorny questions about what exactly it means to say that people of a certain color 'made' a national 'heritage', suppose a white male student in a history class argues that Howard Zinn's *People's History of the United States* should not be on the curriculum because it is bad history. A teacher schooled in 'white-privilege analysis' might have a knee-jerk inclination to try to convince him that his objection is a symptom of 'white fragility' —i.e., the objection to Zinn's retelling of American history stems from a 'privileged' expectation that history be written by white oppressors rather than from the perspective of the historically disenfranchised. But it may alternatively be the case that the white male classroom provocateur believes Zinn's *People's History* is simply not good history, and that he has no objection to books written about the historically disenfranchised so long as they are rigorous, not prone to polemical agendas, do not (as historian Michael Kazin writes) reduce the past to a Manichean fable, and are more objective (which, as Princeton historian Sean Wilentz notes, is not the same as neutral) in the marshalling of evidence

---

56 Jonathan Church, "White Privilege, the Law of Large Numbers, and a Little Bit of Bayes," *The Good Men Project*, August 14, 2016, https://goodmenproject.com/featured-content/white-privilege-law-large-numbers-little-bit-bayes-wcz/.

57 Jonathan Church, "The Problem I Have with the Concept of White Privilege," *The Good Men Project*, March 17, 2017, https://goodmenproject.com/featured-content/the-problem-i-have-with-the-concept-of-white-privilege-wcz/.

58 McIntosh, op.cit., p. 2.

in support of a historical thesis. This is to say nothing of the possibility that the white male student may derive little or no comfort from the mere fact that people of his color 'made' his national heritage or civilization. In sum, white privilege is a red herring when it comes to explaining his objection to Zinn's *People's History*. [59]

In sum, the attempt of Whiteness scholars and activists to reveal, or prove, the reification of structural racial inequality—i.e., racism—in the form of white privilege begins with what, in practice, is an ambiguous premise. Given the long list of examples McIntosh provides of what she considers white privilege—from being able to "arrange to be in the company of people of my race most of the time" to being "pretty sure of finding a publisher for this piece on white privilege" —this inherent conceptual ambiguity is not unrelated to the ever-present risk of concept creep. [60]

Even McIntosh herself observes a source of further ambiguity by imploring us, perhaps inadvertently, to ask: Is privilege necessarily a bad thing? She distinguishes "between positive advantages that we can work to spread, to the point where they are not advantages

---

59   Jonathan Church, "The Problem I Have with the Concept of White Privilege," *The Good Men Project*, March 17, 2017, https://goodmenproject.com/featured-content/the-problem-i-have-with-the-concept-of-white-privilege-wcz/; "An experts' history of Howard Zinn," *Los Angeles Times*, February 1, 2010, https://www.latimes.com/archives/la-xpm-2010-feb-01-la-oe-miller1-2010feb01-story.html; Michael Kazin, "Howard Zinn's History Lessons," *Dissent Magazine*, Spring 2004, https://www.dissentmagazine.org/article/howard-zinns-history-lessons/.

60   Nick Haslam, "Concept Creep: Psychology's Expanding Concepts of Harm and Pathology," *Psychological Inquiry*, Volume 27, Issue 1, 2016. According to Haslam: "I contend that the expansion primarily reflects an ever-increasing sensitivity to harm, reflecting a liberal moral agenda. Its implications are ambivalent, however. Although conceptual change is inevitable and often well motivated, concept creep runs the risk of pathologizing everyday experience and encouraging a sense of virtuous but impotent victimhood." Gregg Henriques, "The Concept of Concept Creep," *Psychology Today*, January 4, 2017, https://www.psychologytoday.com/us/blog/theory-knowledge/201701/the-concept-concept-creep.

at all but simply part of the normal civic and social fabric, and negative types of advantage that unless rejected will always reinforce our present hierarchies."[61] The feeling of belonging, for example, is "an entitlement that none of us should have to earn."[62] But surely we should not want to preserve the "negative 'privilege' that gave me cultural permission not to take darker-skinned-Others seriously" because it "can be seen as arbitrarily conferred dominance and should not be desirable for anyone."[63]

In other words, as the philosopher Lawrence Blum has argued, it is necessary to distinguish between *privileges worth having* and *privileges not worth having*.[64] According to Blum, privileges worth having consist of (1) "spared injustice" privileges and (2) other privileges not related to injustice. Blum describes privileges not worth having as "unjust enrichment" privileges.[65]

When a white person is spared the injustice of being stopped by a police officer without cause, this "privilege" is not something that we want to take away from him. Rather, it is like a right that should be granted to all people in society, white and nonwhite. The same holds for other privileges not related to injustice, such as being able to speak a native language. It would surely be perverse to insist that Americans should stop speaking English in deference to Spanish-speaking immigrants, though a humane society would surely endeavor to make accommodations for people who cannot speak English. Privileges that members of a majority culture enjoy are like rights that should be granted to all citizens of a society: those who were born into the culture, and those seeking to assimilate. As philosopher Lewis Gordon explains:

---

61 McIntosh, Op.Cit., p. 10.

62 Op.Cit., p. 10.

63 Op.Cit., p. 10.

64 Lawrence Blum, "'White privilege': A Mild Critique," *Theory and Research in Education*, 2008, Vol 6 (3), p. 310.

65 Ibid., pp. 310-311.

> A privilege is something that not everyone needs, but a right is the opposite. Given this distinction, an insidious dimension of the white-privilege argument emerges. It requires condemning whites for possessing, in the concrete, features of contemporary life that should be available to all, and if this is correct, how can whites be expected to give up such things?[66]

In contrast, privileges not worth having are the kind of advantages that come at the expense of nonwhite people. Classic examples include the effects of redlining on generational wealth inequality between whites and nonwhites, disproportionate use of police force on white and nonwhite people, and the unjust enrichment that white people have derived from the historical exclusion of nonwhite people from the competition for jobs, homes, and other perquisites of participation in civil society. Undoubtedly, benefits derived from exclusionary practices are privileges not worth having.

In sum, the case of white privilege illustrates the conceptual ambiguities that can arise from the weakening of epistemic discipline in Whiteness Studies. One of the main consequences of epistemic weakening, in combination with an unmitigated zeal attached to its mission, is dogmatism.

The Risk of "Woke" Dogmatism

Whiteness Theory seeks to expose how the reified social expectations that underlie the development of Whiteness as property and give rise to white privilege are, in fact, contingent on the cultural milieu in which we are raised—i.e., they are "socially constructed." The ways that people relate to each other are an offshoot of history, not nature. The expectations we have of people who are members of

---

66 From the Introduction to *"I Don't See Color:" Personal and Critical Perspectives on White Privilege*, edited by Bettina Bergo and Tracey Nicholls, (University Park, PA: The Pennsylvania State University Press, 2015).

different identity groups—e.g., white and black—are expectations that members of one group invented, deliberately or unwittingly or both, as a tool with which to dominate members of the other group. As such, Whiteness Studies is a field heavily influenced by postmodern inquiries into the historical interplay between power and knowledge. This influence makes Whiteness Studies highly susceptible, especially in its activist form, to the influence of "woke" ideology.

"Woke" ideology is a contentious term that many commentators have attempted to define, but it tends to be associated with militant-prone activism on behalf of a "consciousness raising" agenda that pushes crypto-normative left-wing political, social, and cultural goals. Its intellectual paradigm is Critical Social Justice. Its intellectual heritage consists of a potpourri of ideas drawn from postmodernism, neo-Marxism, and Critical Theory. The Critical Social Justice paradigm defines oppression in terms of social stratification along the lines of racial, sexual, and other identity groups. The stratification emerges from, manifests, and is sustained by ossified institutional arrangements that systematically allocate resources inequitably to different identity groups.[67]

This reality remains in place because we speak and act in ways that reinforce social norms, customs, beliefs, habits, and behavioral proclivities that underlie the "social construction" of group identity—e.g., racial identity. As such, we unwittingly act out, or perform, "roles" in society that align with the reified expectations attached to our racial, sexual, and other identities. These roles are not one-dimensional, but intersectional.[68] For example, a white gay disabled

---

67   Critical Social Justice, Background, https://www.progressispossible.org/worldviews/critical-social-justice/. *UMBC, The Women's Center*, https://womenscenter.umbc.edu/critical-social-justice/; Kristin Hermes, "Critical social justice is on the rise," *Philanthropy Daily: a journal of the Center for Civil Society*, July 13, 2021, https://philanthropydaily.com/critical-social-justice-is-on-the-rise/; Helen Pluckrose, *The Counterweight Handbook,* (Great Britain: Swift Press, 2024; United States: Pitchstone Publishing, 2024).

68   Crenshaw, Kimberle, "Demarginalizing the Intersection of Race and Sex: A Black Feminist Critique of Antidiscrimination Doctrine, Feminist Theory

man has a different "lived experience" from a black straight able man, but these experiences nonetheless reflect group characteristics that interact dynamically, and consistently, in historically conditioned ways.

As we perform our roles as members of identity groups, we serve as vessels for ruling class ideologies and discourse. Woke activism, then, is strategically focused on the critique of speech and acts that allegedly perpetuate these ideological, discursive, and performative practices, thus upholding, preserving, and enforcing what are seen as irredeemable, historically grounded social institutions that vindicate social stratification and oppression. The speech and acts under assault are the expression of a kind of "manufactured consent"[69] in the form of "false consciousness" —i.e., ideological sublimation that materializes through the performative and discursive practices that keep oppression in place.

The intellectual heritage that informs this paradigm draws from, among many other things, the neo-Marxian Gramscian idea that ruling class ideologies calcify into a "cultural hegemony" that pervades and permeates cultural institutions. "Woke" activists must engage in a "war of position" as part of what the New Right has characterized as a "long march through the institutions."[70] Gramscian neo-Marxism also draws from the Critical Theory of the Frankfurt School because it attempts to diagnose the institutional foundations of "false consciousness" —the ways in which ruling class ideologies, as expressed in media, movies, books, television, schools, workplaces, political institutions, and other cultural venues teach us

---

and Antiracist Politics," *University of Chicago Legal Forum*, Volume 1989, Issue 1, Article 8, http://chicagounbound.uchicago.edu/cgi/viewcontent. cgi?article=1052&context=uclf.

69 Edward S. Herman and Noam Chomsky, *Manufacturing Consent: The Political Economy of Mass Media,* (New York: Pantheon Books, 1988, 2002).

70 Christopher F. Rufo, *America's Cultural Revolution: How the Radical Left Conquered Everything,* (New York: Broadside Books, 2023).

to think and act in ways that acclimate us to oppressive hierarchies.[71]

Finally, Critical Social Justice draws from postmodern philosophy in how it tries to decenter (or even demolish) discourses that allegedly devalue and thus oppress identity groups that live on the margins of an extant society. The key idea from postmodernism is about how truth and power interact. The contention is not necessarily that truth and power are indistinguishable, but that power influences what we understand or accept to be true. This power-knowledge interplay creates narratives that constrict and circumscribe, devalue and subjugate, the emancipatory impulses of people lower in the social hierarchy by virtue of their group identity.

In principle, these ideas about oppression and marginalization are not necessarily illegitimate or faulty. The problem arises when scholars and activists become fanatically obsessed with critiques of reason and objectivity on the assumption that reason and objectivity are compromised as mere expressions of power in themselves, rather than simply being potentially susceptible to such debasement. As such, dialogue degenerates into irreconcilable debates, reason devolves into rhetoric, and truth becomes indecipherable from falsehood. Instead of trying to reason things out, we think that our only option is to fight it out, especially if "woke" ressentiment[72] breeds a culture of victimhood. When we reach that point, "woke" activism galvanizes the reactionary forces of postmodern conservatism, and we are left with so-called "culture war" partisanship in which both

---

71 Max Horkheimer and Theodor Adorno, "The Culture Industry" from *Dialectic of Enlightenment*, https://www.marxists.org/reference/archive/adorno/1944/culture-industry.htm.

72 "Friedrich Nietzsche," *Stanford Encyclopedia of Philosophy,* https://plato.stanford.edu/entries/nietzsche/. Ressentiment stems from Nietzsche's conception of a "slave revolt in morality" according to which "[p]eople who suffered from oppression at the hands of the noble, excellent, (but uninhibited) people valorized by good/bad morality—and who were denied any effective recourse against them by relative powerlessness—developed a persistent, corrosive emotional pattern of resentful hatred against their enemies, which Nietzsche calls ressentiment."

sides seek power over truth rather than truth over power.[73]

This critical orientation is not fruitless. In *The Fire Next Time*, a foundational text in Whiteness Studies, James Baldwin provides a compelling account of how the history of racial inequality in American history created "white" social expectations about how black Americans fit into American society.[74] These expectations severely limited the aspirations of black Americans in mid-20th century America. In the same vein, W.E.B. DuBois explained the importance of "double consciousness" to black survival in a "white" society in which it was necessary for black people to not only understand their own capacities for engaging in social life, but also to understand the expectations of white people, which had the additional disadvantage that it "yields him no true self-consciousness, but only lets him see himself through the revelation of the other world."[75]

However, it is a risk of any paradigm that it may become a form of orthodoxy. When a paradigm becomes a dogma rather than a flexible framework, the attempt to convince the uninitiated can morph into a militant campaign to preach rather than teach. The purity of belief among true believers galvanizes a crusade to politicize

---

73   Matthew McManus, *The Rise of Postmodern Conservatism: Neoliberalism, Post-Modern Culture, and Reactionary Politics,* (Palgrave MacMillan, 2020).

74   James Baldwin, *The Fire Next Time,* (New York: The Dial Press, 1963).

75   W.E.B. DuBois, *The Souls of Black Folk,* (New York: Barnes & Noble Books, 1903). "After the Egyptian and Indian, the Greek and Roman, the Teuton and Mongolian, the Negro is a sort of seventh son, born with a veil, and gifted with second-sight in this American world, – a world which yields him no true self-consciousness, but only lets him see himself through the revelation of the other world. It is a peculiar sensation, this double-consciousness, this sense of always looking at one's self through the eyes of others, of measuring one's soul by the tape of a world that looks on in amused contempt and pity. One ever feels his two-ness, – an American, a Negro; two souls, two thoughts, two unreconciled strivings; two warring ideals in one dark body, whose dogged strength alone keeps it from being torn asunder."
See: https://plato.stanford.edu/entries/double-consciousness/
#DoubCConsSoulBlacFolk.

that brooks no dissent. One need only be reminded of the Black Lives Matter protesters who surrounded a white woman outside a Washington, D.C. restaurant in August 2020—demanding that she raise her fist to express her solidarity with their cause, insisting that "white silence is violence" —to see how pedagogy can inspire pros-elytization.[76]

The entry of the political into the realm of the pedagogi-cal—i.e., when we take the postmodern turn to suggest that all ed-ucation is political—runs the serious risk of failing to distinguish between objectivity and neutrality. It is an article of faith among adherents to (critical) Whiteness Studies in particular, and among postmodern intellectuals in general, that neutrality is not only prac-tically infeasible if not impossible, but also an ideological aspect of Whiteness that serves to reify "white" norms as the only acceptable norms. It may well be the case that we must concede that a hard distinction between facts and value is a farce, as 20th century devel-opments in the philosophy of language seem to have adequately demonstrated.[77] A loss of confidence in neutrality, however, does not produce an argument for a loss of confidence in objectivity.

Objective inquiry is the use of reason in a good faith effort to marshal facts in pursuit of an argument about the nature of reality. It is, however, an important feature of good faith objective inquiry to acknowledge that truth is not only accessible but also elusive. There is a distinction between truth and certainty. On the one hand, the humility that comes with objective inquiry should make us more open-minded, and thus receptive to questions about the extent to which ideas do a "white" service to white supremacy. On the oth-er hand, the same humility should compel us to question whether

---

76 Fredrick Kunkle, "Protesters Heckle D.C. Diners, Triggering Backlash After Heckling Woman," *The Washington Post*, August 25, 2020, https://www.washingtonpost.com/dc-md-va/2020/08/25/dc-protesters-blm-din-er-confrontation/.

77 Hilary Putnam, *The Collapse of the Fact/Value Dichotomy and Other Essays,* (Cambridge: Harvard University Press, 2004).

those same ideas may not be "white." There is much truth in the claim that beliefs about the inherent qualities of people are historically contingent rather than immutable, and beliefs about what it means to be "white" or "black" help to explain racial inequality. There is also much truth in the claim that not all norms are "white" simply because white people adhere to them.

Unfortunately, proponents of (critical) Whiteness Studies too often seem so interested in the critique of Whiteness that they cannot help but see Whiteness everywhere and anywhere. Like hardcore Marxists who believe that all social problems boil down to contradictions in the capitalist mode of production, a fundamental presupposition of Whiteness scholars is that the problem of racism and racial inequality boils down to Whiteness as a set of hidden "white" ideas which underlie white supremacy. It is only by an ongoing practice of "decentering" and "deconstructing" Whiteness that we can make adequate progress in the struggle to undo white supremacy and achieve racial equality. As Ian Haney Lopez writes in *White by Law*, "there is no other way."[78]

Concluding Remarks

One important concern connected to the arguments presented in this chapter is that the theory and praxis of Whiteness Studies tend to cultivate a singular, dogmatic mindset that not only ignores the fallacies of begging the question, reification, and ambiguity, but also gives rise to a paradox that is familiar to critics of contemporary identity politics. The central paradox of contemporary identity politics is that its demand for more diverse racial, ethnic, gendered, and other forms of identity-based representation in societal institutions comes at the expense of viewpoint diversity.

This is not what is supposed to happen. The motivation for

---

78 Ian Haney Lopez, *White by Law*, New York University Press (New York and London), 2006, pp. 121, 126.

more diverse representation is a presumption that more inclusive representation yields more viewpoints, which necessarily improves the effort to, in this case, decenter Whiteness and address inequality across racial, ethnic, gender, and other forms of social identity. But a contradiction arises from an implicit expectation that the "lived experience" of a more diverse set of representatives will enrich our understanding not of the human condition more broadly, but of human oppression more narrowly.

Proponents of identity politics implicitly, if not explicitly, see human oppression not simply as *one important feature* of the human condition, but as *the fundamental feature* of the human condition. Moreover, they conceive of oppression in rigid, narrow terms as the experience of being subjugated by the use we make of words to communicate with each other, and by the stories we tell about the way we live. As a result, viewpoints are deemed valid, or palatable, only if they reinforce an understanding of social relations as a binary construction of in-group oppressors and out-group oppressed.

In this view, knowledge is necessarily political. One's knowledge reflects his standpoint within the social hierarchy based on the group of which the individual is a member. The criterion by which ideas are deemed valid is whether the "lived experience" of those who offer the ideas sheds light on how the oppressor-group victimizes an oppressed group. The only "lived experiences" that count are those which fit neatly into a "woke" discourse whereby an in-group oppresses an out-group. As Sandra Harding argues, standpoint epistemology—the idea that lived experience provides a unique perspective on the world and thus contributes to our knowledge of the world we inhabit—can provide us with more objective knowledge about the oppression dynamics suffered by marginalized groups.[79] But the purpose is not simply to know, but to act. To in-

---

79 "Feminist Standpoint Theory," https://iep.utm.edu/fem-stan/. "Feminist Epistemology and Philosophy of Science," https://plato.stanford.edu/entries/feminism-epistemology/.

voke the words of the Romantic philosopher J. G. Fichte, "we do not act because we know, but we know because we are called upon to act." It might also be said that we are called upon to act because we feel oppressed.

As noted, the intellectual paradigm that galvanizes "woke" identity politics is Critical Social Justice, according to which social justice activism is conceived exclusively in terms of "decentering" and "deconstructing" the ideas, beliefs, habits, norms, customs, discourses, and behaviors that normalize oppressive social stratification along racial, ethnic, gender, and other identity-based lines. The intellectual heritage of this "woke" identity politics is a potpourri of ideas from postmodern philosophy, neo-Marxism, and readapted Critical Theory about how language, culture, and ideology function to institutionalize and ossify the historical development of oppressive social hierarchies.

This ostensible mission to dissolve oppressive social hierarchies seems so clean and intuitive at first glance as to be without fault. Moreover, the intellectual history that inspires identity politics is formidable and not easily dismissed. It thus seems unobjectionable that, in the pursuit of justice, we defer to marginalized perspectives, as well as those who have studied such perspectives, in our attempt to arrive at a conception and realization of social justice in the world. The more we listen, the more we learn. The more we learn, the more tools we have at our disposal to build a better society.

But listening is only a necessary condition for understanding. It is not sufficient. As anyone conversant with the history of philosophy knows, the nature of justice is not so straightforward. Centuries of inquiry by innumerable eminent philosophers have yet to yield a definitive and all-encompassing conception of justice on which everyone can agree. It is no easy task to figure out what justice is and how to achieve it. How is it, then, that so-called "social justice warriors" so prevalent in identity politics activism are so sure that they have it all figured out?[80]

The answer is that they do not. But commitment to dissolving the institutional pillars of oppression quite understandably inspires a piety that makes true believers susceptible to the myopic sanctimony of fanaticism, and naturally, there are many true believers in the community of "woke" social justice activists, ideologues, and intellectuals. It is unsurprising, then, that social justice activists should feel compelled to be allies to oppressed people rather than to their oppressors, and to assume that the greater the number of marginalized identities with which they form alliances, the more ideas they will be able to retrieve and incorporate into the effort to undo social injustice.

The problem, however, is that a kind of intellectual imperialism arises in which it becomes seemingly impossible in practice to conceive of any detail of social life in terms other than whether it reinforces or undermines not only appreciation of the form of oppression in which one is interested, but also the way in which we are expected to understand that form of oppression.

The result is a dogma rather than a framework, whereby the impulse for action comes from choosing sides rather than from choosing a framework of analysis that is most well-adapted to the facts at hand. The dogma mandates that we choose the side of the oppressed group and blame everything on the oppressor group. The only viewpoints deemed valid and acceptable are those which reinforce an understanding of social relations as a binary construction of oppressors and oppressors, and which embrace the belief that a binary conflict between oppressors and oppressed is *the fundamental* feature of society, rather than being *one important* feature among others. This impassioned singularity of purpose reflects a laudatory

---

80   I explore this theme is more detail here: Jonathan Church, "The Specter of Marxism Haunts the Social Justice Movement," *The Good Men Project,* July 9, 2017, https://goodmenproject.com/featured-content/the-specter-of-marxism-haunts-the-social-justice-movement-wcz/.

commitment to decentering Whiteness as an essential contribution to ending racism and racial inequality. But the same zeal that galvanizes the scrutiny of Whiteness also risks weakening the epistemic discipline necessary to retain credibility.

4

CRITICAL RACE THEORY, ANTI-OPPRESSION IDEOLOGY, AND THE CAPTURE OF MENTAL HEALTH

JON MILLS

The Antiracist Capture of Education and Accreditation

There has been a recent movement across several professional mental health organizations including the fields of social work, counselling, psychotherapy, psychology, and medicine advocating for antiracist policies in clinical education, training, supervision, and praxis. Antiracism training and pedagogy have been introduced at local, state, and national levels in both public institutions and private industry, where universities have adopted curriculum changes in degree programs, and where regulatory bodies now require mandatory classes and continuing education credits in order to achieve and maintain licensure. Some disciplines have already adopted ethical mandates requiring antiracism to be a primary locus of clinical practice while serving the public.

Changes introduced by the Educational Policy and Accreditation Standards (EPAS) adopted by the Council on Social Work Education (CSWE) in 2022, which governs social work education in the United States, now requires social workers to demonstrate antiracist interventions in order to get a license to practice. This was predated by the American Counseling Association's (2015) multicultural counseling competencies guidelines and the American School Counselor Association's (2021) ethical guidelines ensuring that the role of school counselors is to "initiate and/or participate in 'courageous conversations' that move to discomfort on topics of injustice, racism, privilege, oppression and related issues [and] reflect on feelings and sources of personal resistance that might arise in exploring topics of racism, privilege, oppression, marginalization and bias." In turn, antiracist and anti-oppressive mandates *must be taught* in higher education in order for social work programs to retain their accreditation. These policies and practices have also been adopted by the Canadian Association for Social Workers, which revised its Code of Ethics in 2024 to embrace antiracism principles in education and training with an emphasis on anti-Black racism, new black justice strategies, and reparations for those of African descent (CASW, 2024). Under the rubric of Diversity, Equity and Inclusion (DEI) initiatives, the American Psychological Association (APA) has also changed its strategic plan to prioritize social justice as a cardinal focus that is specifically applied to the accreditation of all APA doctoral programs (APA, 2022, 2023), which are likely to result in significant forthcoming changes in the revised ethical principles for psychologists.

The turn toward antiracism pedagogy and training in mental health education under the auspices of social justice activism (Meca et al., 2022) threatens to introduce many unintended consequences in the once noble pursuit of helping the disadvantaged, poor, underprivileged, and those who suffer. No longer is the focus of social work, psychology, psychotherapy, or mental health counseling on the individual, couple, or family unit who present with unique intrapsychic, interpersonal, psychosocial, and familial conflicts and difficulties in adjustment, but rather the purported *cause* of others' hardship and pathology is dislocated to a racist society that subjugates their existence. In other words, antiracist agendas in education and professional training target a perceived dominant identity group with so-called privilege and power based on the color of their skin or social advantage rooted in a psychology of blame.

Throughout this chapter, I will argue that antiracism discourse within the health professions is based in fundamental prejudices antiracist advocates claim to be fighting to militate against, ameliorate, rehabilitate, and heal. Instead, they serve as an inverse form of racism that hypocritically perpetrate a double standard. As a result, antiracism philosophy has been co-opted and distorted from its original intention to educate and combat racism as a humanistic ideal only to proclaim its societal-wide instantiation is entrenched in white supremacy that fully intends to keep racialized others oppressed if not enslaved by white normativity. Given that modern multicultural society in the United States, Canada, and the United Kingdom are among the most ethnically diverse and democratically integrated social collectives in the Western world, attributing white supremacy norms to the cryptic conspiratorial machinations operative in society appears far-fetched at best if not delusional. Before critiquing this mindset in more detail, let me suggest that calling people white supremacists for simply being white is an insidious form of racist propaganda that uses the concepts of race and "whiteness" as dog whistles to vilify and scapegoat a heterogeneous group of peoples falsely accused of unearned privilege and hegemony despite the fact that there is no biology of race (Baker, 2021), as it is merely a social construction, and whiteness appears nowhere on the genome.

Antiracism Rhetoric as Socio-Political Bias

According to antiracist mentality (DiAngelo, 2018; Kendi, 2019), it is not enough to be against racism and condemn it when personally encountered, what most people in the helping professions profess and do, rather you must be an antiracist activist or you are *ipso facto* deemed a racist. Or as Ibram X. Kendi (2019) puts it: "The claim of 'not racist' neutrality is a mask for racism" (p. 2). But when whites—those of European ancestry and Jews—are arbitrarily labelled racist colonizers of all other racial groups and ethnicities, despite wide disparities in class, education, wealth, and equity, this only generates false dichotomies, spreads lies, fuels prejudice and animosities, and hence creates more unwarranted social divisions based in a simple economy of difference and blame. When white society becomes the fantasized causal agent that is *a fortiori* responsible for all of the historical and *current* suffering and disenfranchisement of self-identified minority groups, then we have a very dangerous form of political propaganda that threatens the stability and civility of social relations. These are the premises of critical race theory (CRT), which have become popularized in antiracism education, and form a subset of identity politics that have been adopted more widely through critical social justice theory (CSJ) or what has come to be referred to pejoratively as "woke" ideology. When CSJ becomes dogma within educational paradigms, it conditions the next generation of graduates entering the workforce who will go on to preach the gospel and try to convert the masses.

Once an obscure legal theory not without sophistication (see Lawrence, 1987), CRT has now become annexed in popular culture and used to justify antiracism pedagogy and training as a progressive form of socio-political bias broaching left-wing authoritarianism masquerading as social justice and virtue (Frisby et al. 2023; Krispenz & Bertrams, 2024). In its siphoned hermeneutic version interpreted through the postmodern lens of identity politics, CRT purports two main ontological propositions: (1) White Supremacy governs contemporary society, which is systemically, structurally, and institutionally racist; and (2) Whiteness (including those identified as white) is an infectious disease that oppresses minority or non-normative alterity based in power, privilege, capital, and acts of arbitrary discrimination. In Robin DiAngelo's (2018) words, "positive white identity is an impossible goal. White identity is inherently racist; white people do not exist outside the system of white supremacy . . . Rather, I strive to be 'less white'" (p. 182). Given there is no empirical evidence to support such broad generalizations, as most Caucasians and Jews would be morally offended to be equated with white supremacism or nationalist bigotry, we may conclude that such accusations, modes of thinking, and dispositional attitudes are logically fallacious, what in philosophy we call a non sequitur: premises are asserted as facts when there is no proof or verity for conclusions that are already presupposed. John McWhorter (2021) calls this "woke racism," or what we may simply call new reactionary racism (Mills, 2022), namely, antiwhite hate (Drakulich, Fay-Ramirez, & Benier, 2022).

The new racial hysteria spawning "whiteness studies" (see Engles, 2006, for a book-length bibliography) infiltrating mental health discourse has become prominent in social work, psychology, counseling, and psychoanalysis where "white supremacy," "white privilege," and "white fragility" are simply taken for granted (Altman, 2021; Morgan, 2021; O'Loughlin, 2020; Woods, 2020). The same presumptions apply to attributing "systemic racism" to society at large (see APA, 2021; BACP, 2022), which has corrupted American psychoanalysis in particular (Badenhorst, 2021; Corpt & Richard, 2022; Dunlap, 2022; Holmes et al., 2023; Jenkins, 2022; Mills, 2023a,b). These terms (as bona fide social phenomena) are assumed to be true without even thinking about them—thrown around perfunctorily as if they are undisputed facts that exist as objective properties of material reality when there is no evidence to make such broad sweeping generalizations *in toto.*

Afro-pessimism, anticolonial antipathy, and decolonial rhetoric saturate the literature in the social sciences and humanities (Báez-Powell, 2023; Beshara, 2019; Dunlap, 2022; Gaztambide et al., 2024; Marriott, 2021; Thakur, 2020; Tummala-Narra, 2022; Wood, 2020) with an emphasis on antiracist messaging and pedagogical reform (Badenhorst, 2021; Fuentes et al., 2023; Lynch, 2024; Malamed, 2022; Mills, 2024a; Saketopoulou, 2023) derived from CRT, where microaggressions, implicit bias, intersectionality of identities, the social construction of gender, trans-normality, and the "queering" of any social phenomena is seen as a legitimate form of counter-normative resistance. This new discourse in mental health communities clamor for social activism and transformative community justice (Rao, 2024; Rosenberg, 2022; Wheeler, 2022) with an insistence on elevating decolonial and antiracist ideology, training, and clinical praxis (Comas-Díaz, Adames, & Chavez-Dueñas, 2024; Gaztambide, 2024). But we may question how a philosophy of antithesis and negation of white people will eradicate injustices perpetrated by colonizers from the past. Surely whites today have nothing to do with the actions of their ancestors. This is particularly troublesome given that the history of imperialism precedes European colonization with Arab, Asian, and African empires colonizing cultures long before modern times.

When antiracism education is weaponized to demoralize people in the name of social justice, then we must acknowledge, resist, and reject the untrue, unethical, and immoral posturing such an ideology infests on mental health education, training, and service delivery, which inevitably infects the public at large. It must be openly challenged at all costs or else the helping professions will be transformed into an Orwellian state that harms the masses based in gaslighting, shaming, guilt inducement, bad faith, and traumatic condemnation. Social collectives seeking treatment for mental health issues should never be subjected to identity politics or CSJ activism that favor some populations while devaluing others. This is not egalitarian, humanistic, empathic nor compassionate; but rather indecent, discriminatory, dehumanizing, and harmful. If the next generation of social workers and mental health professionals are trained to think and act this way with the public, then we will predictably see (1) a decline in trust toward the helping professions, (2) an increase in ethics complaints to regulatory bodies, and (3) a spate of lawsuits for psychological damages to vulnerable patients who were emotionally abused by incompetent practitioners.

Social Woke Propaganda

It is not surprising that the field of social work would be the first to turn woke, as social justice initiatives and helping the disadvantaged classes of society had always been its priority since psychoanalysis offered free clinics to the public (Danto, 2005; Graybow, 2017). Brittany Lynch (2024) has recently embraced the call for an antiracist social work mission in education that regurgitates the same CSJ rationale I have just summarized. But we may ask, How does calling out white people on the US history of white supremacy, slavery, white privilege, and their "resistance to learning/discussing antiracist content . . . be perpetrating racism" (p. 207)? Who would not become resistive or defensive if they are falsely accused of a moral crime? Blaming white (Anglo, Caucasian, Jewish) social work students for others' behavior in the past is not civil nor productive, as it generates unnecessary interpersonal discomfort, anxiety, shame, guilt, ostracism, and retaliatory aggression, as it is obscenely offensive. Furthermore, it is morally unjust to sentence and punish an identity group simply based on the color of their skin or ancestry. No one should have to atone for the historical transgressions of others. And this is the very same argument Martin Luther King, Jr. used to justify why we should judge people based on the integrity of their character. This retrograde ideology in social work only reinforces the type of discrimination it has always wanted to ameliorate.

Lynch's (2024) call toward antiracist social work education in curriculum modification, course content and design, classroom environment and instruction, and field placement, training, and supervision that utilizes "CRT as a guiding theoretical framework across courses" (p. 211) is not teaching critical thinking skills or heterodox viewpoint diversity, but rather uncritical CSJ indoctrination. When "anti-racism must be a central tenet" (p. 216) of social work pedagogy and practice, then the field has devolved into ideological brainwashing that displaces its original core values of helping all members of society who are in need regardless of who they are. If antiracism becomes the "central tenet" of contemporary social work, then it will predictably bring about public distrust and the inevitability of the demise of the credibility of the profession. Lecturing white people on their so-called bigoted superiority, privilege, and contribution to a racist society for not embracing the cult of antiracist activism is a sure way to discredit the profession. Who will trust you let alone seek out your help if they know you have a biased agenda? Nor could anyone feel safe in being honest and authentic in their disclosures if they fear being reproached by the morality police. "Weaving anti-racism principles into *all* social work courses" (p. 216) regardless of content or context is merely a progressive political form of ideological conversion therapy.

When Lynch advocates for MSW programs that have "BIPOC student only space" as a means of "de-centering Whiteness" (p. 217), then she is advocating for institutionalized segregation, what Reverand King worked so hard to dismantle, which is a regressive embarrassment to civil rights. Although billed as a battle cry of liberation praxis for anti-oppression, antiracism ideology has a perverted internal logic based on projection of blame and negation of white alterity who are perceived to have advantage and dominance without offering empirical demonstration to support such bald assertions. I am sure there are many disadvantaged impoverished whites who would beg to differ. Here Lynch commits an informal fallacy of logic known as *petitio principii*, namely, begging the question. Not to mention the fact that south and east Asian families are the highest income earners in the United States over their counterparts (Mukhopadhyay, 2023). And given that rates for addictions, mental illness, and suicide are the highest among working class middle-aged white men (Case & Deaton, 2020), the fantasy of white oppression holds little water.

White collectives *en masse* do not act superior to others nor are they oppressing anyone. How can the polarization of peoples based on race be helpful in a democratic multicultural society let alone be educational? The new EPAS mission on turning social worker instruction into antiracist DEI proselytism needs to be rebuked by students, professional membership groups, and the public. If regulatory overreach prescribes educational, accreditation, and practice mandates that are unethical, it will have a chilling effect on the integrity of the profession that will predictably bring it into disrepute.

Antisemitism in Social Work Education

Naomi Farber (2023) has been a vocal critic of antiracist DEI bile that has captured the field of social work in the academy and graduate education, such as the Group for Advancement of Doctoral Education (GADE), research, such as the Society for Social Work Research (SSWR), professional organizations, such as the National Association of Social Workers (NASW), and in accreditation bodies, such as the Council on Social Work Education (CSWE) that wants to replace tradition with activism. All of these institutions in some form or another are issuing mission statements, strategic plans, ethical mandates, and practice requirements that press into service antiracist commitments, anti-oppressive pedagogy, decolonial group-think, DEI enterprises that prioritize the lives of black, indigenous, and people of color (BIPOC)—a most condescending acronym that collapses all diverse peoples into a basket category, as if they are all the same, when they are quite heterogeneous and qualitatively different from one another as individuals—while discriminating against whites for simply being white in order to dismantle so-called systemic racism and white supremacy under the rubric of social justice.

Identarianism in social work education has become so skewed, prejudiced, and distorted in its obsessive fixation on race, ethnicity, sexual and gender inclusiveness, intersectional positionality, and the need to accuse white populations for all the ills of human suffering based in a false binary invective of oppressor and oppressed, that we may readily observe a climate of institutional programing based on a cult of indoctrination. It does not seem to dawn on the profession that when using an oppressive approach to pedagogy that teaches one group is morally evil, while another group is an innocent victim of supremacist and colonial domination, that this dichotomous thinking is an illogical, unethical, unsophisticated form of reactionary antiwhite and antisemitic hate. Besides the widespread gaslighting of students based on untenable premises and emotional polemics, these progressive (illiberal) instructional creeds embrace an educational philosophy based on lies.

Since Hamas' 2023 terrorist attack on Israel, antizionism, antisemitism, and Jew-hatred have spread like a plague throughout the world. It has also been prominent in the academy, medicine, and social work education (Cox, 2021; Cox & Marlowe, 2023; Farber & Fram, 2024), which have deleteriously affected the education, wellness, and safety of Jewish students who have been and are increasing subjected to harassment, denigration, and violence as we have witnessed with the pro-Palestinian campus protest movements. Jews are routinely subjected to a double standard where they are deemed to be white imperial colonizers and oppressors (Hodge & Boddie, 2022) when they are a minority fraction of the world population having indigenous ancestry among Arab lands (Mendes, 2023) with a long history of experiencing persecution, diasporas, and genocide. As a result, they have been excluded, devalued, and cancelled for their identity, are marginalized by minority and progressive voices, feel more isolated, fearful, and self-censor, are shunned by teachers, academic staff, supervisors, and peers, discriminated against being selected for field placements, and are rejected by fellow professionals (Poizner et al., 2022). A prime case example of this is an organization called "Chicago Anti-Racist Therapists," which compiled an online antizionist blacklist of mental health practitioners who were all Jewish (Deutch, 2024; Resnick, 2024; Satel, 2024), a surreal McCarthyite practice of antisemitism dating from antiquity to Nazism.

Farber (2023) is equally concerned with the "widespread academic anti-intellectualism and rejection of truth and objectivity" (p. 19) that threatens to brainwash incoming generations with social justice discourse and plummet the field into an abyss of incompetence where graduates will not be trained to help the masses impartially with dignity and compassion. Rather, if masters and doctoral level practitioners are armed with political activist swords when encountering the public, it bears repeating, we may anticipate a wave of professional complaints, which may further open up accredited programs and regulatory bodies to lawsuits for engendering emotional abuse directed toward vulnerable populations from biased and egregious maltreatment by antiracist zealots. It goes without saying that professional abuse of any form should lead to the revocation of one's license to practice, but if such abuse is condoned—let alone mandated—by a regulatory body, then the whole discipline becomes complicit in bad faith, breach of trust, and institutionalized perpetration of public harm.

Decolonial Racism

Recently, the American Psychological Association has embraced a decolonial liberation psychology (Bryant, 2023; Mills, 2024a,b;

2023d) while the British Association for Counselling and Psychotherapy (BACP) plan to revamp its Ethical Framework to promote CJS ideology including calls to decolonize the profession (Hall, 2024; Morahan & Reeves, 2024). We can no more decolonize contemporary Western society as we can erase history. The whole premise is illogical based on a postmodern ruse to disrupt, displace, deconstruct, and vitiate rational discourse for emotional hyperbole. Even the founder of postcolonial theory, Edward Said (1993), rejects racial and cultural binaries based on the hybridized nature of contemporary life: "Partly because of empire, all cultures are involved in one another; none is single and pure, all are hybrid, heterogenous, extraordinarily differentiated, and unmonolithic" (p. xv). Given our modern globalized world of interconnectedness, history may only be subsumed in our current social ontologies but never eradicated. These revolutionary decolonial fantasies of turning the tides on illusory white oppression are based in grievance, envy, and *ressentiment*, but they will have to overturn a system of democratic liberty in order to be successful. Convincing the social masses they are being oppressed by white dominants will predictably lead to failure as this will only solidify splitting, social division, and rancor that erodes collective identifications with universal values and spurs on more alienation and discord. Here we may be concerned that society will become a borderline personality willing to project all its hateful, sadistic, and destructive impulses onto imaginary bad objects that will bring about a mutual self-destruction rather than mutual recognition, reconciliation, and accord.

A few professional organizations have formed as public critics of DEI in healthcare including Do No Harm, a medical coalition in the US that has testified in Congress on the dangers of DEI, antisemitism, and identity politics in medicine, as well as Critical Therapy Antidote in the UK, a mental health collective concerned about preserving the integrity and healing ethos of traditional therapies, and more recently the Open Therapy Institute in New York

City that combats socio-political bias in mental healthcare, provides therapy referrals to overlooked populations, and training for professionals including promoting research, scholarship, and providing other resources to those negatively affected by progressive social justice causes. These organization have taken principled moral stances against CSJ indoctrination in the helping professions and serve as exemplars of promoting reason, equality, universal humanistic values, and egalitarian treatment of all patients regardless of race, political affiliation, or identity.

It should be noted, as well, that many notable figures among the black intelligentsia adamantly reject CJS ideology reflected in antiracism education including Thomas Sowell, Glenn Loury, John McWhorter, Coleman Hughes, and Wilfred Reilly, just to name a few. The Equiano Project, a British based debate, discussion, and ideas forum on race and society, are also a recognized public outreach collaborative that is against racial identity politics for the simple fact that CSJ and decolonial rhetoric sustain racism and social divisions.

Antiracism or decolonial pedagogy is an exercise in reverse racism, which is a good way to drive away students interested in the helping professions to begin with. CRT propaganda reinforces victimization culture, subordinates individual autonomy, freedom, agency, and personal accountability for existential choices one makes in life. When social collectives are encouraged by educators to view themselves as victims of oppression, who are therefore entitled to compensation, special treatment, and excused of any personal responsibility for their attitudes, behaviors, and expectations from others, this type of emotional prejudice ultimately harms society. It does not teach the youth how to think critically, to embrace alternative perspectives in phenomenology, epistemology, and social reality, or become adaptive and successful in navigating the vicissitudes of the real world where no one is entitled to special status without merit, civility, and humility, where mutual politeness, respect, prudence, and courtesy are proper virtues—not merely ethical posturing—based in a philosophy of universal egalitarian humanism.

The Psychopathology of DEI

Having previously critiqued the psychopathology of DEI (discrimination, exclusion, and indoctrination) in popular culture (Mills, 2024c), I am reminded of a colleague forced to attend a mandatory workplace antiracism seminar who told me the following. Amongst a mixed-racial audience, one facilitator opened the session by asking the participants what they knew about white privilege. Many of the white men in attendance became defensive: their faces turned red, either in embarrassment or anger, remained silent, self-censored, or looked on with an impassive stare. The facilitator took this as evidence of privilege due to a lack of acknowledgement or engagement and went on to say that white people should feel responsible for white power differentials and promoting poverty. The colleague said that the general impression in the room was that of an infantilizing scolding where "she tried to guilt us into believing we are responsible for other's poverty and lack of privilege." A second co-facilitator stated that since it is impossible not to be racist in a society dominated by white supremacy, white people are innately racist. Some black people started high-fiving one another, while whites felt totally dehumanized. Some people started to cry and left the room. There was no agenda—no goals or objectives to guide any meaningful dialogue or discussion, only to harangue and "lecture down to us." The struggle session was a complete and utter paroxysm of antiwhite racism, where most white staff felt cornered, devalued, and mind-controlled: "They were firing at us, telling us how flawed we were." And all of these teaching were culled from the wisdom of CRT.

It does not take much to imagine how interpersonally shaming or potentially hurtful such emotional diatribes can have on people.

When academics announce their race, ethnicity, sex, social class, disability status, gender identity, and pronouns as being germane to their teaching, research, or scholarship, we should be alerted to their bias, especially when it is touted as a qualification to combat white supremacy, systemic racism, settler colonialism and so forth, whether in the academy, society, or science. Signaling race and markers of group identification undermines scientific independence, neutrality, impartiality, and intellectual freedom for the imposition of political ideology kowtowing to the wishes of the aggrieved steeped in identity fetishism and those in search of usurping power (cf. Fuentes et al., 2024). A most preposterous sham that is currently swindling a moment of acceptability is to call "white epistemology" or the "white racial frame" "racist science," such as in STEM studies. The notion that "white science" is racist is a vacuous farce. Most ridiculous is the notion that the subject of mathematics should be taught in school that it is based in white supremacy (Klainerman, 2021) despite the fact that major advances in the field have historically come from Egyptians, Babylonians, Greeks, Chinese, Indians, and Arabs—and whatever ethnicity, mathematicians tend to get similar results (Mills, 2023c).

The Corruption of Traditional Psychotherapies

A more recent politically corrupt takeover of a once esteemed neutral establishment is the APA's wholesale endorsement of antiracist propaganda that glistens the pages of its official journals by demeaning whites based in CRT. We are now told in the *American Psychologist*, APA's flagship journal, that the concept of *professionalism* is based in white supremacy, *relativism* trumps *universal* truth claims, *subjectivity* overrides *objectivity*, that personal lived *experience* is more important than *empirical* reality, and that *collective* minority group identity based on race, ethnicity, and the like eclipses the *individualist* notion of agency, freedom, choice, and taking existential responsibility for one's life. Derald Sue, Helen Neville, and Laura Smith (2024) rely on the usual CRT tropes of asserting (with no evidence) that the disciplines of counseling and psychotherapy are racist—due to white supremacy of course, and that cultural racism in psychology is perpetuated by the notion of "professionalism" —as if we should never have professions, professional standards to protect the public, codes of competence, and accountability as a discipline. We are then advised that we should abandon the Enlightenment notions of reason, science, logos, evidence, the experimental method, and objectivity for the philosophical doctrine of "relativism," which assumes that any claims to truth and reality are as equally valid as any other, an absurd notion that is simply incredulous yet given some semblance of reliability when it applies to the lives of people of color (POC) simply because they tell us so. If everything is relative, then there are no absolute truths, facts, or universals, hence no objective properties of the universe. Here I suppose the laws of physics no longer apply simply because someone thinks they can fly. If there are no universal facts or values then there is no epistemic or material reality independent of one's mind. Tell that to the doctor next time a brick falls on your head.

Sue et al.'s (2024) paper appears to be written as a hoax article, but it is not. We are told that "universalism promotes racial color blindness" when universality merely applies to all people regardless of the color of their skin; that "individualism blames the victim" when all individuals are autonomous agents capable of free choice that has nothing to do with victimization; that "objectivity leads to demonization and objectification" when objectivity refers to the epistemic correspondence and justification of what we know about facts in the world; and "empiricism denies the lived reality of POC" when extraspective empirical observation is not to be equated with subjective phenomenology, both of which are operative simultaneously (p. 596). Sue et al. (2024) also refer to the "myth of meritocracy" (p. 598), as if POC are not capable of merit, success, excellence, or achievement. Suggesting that minority groups are helpless passive victims incapable of defending their ideas, lives, or taking accountability for their existence is an indecent condescension and infantilization of alterity. The false bifurcation and dichotomous reasoning behind these propositions are none other than feckless fallacies if not a projection of cultural relativism.

Not only are these ontological and epistemological mischaracterizations of philosophy and science, but they extend to how therapy is erroneously depicted and conducted. We are told that white racism permeates all forms of therapy and are

> manifested in (a) treating individuals as the psychosocial unit of identity, (b) defining problems as residing in clients, (c) placing responsibility for change upon clients, (d) downplaying systemic forces (cultural and sociopolitical), (e) focusing on remediation rather than prevention, (f) defining departures from conventional norms as disorders, and (g) interpreting differences from White/European heteronormative and patriarchal customs as pathological (p. 595).

Let us examine each of these predicates in turn: (a) we do treat people as individuals with their own identities, histories, and problems, that is how therapists relate to their clients in order to help them; (b) of course problems reside within the psyche, as they do in external social environments, or people would not be seeking out therapy to begin with; (c) existential responsibility for choice, action, and volition are within the parameters of possibility as agents of change in order to live a more adaptive and meaningful life, as no one else is going to change clients' internal conflicts, attitudes, or behaviors for them; (d) accepting overdetermination of social forces does not mean they are downplayed, only that they are not the direct cause of change over personal agency; (e) both remediation and future prevention of psychological difficulties are part of therapeutic action; (f) normativity, non-normativity, and disorders all exist, as they are not merely social constructions; and (g) cultural differences from Western/European customs and hermeneutics do not make them pathological, but that does not mean there is no such thing as psychopathology. These philosophical assumptions and therapeutic prescriptions on how to conduct mental health treatment violates the leading premises, clinical techniques, and competencies of the traditional therapies (Thomas, 2023), is not aligned with evidence-based practice, and is a salient distortion of how therapy actually transpires and should be taught.

When the discipline of psychology is willing to place subjective experience over objective fact, such as personal feelings or beliefs over scientific evidence about ontological reality, minority identity formation over broader collective universality, such as the notion that we are all embodied in space and time, have consciousness, and are mortal, as bioscience will tell you, and that racialized groups are victims that have no personal agency or choice to alter the course of their lives based in white hegemony, then you are asking rational, conscientious, and pragmatic people to adopt a delusional view of the world.

Sue and colleagues' paper is one of the most philosophically unsophisticated, embarrassing, and naïve articles that has likely ever been published in the journal based in shabby sophistry and a distortion of facts grounded in CJS ideology. It furthermore is a politically biased racist tract the profession claims to be combatting. As an academic philosopher by training, these arguments deserve what Plato refers to in the *Gorgias* as a refutation by laughter. But more dangerously, allowing this article to be published in the APA's premiere journal shows how ideologically captured the organization has become.

Concluding Reflections

If the premises and arguments put forward by antiracist frameworks are not allowed to be critiqued and debated within higher education, let alone clinical pedagogy, and in professional public space such as at conferences, journals, and periodicals due to censorship or cancelation, then we will be fostering a learning environment based on prejudice, cult programming, and indoctrination that will predictably have a deleterious effect on professional training and its impact on society. Focusing on racialized collectives based on essentialized or reified identities determined by biology, race, gender, sex, or intersectional hybridity is to commit the most reductive and dogmatic ontological fallacy that strips away a person's unique individuality, freedom, and subjective agency. Nothing could be more offensive than to assume a race or cultural category determines selfhood or could remotely speak to the private parameters of the life within.

Race hysteria and critical social justice creed have managed to snow the academy and professional organizations through the dissemination of DEI gospel. A no confidence vote should be levelled against administrative programs, accreditation bodies, and licensing boards that peddle antiracist snake oil attempting to wash the brain of heterodox independent thinking, toxicity that should be entirely divorced from mandatory instruction, training, and professional requirements.

When racial essentializing and identity politics are used as weapons to demonize difference and cry foul due to white power imbalances, this stokes conflict, resentment, indignation, and rage, reinforces prejudice and antipathy for the Other, and alienates groups of peoples from different cultures, ethnicities, genders, and sexualities that live and participate in the same communities—all of whom want basic respect for universal egalitarian ideals (Mills, 2024c). Accusing white people and Jews of being colonial white supremacist oppressors who have unearned privilege over all other people of a different hue is an insidious form of racism imposed on alterity in the past. This hatred has no chance of cultivating emotional connection and solidarity between different groups, races, and ethnicities. It will predictably lead to more segregation, discrimination, and repugnance simply based on difference alone. Although these are sensitive and nuanced issues, the cult of victimization, splitting, either-or thinking, and infantile blame does not promote peaceful relations, recognition, or mutual understanding, nor does it serve the goal of higher education.

References

Altman, Neil (2021). *White Privilege*. London: Routledge.

American Counseling Association (2015). "Multicultural and Social Justice Counseling Competencies," *Association for Multicultural Counseling and Development*. Endorsed July 20.

American Psychological Association (2023). "Impact in Action: Reflecting on APA's Strategic Plan and Progress," https://www.apa.org/about/apa/strategic-plan/update-apa-strategic-plan.pdf.

____ (2022). "Psychology's Role in Dismantling Systemic Racism: Racial Equity Action Plan," https://www.apa.org/about/apa/addressing-racism/racial-equity-action-plan.pdf.

____ (2021). "APA Apologizes for Longstanding Contributions to Systemic Racism," *America Psychological Association*, October 29. https://www.apa.org/news/press/releases/2021/10/apology-systemic-racism.

American School Counselor Association (2021). "The School Counselor and Anti-Racist Practices," https://www.school-counselor.org/Standards-Positions/Position-Statements/ASCA-Position-Statements/The-School-Counselor-and-Anti-Racist-Practices.

Amos, Andrew (2024). "The Gender-Affirming Model of Care is Incompatible with Competent, Ethical Medical Practice," *Australasian Psychiatry*, Online first, March 19. https://doi.org/10.1177/10398562241239478.

BACP (2022). "Race for the Soul of the Profession—Tackling Racial Inequalities in the Counselling Professions," *British Association for Counselling and Psychotherapy*, May 19. https://www.bacp.co.uk/media/15293/bacp-presidents-paper-race-for-the-soul-may22.pdf

Badenhorst, Pauli (2021). "Predatory White Antiracism," *Psychoanalysis, Culture & Society*, 26, 284–303.

Báez-Powell, Natalia N. (2023). "Decolonizing my Therapeutic Identity: Going Beyond the Surface," *Psychoanalysis, Culture & Society*, 28 (3): 476-486.

Baker, Beth (2021). "Race and Biology," *BioScience*, 71(2): 119–126. https://doi.org/10.1093/biosci/biaa157.

Beshara, Robert (2019). *Decolonial Psychoanalysis: Towards Critical Islamophobia Studies*. London: Routledge.

Bryant, Thema S. (2023). "Psychologists Must Embrace Decolonial Psychology," *Monitor on Psychology*, 54 (7): 8.

Canadian Association of Social Workers (2024). "CASW Affirms Social Work Call-to-Action in Canada's New Black Justice Strategy," July 11. https://www.casw-acts.ca/en/casw-affirms-social-work-call-action-canadas-new-black-justice-strategy.

Case, Anne, & Deaton, Angus (2020). *Deaths of Despair and the Future of Capitalism*. Princeton, NJ: Princeton University Press.

Corpt, Elizabeth & Annette Richard (2022). "Racism and Other Traumatic Inequalities: Editors' Introduction," *Psychoanalysis, Self and Context*, 17:2, 137-140.

Council on Social Work Education (CSWE). (2021). *Educational policy and accreditation standards.* Council on Social Work Education Commission on Accreditation, Commission on Educational Policy. https://www.cswe.org/accreditation/policies-process/2022epas/.

Cox, Carole (2021). "Addressing Anti-Semitism in Social Work Education," *Journal of Religion and Spirituality in Social Work: Social Thought*, 40 (2): 111-125.

Cox, Carole & Marlowe, Dana (2023). "Antisemitism in Social Work Findings from an Exploratory National Survey," *Journal of Religion & Spirituality in Social Work: Social Thought*, 43(1): 3–17. https://doi.org/10.1080/15426432.2023.2289435.

Danto, Elizabeth Ann (2005). *Freud's Free Clinics: Psychoanalysis and Social Justice, 1918-1938*. New York: Columbia University Press.

Deutch, Gabby (2024). "'Opposite of Inclusive': A Look Inside the Increasingly Hostile Environment for Jewish Therapists," *Jewish Insider*, May 30. https://jewishinsider.com/2024/05/therapy-jewish-mental-health-professionals-oct-7-war-gaza-antisemitism/.

DiAngelo, Robin (2018). *White Fragility: Why it's so Hard for White People to Talk About Racism*. Boston: Beacon Press.

Drakulich, K., Fay-Ramirez, S., & Benier, K. (2022). "The Neighborhood Context of Perceived and Reported Anti-White Hate Crimes," *Race and Justice*, 12(1): 3-27.

Dunlap, Constance E. (2022). "A Renewed Appeal for Vigorous and Positive Action: Commentary on Dennis," *Psychoanalysis, Self and Context*, 17 (2): 174–180.

Engles, Tim (Ed.) (2006). *Towards a Bibliography of Critical Whiteness Studies*. Champaign, IL: University of Illinois at Urbana-Champaign.

Farber, Naomi (2023). "The Dystopian World of Social Work Education," *Academic Questions*, 36(4): 17-25.

Farber, Naomi B., & Fram, Martah Stella (2024). "The Danger of Ideology: Social Work, Israel, and Anti-Semitism," *Social Work*, 69(2): 204-206. https://doi.org/10.1093/sw/swad052.

Frisby, Craig L., Richard E. Redding, William T. O'Donohue, & Scott O. Lilienfeld (Eds.) (2023). *Ideological and Political Bias in Psychology: Nature, Scope, and Solutions*. Cham, SZ: Springer.

Fuentes, Milton A., David G. Zelaya, Edward A. Delgado-Romero, & Mamona Butt (2023). "Open Science: Friend, Foe, or Both to an Antiracist Psychology?" *Psychological Review*, Vol. 130, No. 5, 1351–1359.

Gaztambide, D. J. (2024). *Decolonizing Psychoanalytic Technique: Putting Freud on Fanon's Couch*. Cham, SZ : Palgrave Macmillan.

Gaztambide, D. J., Feliciano-Graniela, F. E., Luiggi-Hernández, J., & Escobar, E. V. M. (2024). "Decolonizing Psychoanalysis: Anti-Blackness, Coloniality, and a New Premise for Psychoanalytic Treatment," In L. Comas-Díaz, H. Y. Adames, & N. Y. Chavez-Dueñas (Eds.), *Decolonial Psychology: Toward Anticolonial Theories, Research, Training, and Practice* (pp. 321–343). Washington, DC: American Psychological Association.

Graybow, Scott (Ed.) (2017). *Progressive Psychoanalysis as a Social Justice Movement*. Cambridge, UK: Cambridge Scholars Publishing.

Hall, Sue Parker (2024). "What Do You Want, BACP Members — an Ethical Framework or a Political Framework for Practice?" *Critical Therapy Antidote,* April, 12. https://criticaltherapyanti-dote.org/2024/04/12/what-do-you-want-bacp-members-an-ethical-framework-or-a-political-framework-for-practice/.

Hodge, D. R., & Boddie, S. C. (2022). "Are Practitioners Equipped to Work with and Advocate for Members of the American Jewish Community? An Analysis of Discourse-Shaping Periodicals," *Families in Society,* 103(3): 358-369.

Holmes, Dorothy E., Anton Hart, Dionne R. Powell, & Beverly J. Stoute (2023). "Final Report: The Holmes Commission on Racial Equality in American Psychoanalysis," *American Psychoanalytic Association,* June 19.

Jenkins, Lee (2022). "Meditations on Psychoanalysis, Race, and The Divided Self," *The Psychoanalytic Review,* 109 (1): 13-33.

Kendi, Ibram X. (2019). *How to Be an Antiracist.* New York: One World.

Klainerman, Sergiu (2021). "There is No Such Thing as 'White' Math," (Podcast), *Common Sense with Bari Weiss,* March 1. https://bariweiss.substack.com/p/there-is-no-such-thing-as-white-math.

Krispenz, Ann & Alex Bertrams (2024). "Understanding Left-Wing Authoritarianism: Relations to the Dark Personality Traits, Altruism, and Social Justice Commitment," *Current Psychology,* 43:2714–2730.

Lawrence, Charles R. (1987). "The Id, the Ego, and Equal Protection: Reckoning with Unconscious Racism," *Stanford Law Review,* 9: 317-388.

Lynch, Brittany (2024). "Anti-Racist Social Work Education: "Ready or Not, Here I Come, You Can't Hide . . .", *Journal of Teaching in Social Work*, 44:2, 204-223, DOI: 10.1080/08841233.2024.2316350.

Malamed, Charla Ruby (2022). "Does Your Institute Have an Anti-Racism Commitment? Interrogating Anti-Racism Commitments in Psychoanalytic Institutes," *Psychoanalysis, Culture & Society*, Online first: 1-11. https://doi.org/10.1057/s41282-022-00285-1.

Marriott, David S. (2021). *Lacan Noir: Lacan and Afro-Pessimism*. Cham, SZ: Palgrave Macmillan.

McWhorter, John (2021). *Woke Racism: How a New Religion Has Betrayed Black America*. New York: Penguin Random House.

Meca, A., Sparkman-Key, N. M., Johnson, K. F., & Tarver, S. Z. (2022). Introduction. In K. F. Johnson, N. M. Sparkman-Key, A. Meca, & S. Z. Tarver (Eds.), *Developing Anti-Racist Practices In the Helping Professions: Inclusive Theory, Pedagogy, and Application* .(pp. 1–11). Palgrave Macmillan/Springer Nature. https://doi.org/10.1007/978-3-030-95451-2_1.

Mendes, Phillip (2023). "Empowering the Lived Experience Voices of Arabs but not Jews: The Attempted Subversion of Universal Social Work Values by the Extremist Boycott, Divestment and Sanctions (BDS) Movement," *Migration und Soziale Arbeit*, 1: 35-44.

Mills, Jon (2024a). "How the American Psychological Association is Harming Society,"*New English Review*, April 1. https://www.newenglishreview.org/articles/how-the-american-psychological-association-is-harming-society/.

_____ (2024b). What Happened to the American Psychological Association? *Merion West*, January 17. https://merionwest.com/2024/01/17/what-happened-to-the-american-psychological-association/.

_____ (2024c). "Discrimination, Exclusion, Indoctrination: The Psychopathology of DEI," *The Equiano Project*, April 15. https://theequianoproject.substack.com/p/discrimination-exclusion-indoctrination.

_____ (2023a). "The Toxicity of Racial Politics in American Psychoanalysis: A Critique of BIPOC Experiences in Division 39 and the Holmes Commission Reports," *Unsafe Science*, September 8. https://unsafescience.substack.com/p/the-toxicity-of-racial-politics-in.

_____ (2023b). "Burning Down the House—The Crisis in American Psychoanalysis: How Wokeism and Identity Politics are Destroying the Profession and Marginalizing Jews.," *Fathom Journal*, May 30. https://fathomjournal.org/burning-down-the-house-the-crisis-in-american-psychoanalysis-how-wokeism-and-identity-politics-are-destroying-the-profession-and-marginalising-jews/.

_____ (2023c). "On Whiteness, Racial Rhetoric, Identity Politics, and Critical Race Theory: A Crucial Moment in American Psychoanalysis," In Fred Busch (Ed.), *Psychoanalysis at the Crossroads: An International Perspective*, pp. 199-212. London: Routledge.

_____ (2023d). "Antisemitism in the APA? The Case of Lara Sheehi," *Areo Magazine*, February 7.

_____ (2022). "Woke Psychology and New Racism," *New Grapevine Magazine*, July 6, 2022, 62-63. https://grapevinemagazine.ca/articles/woke-psychology-and-new-racism.

Morahan, M, & Reeves, A. (2024). "Reshaping the Ethical Framework," *Therapy Today*, Vol 35 (2): 42-44.

Morgan, Helen (2021). *The Work of Whiteness*. London: Routledge.

Mukhopadhyay, Sounak (2023). "Indians are Highest-Earning Ethnic Group in USA: Harsh Goenka Explains Why," *Mint*, January 15. https://www.livemint.com/news/india/indians-are-highest-earning-ethnic-group-in-usa-harsh-goenka-explains-why-11673748104413.html.

O'Loughlin, Michael (2020). "Whiteness and the Psychoanalytic Imagination," *Contemporary Psychoanalysis*, 56(2-3): 353-374.

Poizner, Annette, Love, Stacey, Spindel, Andria, Primerano, Jesse, Alloul, Elisa, Katzman, Rebecca & Walker, Robert. (2022). "Exclusion, Isolation, and Rejection: Emerging Anecdotal Reports of Jews Studying Social Work—Preliminary Findings," *Journal of Contemporary Antisemitism*, 5(2): 97-110. https://doi.org/10.26613/jca.5.2.118.

Rao, Jyoti M. (2024). "Social Justice Activism as Interpretation in a Loewaldian World," *Journal of the American Psychoanalytic Association*, 71(6), 1149-1173.

Resnick, Allison (2024). "Jewish Therapists Boycotted in Chicago Respond," *Kesher: Journal of the Association of Jewish Psychologists*, 1(1): 19-23.

Rosenberg, Joyce M. (2022). "A Call for Inclusiveness in the Psychoanalytic Community,." *The Psychoanalytic Review*, 109 (1): 35-38.

Said, Edward W. (1993). *Culture and Imperialism*. New York: Vintage.

Saketopoulou, Avgi (2023). "Anti-Racism Racism: Trauma, Traumatism, Traumatophilia," *Journal of the American Psychoanalytic Association*, 70 (6): 1071-1109.

Satel, Sally (2024). "Inside the Campaign to Blacklist 'Zionist' Therapists," *The Free Press*, August 12. https://www.thefp.com/p/campaign-to-blacklist-zionist-therapists.

Sedgwick, James M. (2022). "Therapy and Diversity—An (Un)therapeutic Relationship?" *European Journal of Psychotherapy & Counselling*, Online first, 1-15.

Sue, Derald Wing, Neville, Helen A., & Smith, Laura (2024). "Racism in Counseling and Psychotherapy: Illuminate and Disarm," *American Psychologist*, 79(4): 593-605.

Thakur, Gautam Basu (2020). *Postcolonial Lack: Identity, Culture, Surplus*. Albany, NY: State University of New York Press.

Thomas, Val (Ed.) (2023). *Cynical Therapies: Perspectives on the Antitherapeutic Nature of Critical Social Justice*. Milton Keynes, UK: Ocean Reeve Publishing.

Tummala-Narra, P. (2022). "Can We Decolonize Psychoanalytic Theory and Practice?" *Psychoanalytic Dialogues*, 32(3): 217–234.

Wheeler, Kalen (2022). "Still-Evolving Thoughts on Transformative Justice and Community Psychoanalysis," *Division | Review: A Quarterly Psychoanalytic Forum*, 28 (Winter): 35-38.

Wood, D.A. (2020). *Epistemic Decolonization: A Critical Investigation into the Anticolonial Politics of Knowledge*. Cham SZ: Palgrave Macmillan.

Woods, Alexandra (2020). "The Work Before Us: Whiteness and the Psychoanalytic Institute," *Psychoanalysis, Culture & Society*, 25: 230–249.

5

How Transwomen Became Women—The Transition of "Gender" from Meaningful to Meaningless

Bret Alderman

I.

The word *gender* is a descendant of the Proto-Indo-European root *gene*, which means to birth or beget. Other progeny of *gene* includes the words *genealogy, eugenics, genesis, genius, genocide, genre, genuine,* and, most notably *genitals* (Online etymology, n.d.). This last word is most notable because genitals are the primary though not infallible indicators of sex, and the changing relationship between the concepts of sex and gender has become a topic of fierce debate, one with far-reaching cultural, legal, medical, and political consequences. The aforementioned etymology of gender suggests that it is intrinsically linked to sex, and the two terms have historically been used synonymously and continue to be used in this way to the present day. Yet this particular usage is not as ancient as its Proto-Indo-European roots suggest. As a synonym for sex, it has only been in use in English since the early 15th century (Online etymology, n.d.).

Other aspects of *gender*'s etymological lineage warrant mention here and include the Latin *genus*, as well as Old French *gendre* and *genre*. The Latin line of descent comprises meanings like *race, stock, family, kind, rank,* and *order,* and the Old French contains similar meanings like *kind, species,* and *character* (Online etymology, n.d.). This Latin-based line of descent suggests not only birthing and begetting, but also the act of classification, ordering, or placing within a taxonomy.

Yet there has arisen another usage, according to which the term *gender* means something quite different than *sex*. This usage implies that, historical and present-day conventions aside, the link between sex and gender has been severed or rendered inoperative, so much so that a person's sex can in fact be the opposite of their gender: An adult human male can be a woman. An adult human female can be a man. Such individuals who possess genders that are the opposite of their sex are described by way of the prefix 'trans.' Derived from the Latin, this prefix means *across, beyond, through, on the other side of.* Such individuals with a sex that does not correspond to their gender have transitioned, crossed from one condition to another, moved beyond a previous state to inhabit a different one.

How is such a transition accomplished? An informed reader might respond that transition involves the taking of hormones and various medical procedures including the radical reconfiguration or amputation of genitals and sometimes mammary glands, procedures that, euphemistically described as *gender affirming care,* have become a massive, multimillion dollar industry. Yet it should be noted that such procedures are inevitably preceded by something far more simple and seemingly innocuous: a performative utterance. A performative utterance, to be defined in greater detail further on, is an utterance become action (Austin, 1975). What this means is that transition is enacted by way of a declaration. A person changes gender via decree or fiat. It is as simple as stating one's 'preferred pronouns,' as simple as announcing how one identifies. Such declarations generally come before changes to the physical body (which are not always carried out), which suggests that gender transition is first and foremost a linguistic matter.

But can anybody truly transition? Or is it perhaps that the word *gender* itself has transitioned? Something about it has surely changed. And is it also possible that this change forms part of a broader transformation in how we understand language itself? My own answer to this question is *Yes*. This *yes* is also the thesis of the present essay: The transitioning of the word *gender* has a great deal to do with a change in how language in general is understood and this change has a name: the linguistic turn.

II.

Coined in 1953 by Gustav Bergmann, the phrase 'the linguistic turn' was popularized by the American philosopher Richard Rorty's publication in 1967 of an anthology by that same name (Neal, 2007). This coinage has come to allude to a pervasive shift in Western philosophy, humanities, and social sciences: beginning in the early teens of the twentieth century, there was a growing acceptance of the idea that language, rather than merely describing or reflecting the world, in some sense, formed it (Levenson, 2011). With such early twentieth century figures as the linguist Ferdinand de Saussure and the philosophers Ludwig Wittgenstein and Martin Heidegger there arose an interest in the formative power of language that would later come to form the turn (Levenson, 2011). With growing influence, this interest profoundly affected the entire intellectual milieu of a variety of disciplines, and many writers see it as being essential to, and, in part, generative of, the postmodern sensibility, with its skeptical stance towards grand meta-narratives, and suspicion of essentialism and philosophical universals (Fairlamb, 1994; Gendlin & Kleinberg-Levin, 1997; Reason & Bradbury, 2006).

Painted in the broadest of strokes and with primary colors,

this sensibility envisions a world in which language cannot reflect a reality outside of itself, but can only reflect the historical, cultural, and linguistic predispositions of the language user. Therefore, there are no criteria for knowing what phenomena are like, independent of the knowledge of how words are used, and there can be no way to evaluate the accuracy of descriptions (Rorty, 1979). Since our experience is always mediated by language, which is itself a product of our particular culture and moment in history, there are no truth claims that can be said to transcend this cultural, historical, and linguistic context (Brandom, 2000). What counts as true or valid is a product of existing consensus-based habit more than anything else. It has little to do with how any given claim might correspond to an actual state of affairs (Norris, 1996). Language, disengaged from a referent, cannot accurately represent anything: neither universal constants in nature, nor minute, intimate human particulars. The resultant worldview is a profoundly relativistic one in which no perspective can rightly claim more validity than any other (Dillon, 1995).

But what does this phrase 'disengaged from a referent' really mean? Saussure's revolutionary volume *Course in General Linguistics* (Saussure et al., 1986) will help supply an answer. It not only transformed his own field, but would later form the primary impetus for structuralism, an intellectual movement that exerts a formidable influence on the humanities and social sciences to this day. In that work, he states that "the only true object of study in linguistics is the language, considered in itself and for its own sake." The statement, upon first glance, might seem like a truism, something so obvious as to be unworthy of mention, but for Saussure, the phrase 'in itself and for its own sake' implied a radical askesis, an ascetic discipline of mind that demanded the exclusion of much that had heretofore been included within the purview of linguistics. Saussure stated that "our definition of a language assumes that we disregard everything which does not belong to its structure as a system; in short everything that is designated by the term 'external linguistics'" (Saussure et al., 1986, p. 21). He goes on to enumerate these disregarded externalities, and includes within them questions of ethnology—the relation between the history of a language and the history of a civilization. Then, he adds to the list political history and relations, such as those between any given tongue and an institution, like the Catholic church. Then, also to be disregarded are the geographical extension of a language, as well as how it splits off into various dialects.

All of these externalities, and others, he recognized as important subject matter for linguistics, but not for his own project. For Saussure's concern, and what made his approach so innovative and fecund, was to understand language as a self-enclosed system, a "self-contained whole" (Saussure, 1986, p. 10). This was what he called giving linguistic structure *pride of place*. In more contemporary parlance, this might be expressed as a *privileging* of structure over all other characteristics. The father of structuralism was explicit both in the fact of this privileging, as well as its motivation. His intent was to found a truly new approach to understanding language, a new science of signs, a semiology, or what has now become known as semiotics.

This new science Saussure contrasted with another approach, one for which language "reduced to its essentials, is a nomenclature: a list of terms corresponding to a list of things" (p. 65). And it was exactly this correspondence between terms and things that he was determined to set aside because, in his view, "it leads one to assume that the link between a name and a thing is something quite unproblematic, which is far from being the case" (p. 66). Much of the subsequent development of postmodern thought inspired by Saussure can be described as an argument as to just how problematic this link between names and things or words and referents actually is.

Contrary to such a school of thought that reduced language to nomenclature, Saussure emphasized the importance of the link between signs themselves. He considered *meaning* to be the effect of intra-linguistic as opposed to extra-linguistic relations. A result of this approach, in the words of Saussure's translator, Roy Harris, was the belief that "the concepts we use are creations of the language we speak" (p. ix) and that "men's understanding of reality came to be seen as revolving about their social use of verbal signs" (p. ix). What we think of as real is *socially constructed*. Meaningful distinctions are not so much *observed in* the world as much as they are *assigned to* it. The idea of social construction will find its way into numerous disciplines that he helped to influence and that will bear heavily upon a new sense of the word *gender* as understood by a generation of feminists (Lawford-Smith, 2022).

A final element of Saussure's thought that warrants brief mention here is what is called the arbitrariness of the sign. This arbitrariness resides in the fact that the way a word sounds has little to do with what it means. The sound pattern, what he referred to as the *signifier* has no intrinsic relationship to the *signified*, the word's meaning. The relationship is simply a matter of convention. Once agreed upon and accepted in general usage, any set of sounds can be made to signify any other concept. In English we use the signifier *sea* to speak of the same signified that in Spanish is spoken of with the signifier *mar*. In French, German, Swahili, Farsi, and other languages, yet other signifiers, with remarkably different sound patterns, are used to speak of essentially the same concept. "The language we use is a convention," said structuralism's originator, "and it makes no difference what exactly the nature of the agreed sign is" (Saussure, et al., 1986, p. 10).

Although his approach—a quite conscientious and pragmatic delimitation of an area of study—had a certain theoretical justification, it implicitly calls into question what relationship, if any, the system of signs might have with the world within which it is spoken and written. On some accounts, Saussure's exclusion of the referential dimension of language was "strictly a matter of methodological convenience, a heuristic device adopted for the purpose of describing the structural economy of language, that is, the network of relationships and differences that exist at the level of the signifier and the signified" (Norris, 1990, pp. 184-185). It was not intended as a point of dogma as to the absolute dissociability of language in relation to a world to which it ostensibly refers. A similar statement can be made as to the arbitrary aspect of the sign. It may refer to the signified in its relation to the signifier or, on the other hand, it may refer "to the linguistic sign being arbitrarily related to the referents. It is generally assumed that Saussure was referring to the relationship between signifier and signified" (Kugler, 1982, p. 59). Both of these points emphasize what appears to be a fundamental ambiguity—the lack of any clear, discernible explication of the relation between signs and referents. The way in which words refer to the objects of the world appear to be either a point of little interest or a somewhat arbitrary relationship, or perhaps both.

Several decades after the publication of Saussure's *Course*, echoes of his exclusion of the referential dimension of language could still be heard, resoundingly so, in the title of Michel Foucault's *Les Mots et les Choses*, the literal translation of which is *Words and Things*, although the volume was published as *The Order of Things* (1973). The work can, and should, be read in the light of Saussure's assertion that the link between things and the words that name them is problematic. Foucault extends this assertion, applying the principles of structuralist linguistics to areas far outside the realm of its original purview, to the analysis of what he called an *episteme*—a system of thought "that defines the conditions of possibility of all knowledge" (p.168).

Such epistemes are problematic precisely because of the dubious way that they link words with things. A pithy summation of Foucault's complex, challenging work might be: The order of things as we know it is arbitrary and the result of the age in which we live. An image favored by Foucault to address this arbitrariness is that of a grid. It appears and reappears throughout the book. And it is language, conceived as a system of signs, that forms the grid. Such a grid is presented as something like a lattice by which, and through which, humans perceive and articulate their world.

Importantly, it is the linguistic/epistemic grid that determines how we classify what we perceive. Foucault (1973) asks his reader throughout—How are we "able to establish the validity of [any] classification with complete certainty? On what 'table', according to what grid of identities, similitudes, analogies, have we become accustomed to sort out so many different and similar things?" On his account, we are able to sort out so many different and similar things not by virtue of anything immediately apparent or given by perception nor anything determined by an *a priori*. The only ground that might serve to determine the validity of any classification, tellingly, Foucault looks for in the very grid or table that is used to express these taxonomical, classificatory distinctions. An individual perceives similarities and differences based on the criteria she or he already possesses. A person's sense of order, for Foucault, has no existence except in the grid that is created by language, the grid that *is* language.

Jaques Derrida, the founder of a literary-philosophic method known as *deconstruction*, was similarly influenced by Saussure. He is, arguably, along with Foucault, the most quintessentially postmodern theorist of his generation and undoubtedly one of its most influential. The term *deconstruction* itself, which has become commonplace in both academic and popular vernacular, as well as its usage by people who know little or nothing of its origins, testifies to this fact: Its prevalence bespeaks Derrida's cultural impact, perhaps far more than the innumerable citations of his works.

Drawing heavily upon Saussurian linguistics with its focus upon intralinguistic relations, that is to say, its focus upon the creation of meaning by way of the interplay of signs upon signs, he posited what he called an "assemblage" (Derrida, 1973, p. 131), a stratagem that would define, in one form or another, the entirety of his writings. That stratagem or assemblage is known as *différance*, and it allowed him to create a seemingly revolutionary critique that purported to shake the very foundations of Western thought and undermine just about any certitude.

Différance is a neologism that plays upon dual senses of the French verb *différir*—to defer or delay, but also, to differ or to be non-identical. Fundamental to the production of textual meaning, as deferral it alludes to a temporal lag forever at work within language: The conclusive meaning of a word, a phrase, an utterance can never be truly grasped because it is always dependent upon its relation to other words, or signs, the meaning of which cannot yet be made fully present until other words are present as well. According to this logic, the question of meaning is always subject to postponement. Every time we ask what a word, a sentence, or an entire text means, we can only respond by using yet other words, sentences, and texts, which themselves are subject to similar queries. Différance as deferral signifies the "interposition of a delay, the interval of a *spacing* and *temporalizing* that puts off until 'later'" any ultimate, definitive meaning (Derrida, 1973, p. 129).

But the strategic assemblage of différance does not merely allude to deferral, to a semiotic *not yet* forever and always at work within texts. It also alludes to a *differentiation*. *Spacing* is the name for this differentiation. What, precisely, is meant by "spacing" is perhaps most easily understood in terms of the iterability of the sign, the repeatability of words. Although the signifier—the manifest word or linguistic unit, what you see upon the page or hear—may appear seemingly identical from one instance to another; its meaning, its signified, cannot. No word, no phrase, no utterance has an identical meaning from one context to another. In this sense, the absolute, unequivocal repetition of a sign, or any meaningful utterance, is an impossibility—because the very act of repetition is transformative . . . or so the argument goes. Repetition is transformation and no word is ever the same word twice, much like the repetition of a piano chord will never have the same aesthetic effect if it is played within a different measure of a song, or at another tempo, or within another melody. Take any fragment of language, whether it be a single word, an entire phrase, paragraph, or work, then place it in a different context, and its meaning will be altered. Given that contexts are always changing, each time a text or even a single word is read or heard, its meaning will change.

The effect of such a form of thought is profoundly destabilizing. Any meaning communicated in language appears to be ever elusive, like water or sand slipping through the hand that would grasp it. In a manner similar to Saussure, and even more so Foucault, Derrida takes aim at the link between words and things. This is perhaps made no clearer than in his relentless critique of phenomenology, the philosophy which Edmund Husserl initiated with his work *Logical Investigations* (2001). A guiding notion for all philosophers who work within the phenomenological tradition is captured in the phrase *to the things themselves. The things themselves* are the starting place for all phenomenological reflection. Yet for Derrida one can never get to the things themselves at all. Because the meanings of words are established only in relation to other words, "what you will never find in the dictionary is a word that detaches itself from these internal relationships and sends you sailing right out of the dictionary into a mythical, mystical thing in itself 'outside' of language (Derrida & Caputo, 1997, p. 100). Language is omnipresent and its referent is omni-absent. Language is everything and it refers to nothing.

A great deal of Derrida's critique of phenomenology centers around the idea of perception. For him (1973) the idea of a pure and primordial perception as developed by Husserl was untenable: In contrast to the perception that phenomenology envisioned, Derrida contended that "perception does not exist or that what is called perception is not primordial, somehow everything 'begins' by 're-presentation'" (p. 45n). The statement is typical, even prototypical of much postmodernist thought: Everything begins by representation. Everything originates in language and there is no 'thing in itself' that has not been tainted by it. Put differently, as Jürgen Habermas (1987) noted, for Derrida, experience itself "is indebted to an act of representation, perception is indebted to a reproducing recognition" (p. 174).

The upshot of all this is that evidence—understood as that which is perceptible, obvious, clear, or apparent—is always already rendered non-evidential by virtue of the aforementioned indebtedness. Nothing is quite self-evident because what appears self-evident is merely the result of linguistic play, which Derrida exuberantly described as "the affirmation of a world of signs without fault, without truth, and without origin" (1967 [1978], p. 292).

III.

Often ideas that echo through the hallowed halls of academia acquire a certain provocative charm simply by virtue of their surroundings. Up in the proverbial ivory tower where one can survey vast distances at a glance, they acquire a seductive aura. Communicated in an often-obscure idiom, the abstractions of academics can give rise to a vague sense that one is an initiate into an esoteric cult, privy to special knowledge inaccessible to the uninitiated. But provocative assertions put forth in an academic context can appear utterly risible outside of the academy, and rightly so. Such is the case with Foucault's reflections on the arbitrary nature of taxonomies, classifications, and nomenclature, and perhaps nowhere else can this be seen more clearly than in the case of sexed bodies. In theory, things, including human bodies, can be categorized in an infinitely arbitrary manner just as, in theory, perception is so vitiated by language that it ceases to exist in any relevant sense of the word. But in practice, things are a bit different. Faced with the naked truth of naked bodies, can anyone not perceive the obvious differences that lead to such a simple taxonomy as the sex binary? Can anyone in good faith believe that such differences are simply constructed out of nothing, created *ex nihilo*, merely assigned to them rather than being observed?

Writing on a divide within feminism, one commonly articulated in terms of successive 'waves,' Holly Lawford-Smith (2022) addresses such questions in her book *Gender-Critical Feminism*:

> Pointing to the fact of *social construction* [italics added] when the meaning of a thing is pernicious, or hurts people, is often a first step in finding a way to deconstruct it. This is exactly what the second-wavers were trying to do when they first made use of the sex/gender distinction. This strategy makes sense when it's deployed against things like money and universities (although once made, it is not necessarily easy to unmake). But it's absolutely hopeless against things like rocks and trees (p. 43).

Pointing to the historical and cultural dimensions of womanhood—the social norms and expectations associated with being an adult human female—and differentiating them from the purely biological aspects, in short, making the distinction between sex and gender is an approach that served one generation of feminists in their attempts to articulate sex-based oppression and discrimination. The strategy makes sense within a given context, within certain limits. It makes sense if one knows when to stop. But it is hopeless if one fails to understand that "sex is like rocks and trees" (Lawford-Smith, 2022, p. 42). It is a universally human, self-evident binary that, like rocks and trees, is not merely the result of social construction.

For these feminists, unlike those of the third wave—for example Judith Butler to whom we will soon turn our attention—the sex/gender distinction has not become *absolute*. In other words, the two ideas have not become utterly dissociated from one another. Second wave feminists acknowledge the sex/gender distinction, the difference between the two concepts, but in a way that does not fully detach one from the other. Those of the second wave are able to recognize that although the content of female socialization varies across time and place, the category of humans known as female does not, not in any comparable way. In the words of Lawford-Smith (2022):

> Sex is a necessary ingredient in gender, because it tells us what it is that the social meanings are attached to. There is no way to eliminate or displace sex—as some of those committed to gender as an identity want to do—without a massive loss of explanatory power (p. 47).

The point is simple and straightforward: The condition required for the term *gender* to be meaningful is that sex be a part of it. The two need to be attached to one another. Yet the revolution that Saussure inaugurated—one that, like most revolutions took on a life of its own, alien to its original intent—has inspired a generation of academics to envision a world in which social meanings have become utterly, entirely detached from a world of things, a world of objects, including human bodies.

A concise, simple way of addressing this idea of socially-constructed meanings detached from a world of object-referents within feminist discourse is by considering Simone de Beauvoir's oft-cited declaration "One is not born, but rather becomes, a woman." From her canonical work *The Second Sex*, the phrase was clearly intended to draw attention to the fact of female socialization, its unacknowledged depth and breadth, the incalculable degree to which it has determined what is considered to be feminine, what is taken to be essential to the character of women. On Beauvoir's reading, if females were socialized differently, what we take to be their essence or nature would change dramatically. Given the same socialization as boys and men, many differences that appear innate between the sexes could disappear entirely. The point being made, one that is fundamental to both radical and gender-critical feminists, is the extent to which sex-based socialization shapes our understanding of the sex-class 'women.' In subsequent decades after the publication of Beauvoir's work, second wave feminists focused on questions of femininity and masculinity specifically as sets of expectations and stereotypes that they would come to call *gender*, and for many of them it was important to think of these as something separate from questions of biology (Stock, 2023).

Yet *separate from* was not understood as *utterly alien from*. On Beauvoir's account, the *specifically female* body is the referent to which social meanings have become attached, and the nature of this body is significant, although it is also not fully determinant. Biology is not destiny, but it is also not irrelevant:

> Biological data are of extreme importance: they play an all-important role and are an essential element of woman's situation: we will be referring to them in all further accounts. Because the body is the instrument of our hold on the world, the world appears different to us depending on how it is grasped, which explains why we have studied these data so deeply; they are one of the keys that enable us to understand woman. But we refuse the idea that they form a fixed destiny for her. They do not suffice to constitute the basis for a sexual hierarchy; they do not explain why woman is the Other; they do not condemn her forever to this subjugated role (Beauvoir, 2009, p. 44).

It is clear from such passages, and so many others, that Beauvoir's claim that "one is not born, but rather becomes, a woman," is in reference to the socialization that *shapes* a pre-existing female subject. There is no ambiguity as to what is meant by the term *woman*, no difficulty in discerning what or who is being referred to. It is an adult human female.

Yet Judith Butler, a major figure in third wave feminism and the most widely known proponent of Queer Theory, takes Beauvoir's celebrated phrase and makes it into something it is not. Citing it in multiple works (1986, 1990a, 2016), she suggests that it is consonant with her own argument when in fact nothing could be farther from the truth. She conveniently disregards such passages as cited above and asserts that "the female body is the *arbitrary locus* [italics added] of the gender 'woman,' and there is no reason to preclude the possibility of that body becoming the locus of other constructions of gender" (Butler, 1986, p. 35). But there is! There is a reason to preclude any other body than the female one from becoming the locus of the gender 'woman.' The reason is that the term *woman* loses any coherent meaning without that locus. Sex is a necessary ingredient in gender.

Butler reasons, furthermore, that if Beauvoir's claim is valid, "it follows that woman itself is a term in process, a becoming, a constructing that cannot rightfully be said to originate or to end" and that, as such, "it is never possible to finally become a woman" (1986, p. 35). Woman is, apparently, little more than a term in a discourse, without any apparent relation to female bodies, and terms themselves are subject to the never-ending linguistic play that Derrida's deconstruction is founded upon. Woman is something like a flexible, ever-evolving concept that can attach or detach itself from any given body. This is all, of course, an egregious distortion of Beauvoir. Her claim was not 'Anyone, male or female, can become a woman.'

At the same time, the supposed arbitrary relation of the female body and the word *woman* echo Saussure's claims as to the arbitrariness of the sign and his emphasis on socially constructed meanings, as well as Foucault's reflections as to the arbitrariness of taxonomies. Yet, as happens with echoes, Butler's reference to an arbitrary locus also reflects a growing distortion: Each iteration of what is meant by *arbitrary* and what is meant by *construction* sounds so dissimilar to previous iterations as to appear utterly alien.

Question: What is gender if, contrary to the second wave feminists, it is understood as something divorced from sex? Answer: It is performance, or better yet, performativity.

Judith Butler, has arrived at just such a conclusion. For her, such a divorce is quite simple. Drawing heavily upon Foucault, she easily dismisses the sex binary as little more than the result of a historically determined linguistic/epistemic grid. It is certainly not given by the nature of things. Furthermore, she extends this logic to gender and sexuality. In a fit of hyper historicism gone awry, she argues that "sex, gender, and heterosexuality are historical products which have become conjoined and reified as natural over time" (Butler, 1990, p. 525). Such a statement not only dismisses the reality of sex, it dismisses its relation to gender. It is as if Butler, like a gleeful surgeon with bloody hands, separated a pair of conjoined twins and remained indifferent to their survival. Put differently, she has, to use Lawford-Smith's language, displaced sex, and in so doing, the explanatory power of gender has been lost. The word *gender* has now fully transitioned. It means something that it did not. Or perhaps this transition is best conceived as one in which gender, which once meant something, now means nothing.

Whatever is left of its meaning, on her account, has something to do with 'performativity' and her conception of gender as performance has had a remarkable impact upon the popular understanding of what is meant by *gender*. Despite the impact, few people may be familiar with Butler's argument, and even those who are may have a difficult time reproducing it. Butler's writings are notoriously difficult and murky in their conceptualization. When the theme is performativity, she often communicates simple ideas while giving the impression of saying something far more complex.

Performativity does, however, occasionally make its appearance upon the stage of her prose without the sophist's regalia that cloaks it in philosophic complexity. In some essays she expresses herself with a modicum of clarity, as in *Performative Acts and Gender Constitution: An Essay in Phenomenology and Feminist Theory* (Butler, 1990) in which she informs the reader that "the acts by which gender is constituted bear similarities to performative acts within theatrical contexts" (p. 521). The word 'contexts' here is crucial for understanding Butler's argument, for context is exactly what she disregards as will be made clear further on. Yet her reference to theatre is a helpful one: Just as actors upon a stage think of their bodies as the 'instruments' through which they perform their craft, bodies off the stage are also involved in the crafting of identities, the creation of characters, the fictions we take to be real. Both on and off the stage, we create the illusion of a self through stylized action. We *'do'* the body as much as we *are* the body.

Despite Butler's use of the analogy to theatre to explain her concept of gender performativity, it is speech act theory, and more specifically Derrida's modification of it, that Butler uses to support her argument (Miller, 2007). J. L. Austin, a British philosopher of language, along with his student John Searle, developed this theory which, in its original conception, as put forth by Austin in his book *How to Do Things with Words* (1975), introduced the idea of a *performative utterance*: a speech act that does not merely *describe* something but *does* something. Austin argued that certain uses of language serve neither to represent nor to structure reality. Rather, they bring a new state of affairs into being.

The most paradigmatic and oft-cited example of such a performative utterance is marriage vows. When a person says 'I do' at the altar of a marriage ceremony, they are not merely describing what they are doing, they are actually doing it. Within appropriate circumstances and specified social contexts, what Austin called *felicity conditions*, simply saying something brings about a situation that had not existed beforehand: In the act of saying 'I do,' a person becomes married. 'I do' is, in such a setting, a *performative*: an utterance in which to say something is to do something, which Austin contrasts with a *constative*, an utterance that is assertive or descriptive, correctly or incorrectly, of a set of facts. A constative is. A performative does. It brings about what it says. Making a bet or promise, christening a ship, saying 'I quit,' giving an order or warning, apologizing, or taking an oath can also function as a performative.

It is important to note that such phrases are performatives *only* in light of the total situation in which the utterance is issued—the total speech act—which must fulfill the necessary *felicity conditions*. This total situation, furthermore, includes much that could be considered *extralinguistic*, that is to say, it includes the entire setting within which the words are uttered. If a person says the words 'I promise' while reporting another person's speech, as an actor in a play, while reading a poem, or as the punchline to a joke, then the words may not be performatives at all, much like the words 'I do' uttered outside a wedding ceremony may not either. Context and intent are crucial. Without them, the 'abracadabra-like' quality of a performative is not in force. From the Aramaic phrase *avra kehdabra*, which means "I will create as I speak," *abracadabra* is perhaps a good phrase to remember what is meant by *performative* in Austin's original sense of the term.

In his essay *The University Without Condition* (2002), Derrida makes use of, while simultaneously undermining, Austin's understanding of performative and constative utterances. This is somewhat typical of his habitual form of argumentation. He often deconstructs the binaries that, somewhat surreptitiously, he later relies upon to make his point. The deconstructive element of his argument in this case is contained in the phrase *without condition*. This is the element of Austin's speech act theory that Derrida sets aside, and in so doing, he dramatically alters its essential meaning. He renders all of Austin's carefully delineated felicity conditions inoperative. And it is this conditionless version of performativity that Butler adopts as her own, a version that utterly ignores context and intent. In the introduction to *Excitable Speech* (1997), Butler, in reference to the total speech act that defines performatives, states that "there is, however, no easy way to decide on how best to delimit that totality" (p. 3). Where does the total speech act with all of its potentially felicitous conditions begin and end? There is no way of saying in all certainty.

Simultaneously, while eliminating the question of context by undermining any way of delimiting the speech act, she construes any action whatsoever as a form of speech. Austin's *How to Do Things with Words* (1975) becomes in Butler's hands a question of how 'doing things' *are* words. The notion of *speech as act* becomes *act as speech*, or in Butler's words "every act is itself a recitation" (1996, p. 187). This is, perhaps, a less egregious form of Butler's use of speech act theory. The belief that actions, mannerisms, gestures, facial expressions, etc. can be used to communicate is fairly well accepted. Few people would quibble with the notion of body language. The idea that clothes and make up are also forms of communication is likewise uncontroversial. One could also accept the idea that they can act as performatives in certain contexts. Raising a hand or nodding the head, in certain situations, can communicate the idea of an oath or an 'I do,' which are two prototypical instances of performative speech.

Furthermore, it is not difficult to accept the idea that a person might, through gesture, voice, and costume, communicate the idea of womanhood or femaleness. Actors, both male and female, have done this for ages. But it is something quite different to believe that gesture, voice, and costume can *create* the condition of womanhood or femaleness, as if it were something analogous to oath taking. One does not become a woman by saying "I swear I am a woman" or acting in a way that might suggest "No, really, I am." Yet this is what Butler appears to believe. Stripped of its academic attire and stated with maximum economy, Butler's thesis bears a striking resemblance to Peter Pan's thesis (Alderman, 2024). As J.M. Barrie said of his fictional creation: "to him make-believe and true were exactly the same thing" (1911, p. 75). One might say these words of Butler as well.

The absurdity of such a thesis and the grotesque distortion of Austin's speech act theory resides, perhaps first and foremost, in the way it sets aside the entire context—the entire concrete, objective situation in which the utterance occurs—which is what makes a performative utterance a coherent idea. Without this context, the most important felicity condition of all, in fact the only felicity condition that could be relevant is disregarded: biological sex. One must be a woman to perform womanhood, just as one must be a man to perform manhood.

Performative speech without felicity conditions is like gender without sex. It makes little sense. Without biological sex, the concept of gender loses its explanatory power (Lawford-Smith, 2022) and ceases to be a coherent idea. If even men can perform womanhood, and in the act of performing it, become the gender 'woman,' then gender has become a meaningless concept.

Butler's gender performativity is to Austin's performative utterance what the phrase *hocus pocus* is to the word *abracadabra*. There is a surface similarity between them, but little more. Both are employed in the context of conjurers and illusionists. Yet one is directly derived from a real language, Aramaic, whereas the former is an entirely made-up phrase. It is a fabrication that mimics the sound of Latin without actually being Latin. Used by magicians, it is rumored to be copied from the phrase *Hoc est corpus meum*, which means *this is my body*. But simply saying those magical words doesn't make it so.

References

Alderman, B. (2024). *Eternal Youth and the Myth of Deconstruction: An Archetypal Reading of Jacques Derrida And Judith Butler*. Routledge.

Austin, J. L. (1975). *How To Do Things With Words*. Oxford University Press.

Barrie, J. M. (1911). *Peter and Wendy*. Charles Scribner's Sons.

Brandom, R. (2008). *Rorty and His Critics*. Blackwell.

Butler, J. (1986). "Sex and Gender in Simone de Beauvoir's Second Sex," *Yale French Studies,* 72, pp. 35-49.

____ (1990a). *Gender Trouble: Feminism and The Subversion Of Identity.* Routledge.

____ (1990b). "Performative acts and gender constitution: An essay in phenomenology and feminist theory," In S. Case (Ed.), *Performing Feminisms: Feminist Critical Theory and Theatre.* Johns Hopkins University Press.

____ (1996). *Bodies That Matter: On The Discursive Limits of Sex.* Routledge.

____ (1997). *Excitable speech: A politics of the Performative.* Routledge.

____ "Performative acts and gender constitution: An essay in phenomenology and feminist theory," (2016). *Feminist Theory Reader,* 493–504. https://doi.org/10.4324/9781315680675-71.

Derrida, J. (1967). *Writing and Difference* (A. Bass, Trans.). University of Chicago Press.

____ (1973). *Speech And Phenomena, and Other Essays On Husserl's Theory of Signs.* Northwestern University Press.

____ (2002). *Without Alibi* (P. Kamuf, Trans. & Ed.). Stanford University Press.

Derrida, J., & Caputo, J. D. (1997). *Deconstruction In a Nutshell: A Conversation with Jacques Derrida.* Fordham University Press.

Dillon, M. C. (1995). *Semiological Reductionism: A Critique of The Deconstructionist Movement in Postmodern Thought.* State University of New York Press.

Fairlamb, H. L. (1994). *Critical Condition: Postmodernity and the Question of Foundations.* Cambridge: Cambridge University Press.

Foucault, M. (1973). *The Order of Things: An Archaeology of the Human Sciences.* New York: Vintage Books.

Habermas, J. (1987). *The Philosophical Discourse of Modernity: Twelve Lectures.* MIT Press.

Husserl, E. (2001). *Logical Investigations* (Vol. 1, D. Moran, Ed.). Routledge.

Kleinberg-Levin, D. M. (1988). *The Opening of Vision: Nihilism and the Postmodern Situation.* New York: Routledge.

Lawford-Smith, H. (2022). *Gender-critical Feminism.* Oxford University Press.

Levenson, M. H. (2011). *The Cambridge Companion to Modernism.* New York, NY: Cambridge University Press.

Miller, J. H. (2007). "Performativity As Performance/Performativity As Speech Act: Derrida's Special Theory of Performativitym," *South Atlantic Quarterly, 106* (2), 219–235. https://doi.org/10.1215/00382876-2006-022.

Neal, A. (2007). *How Skeptics Do Ethics: A Brief History of the Late Modern Linguistic Turn.* Calgary: University of Calgary Press.

Norris, C. (1990). *What's Wrong With Postmodernism: Critical Theory and the Ends of Philosophy.* New York: Harvester Wheatsheaf.

Online etymology dictionary. Etymonline. (n.d.). Retrieved January 3, 2024 from https://www.etymonline.com/.

Reason, P. & Bradbury, H. (Eds.). (2006). *Handbook of Action Research: Concise Paperback Edition.* Thousand Oaks, CA: Sage Publications.

Saussure, F. d., Bally, C., Sechehaye, A., & Riedlinger, A. (1986). (R. Harris, Trans.) *Course in General Linguistics.* LaSalle, IL: Open Court.

Stock, Kathleen. (2021) *Material Girls: Why Reality Matters for Feminism.* Little, Brown Book Group. Kindle Edition.

6

CRITICAL SOCIAL JUSTICE AND THE TRIUMPH OF AN ILLUSION

JACO VAN ZYL

Introduction

Critical Social Justice (CSJ), often referred to as "Woke ideology," has surged into popular discourse over the past decade. Originally emerging from academic circles, its ideas have swiftly permeated corporate media, entertainment, politics, business, and everyday life. As a totalising theory, it purports to offer an exhaustive explanation of the causes and solutions to all societal ills in the West: these ills are due to disparate outcomes between dominant and minority identity groups. Inequity (unequal outcomes) is due to exploitation and oppression of minority groups by dominant oppressor groups. As a practical theory, CSJ promotes an ideology of revolutionary action as the only solution to so-called social injustice (Boyers, 2019). CSJ tolerates no competing ideologies, as these would only maintain the *status quo,* and asserts that utopian liberation from oppression can only be achieved through the revolutionary dismantling of political, economic, and social systems. "Critical social justice recognises inequality as deeply embedded in the fabric of society (i.e., as structural), and actively seeks to change this" (Sensoy & DiAngelo, 2017, p. 26). It is, in the true sense of the term, a *revolutionary socio-political ideology.*

Psychoanalysis recognises that all ideological pursuits are grounded in deep psychological processes (Becker, 1973). As a socio-political ideology, CSJ is similarly underpinned by unconscious psychological dynamics. In this chapter I explore how CSJ mirrors the psychodynamics of an illusion, driven by a desire to restore a state of primary narcissism through revolutionary action. I will demonstrate how CSJ operationalises this illusion through the primitive psychodynamics of envy, its disavowal of necessary Oedipal imperatives, and the use of narcissistic large-group regression as a strategy to secure this illusion.

Critical Social Justice as Utopian Ideology

Critical Social Justice (CSJ) is a collective term for a body of theories, including Critical Race Theory, Intersectional Feminism, Queer Theory, Gender Studies, Postcolonial Theory, Fat Studies, and Disability Studies (Pluckrose & Lindsay, 2020). Developmentally, CSJ represents a complex adaptation from both postmodernism and Marxism. From *postmodernism,* it adopts a focus on the centrality of power, language, and knowledge, emphasising how these elements pervade and construct everything considered true. Under this view, all accepted truths are seen as socially constructed and laden with assumptions, as determined by those in power—ranging from scientific facts to social identities and their interactions. In CSJ discourse, truth is purely subjective, and the identity of those asserting truth becomes a central point of contention, drawing directly from postmodern theories of power.

In contrast to the sceptical nature of postmodernism, CSJ incorporates both its speculative and applied dimensions derived from *Marxism.* As a speculative social theory, it makes assertive claims about the nature of Western society, characterising it as fundamentally and systemically oppressive to certain identities. As an applied theory, it promotes the moral imperative of revolutionary action to dismantle these structures entirely, aiming to establish a more socially just society. The deconstructive methods of CSJ echo the *immanent criticism* of the Frankfurt School, particularly the work of Freudo-Marxist Herbert Marcuse. Marcuse extended the critique of Western society beyond capitalism through the "subjective turn" in Marxian theory (Whitebook, 2023). This blending of Freudo-Marxism with postmodernism provided later CSJ theorists with the terminology and methods to deconstruct, disrupt, and dismantle society along identitarian lines. Since truth is viewed as constructed by the powerful, CSJ advocates for re-anchoring truth not in consensus reality but in the subjective realm of *lived experience* (Casey, 2023).

Thus, CSJ is not merely a theoretical framework but a practical, applied philosophy aimed at fostering revolutionary action (Marcuse, 2014). Such action is contingent upon cultivating *critical consciousness* among the masses—a heightened awareness (or "wokeness") to the ubiquity of oppression affecting marginalised groups in every interaction, utterance, gesture, and thought within Western society. This critical consciousness is operationalised through *standpoint epistemology* (Harding, 2004). Drawing from the Hegelian master-slave dialectic, Marxian concepts of exploitation, and postmodern ideas of power, standpoint epistemology asserts that knowledge is contingent upon identity. Accordingly, marginalised groups possess unique insights into the dynamics of societal oppression that are inaccessible to dominant groups. Interactions are thus framed through a lens of power differentials, reframing other motivational factors, such as the desire for *achievement* or *affiliation* (McClelland, 1961), as expressions of exploitative power relations instead.

Over recent years, CSJ and its standpoint epistemology have permeated research, media, and public discourse, often through narratives about the "lived experiences" of individuals from marginalised groups. These narratives typically outline the individual's struggles under systemic discrimination, followed by calls for revolutionary change. During restorative "struggle sessions," speakers often begin with, "As a [member of a minority group], I feel . . . " and proceed to share experiences of social failure, accompanied by descriptions of fear, discomfort, and perceived injustice. Such accounts are taken at face value, with an assumption of homogeneity in the experiences of all group members. CSJ frameworks predetermine orthodox narratives of victimhood, asserting that true minorities can only be oppressed, while members of dominant groups can only be oppressors. Consequently, it prioritises the experiences and demands of marginalised groups, repudiates attempts at verification, and accepts only orthodox identitarian narratives as truth (Casey, 2023).

In CSJ, Western society is seen as comprising two distinct collectives: inherently virtuous victims and inherently exploitative oppressors. These categories are delineated by race, gender, sexual orientation, ability, and, to a lesser extent, age, determining a person's status as either victim or oppressor. Races are not seen as extremely complex groupings with diverse cultural, linguistic, and historical differences, and individuals are not viewed as complex beings with diverse traits but as moral representatives of their identity markers. Following this, guilt or innocence in interactions is predetermined by *identity* rather than by *ethical behaviour*, *intent*, or the *actual consequences* of actions. In any given interaction, CSJ does not ask whether acts of racism, sexism, or homophobia occurred; it presupposes their existence: "The question is not 'Did racism take place?' but rather 'How did racism manifest in that situation?'" (Schroeder & DiAngelo, 2010, p. 244).

This critical consciousness underpins the *grievance discourse* within CSJ, which portrays Western society as fundamentally flawed, scrutinising everything from Enlightenment ideals and the scientific method to art and infrastructure through the most uncharitable lens.

This discourse is exhaustive in its critiques, seeking to dismantle the legacy of the West by problematising its history and achievements.

> There are many approaches to antiracist work; one of them is to try to develop a positive white identity. Those who promote this approach often suggest we develop this positive identity by reclaiming the cultural heritage that was lost during assimilation into whiteness for European ethnics. However, a positive white identity is an impossible goal. White identity is inherently racist; white people do not exist outside the system of white supremacy . . . Rather, I strive to be 'less white' (DiAngelo, 2022, p. 182).

Problematising is a central practice in CSJ, where adherents examine both macro-level structures and minute social interactions for identity-based harm. Through standpoint epistemology, practitioners scrutinise gestures and remarks, identifying subtle prejudices or *microaggressions* that perpetuate systemic inequalities. The priority given to victim groups' comfort, based on their interpretations, has led to a pervasive victimhood culture supported by a sophisticated framework for managing microaggressions (Campbell & Manning, 2018).

The proposed solution to these social ills is not reform but revolution (Whitebook, 1995) —an overhaul involving the dismantling of oppressive structures, whether physical or systemic, and retaliatory actions against a perceived *common enemy* (Lukianoff & Haidt, 2018) characterised as white, male, heterosexual, able-bodied, and sex-congruent. CSJ advocates for a reinstituting of systems that resort to social engineering and broad-based discrimination, justified by their aims to "remedy" social injustice. "The only remedy to racist discrimination is antiracist discrimination. The only remedy to past discrimination is present discrimination. The only remedy to present discrimination is future discrimination" (Kendi, 2023, p. 22).

Like all revolutionary ideologies, CSJ is utopian; it claims to offer a solution to systemic injustice that the current establishment has either failed or refused to deliver. It reduces complex, nuanced realities to absolutist, dogmatic terms, disavowing the tragic elements of human existence by attributing suffering solely to social causes. This ideological promise of direct access to social ideals creates an illusion of a utopia—a society free from prohibition, frustration, and microaggressions, where everyone's needs are met at microscopic levels. To perceptive psychoanalysts, the envisioned society of CSJ bears a striking resemblance to a world where the infant enjoys unfettered access to the gratifying maternal breast: indulgent, unrepressed, and ultimately illusory—an *eutopia*[1] of Critical Social Justice.

The Illusion – A Yearning for Utopia

In psychoanalysis, the human condition is understood as a tragic interplay of partial pleasures and inevitable losses; a reality that can only be acknowledged and integrated, but never escaped. This tragedy begins at birth, as the infant transitions from a state of paradisiacal bliss within the womb to the harsh demands of external reality. Birth initiates the classical Freudian conflict between the Pleasure Principle or instincts and the Reality Principle or reality-based limitations and civilisational prohibitions; a clash that ultimately disrupts a person's primary narcissism as early as infancy. From this moment onward, life as a sentient human will consist of partial wish-fulfilment in the form of frustration, which the individual will experience as privation.

Due to the painful nature of privation, and the occasional moments of pleasure, a belief is created that primary narcissism can be restored, if only the ego could merge with an ideal state associated with the pristine, maternal union, or the state of "primary plenitude" (Chasseguet-Smirgel, 1986, p. 14). As the infant matures, this

---

1 From the Greek *eutopia,* meaning "good place."

belief in the ultimate reunification with the maternal gets modified through defensive manoeuvring, enabling the individual to tolerate gratification delay, partial satisfaction, and even negation of gratification. Defensive manoeuvring is present at both the individual and collective level, forming the basis of civilisation and a functioning society. Here, illusion plays a crucial role, as it ensures the cooperative endorsement of instinct-privation, while keeping the hope alive of returning to primary narcissism.

> Typically, the illusion is derived from human desires . . .
> [W]e refer to a belief as an illusion when wish-fulfilment
> plays a prominent part in its motivation, and in the process
> we disregard its relationship to reality, just as the illusion
> itself dispenses with accreditations (Freud, 1927, p. 38).

In his elaborate exposition of the role of culture in maintaining functional civilisations, Freud focused on traditional religions as illusory systems aimed at wish-fulfilment, providing psychological comfort while "taming anti-social drives" (Freud, 1927, p. 45).

The harshness of disinterested nature, the certainty of fate (death), and the reality of wish-privation are sources of great frustration and abandonment anxiety. Consequently, civilisations have developed religious systems in which harsh natural forces have been anthropomorphised as human-like gods whom a person can negotiate with and appease; entities capable and willing to respond to our wishes, particularly our wishes for safety and nurturance. Deep existential frustration creates the impetus for defensive strategies to achieve reality-disavowing wish-fulfilment in the ideal.

What needs to be borne in mind is that Freud applied this formulation of illusion to established religious ideologies that have shaped civilisations and have persevered along with them. What traditional religion managed to create, is a system of practices that mediates between the instinctive impulse and eventual wish-fulfilment, ensuring that sexual and aggressive instincts are not impulsively discharged. Mediated wish-fulfilment creates the circumstances to think about, doubt, and reconsider consequences, before going over into action—both for the individual and civilisation.

It is in the conflict between mediated versus unmediated gratification, that religious illusions are to be distinguished from revolutionary ideologies, which employ different defensive strategies to achieve reality-disavowing utopian ideals. While in traditional religions adherents appease, negotiate with, seek guidance from, and plead forgiveness from authority (civilisational and its divine parallel), revolutionary ideologies operationalise the anti-social defences in service of frustrated wishes. The relationship towards authority is different, compared to religious illusion. In traditional religious illusions, the imagined authoritative Other is an ambiguous figure who can respond in punitive or rewarding fashion, whose reasons are up for the believer to discover. Guilt and responsibility tend to predominate in religious illusions, as the subject's own behaviours influence either punishment or reward from the authoritative Other. In revolutionary ideologies harsh realities are associated with a hostile Other who maliciously withholds wish-fulfilment and actively seeks to destroy or torture the subject. Resentment, envy, and hatred predominate his relationship to this authority, which heighten the destructive urge for revolution and emancipation. Other than the complex mediatorial engagement with an illusory authority figure in religion, the nature of revolutionary ideologies is to engage in unmediated, destructive practice that would replace the current structure in its totality, and usher in the wished-for utopia:

> [Religion] has merely given way to ideologies and superstition, or been degraded into mysticism. For there are degrees of Illusion, and a system in which the [mediatorial] dimension of the psyche is preserved does not merit the title to the same extent as the one which abolishes that dimension. It corresponds, rather, to the need for the uniting of ego and ideal via the shortest possible route (Chasseguet-Smirgel, 1985, pp. 216, 217).

Revolutionary ideologies involve a more primitive illusory process employing more primitive defensive strategies. Tenets of the ideology and their execution are aggressively advanced, even to the 'annihilation of anything that stands in its way.' (Chasseguet-Smirgel, 1986, p. 16). Psychoanalytically, these defences include *paranoid splitting, idealising* and *devaluing projections,* and *primitive envy.* These strategies reveal a particular psychological structure in terms of preoedipal psychology, as well as Oedipal psychology. For an exploration of preoedipal dynamics present in CSJ, I will explore the concepts by Melanie Klein, followed by an exploration of its (anti-)oedipal dynamics, as expounded by Freud.

Illusion in Ideological Splits – A Kleinian Perspective

The history of human civilisation is a complex narrative marked by achievements, failures, and adaptations under harsh conditions, contributing significantly to humanity's survival over millennia. Yet, within Critical Social Justice ideology, this historical empathy, particularly towards European civilisations, is repudiated. The West and everything associated with it are viewed as a singularly oppressive force; one whose only acceptable future is eradication. While other civilisations' cultural heritages and histories are celebrated, and their worldviews are accepted as normative, any celebration of European heritage or normalisation of European perspectives is condemned as "white supremacy." As with any cultural worldview according to which cultural experiences are deemed "normal, normative, and ideal," an exception is made with Western or European worldviews, as this is condemned as "white racism or white supremacy" (Collins, 2000, p. 517).

Any acknowledgment of the West's contributions—be it in technological advances or historical improvements in quality of life—is treated with hostile suspicion, seen as an attempt to maintain an oppressive *status quo*. In this framework, Western history is uniquely recast as the narrative of a clear villain, its non-European victims suffering under its colonisation, displacement, and enslavement. In contrast, the histories of other civilisations, including their engagements in imperial conquest, slavery, or genocide, are revisionistically overlooked, even when European nations were the recipients of such aggressions. CSJ re-enacts historical suffering, casting contemporary individuals in roles defined by broad identity markers, assigning moral culpability or victimhood based on these identifiers.

Critical consciousness of CSJ, forensically applied to domains of gender, sexuality, and ability, reflects the psychodynamics familiar in revolutionary socio-political ideologies. To understand the primitive dynamics at play in CSJ, I will consider the psychoanalyst, Melanie Klein's theories on early relational dynamics, such as the schizoid-paranoid and depressive positions, as an interpretive lens.

In early development, the loss of primary narcissism due to separation from the mother initiates instincts aimed at restoring this original state of perceived bliss. In this symbiotic maternal union, the infant's subjective experience dominates, and external objects are engaged with in *part-object* representations. Gratifying elements, such as a breast or a face, are projectively idealised as entirely good, while frustrating elements are projectively expelled as entirely bad. This schizoid-paranoid position employs splitting to protect primary narcissism by isolating and expelling threats (Klein, 1946).

Here, the infant projects unwanted aspects of itself into the mother, who becomes the target of its aggression. Perceived as a threat to its survival, the infant directs hostility toward this "bad" mother, while an "all-good" idealised version of the mother exists to sustain the illusion of unlimited, utopian gratification. Beyond devaluing the object targeted for destruction, idealisation reflects a deep-seated desire for endless satisfaction, conjuring the image of an "inexhaustible and always bountiful breast" (Klein, 1946, p. 4).

Progressing beyond this paranoid position, the infant must develop a "capacity for concern" (Winnicott, 1963) and "gratitude" (Klein, 1957), marking the emergence of the depressive position. This phase involves recognising the mother as a *whole object*—sometimes gratifying, sometimes not—leading to the development of ambivalence. The ability to feel guilt, a fundamental aspect of this position, underpins the capacity for concern. "The synthesis between the loved and hated aspects of the complete object gives rise to feelings of mourning and guilt which imply vital advances in the infant's emotional and intellectual life" (Klein, 1946, p. 2). The infant begins to grasp rudiments of ambivalence and feels a wish to repair the damage it has caused.

However, the drive for unbridled gratification remains, often leading to destructive impulses driven by primitive envy, "the angry feeling that another person possesses and enjoys something desirable—the envious impulse being to take it away or to spoil it" (Klein, 1957, p. 79). Under the Illusion, the infant perceives the idealised Other as omnipotent, possessing what it lacks, namely primary narcissism. This awareness fuels rage, seeking to destroy or spoil any reminder of this deficiency, even if that means devaluing previously cherished objects. Typically, guilt would temper such destructiveness; but when envy has been allowed to dominate, guilt becomes too overwhelming to bear. The infant projects this unbearable guilt into the mother, compelling her to projectively identify with the guilt, while the infant remains self-idealised and indignant. If envious dynamics do not resolve, repair is not integrated and gratitude not experienced, psychological growth can be severely hampered. The proclivity toward envy often leads to the emergence of severe psychopathology, which may find sublimated expression in revolutionary ideologies.

Schizoid-paranoid early dynamics, as seen between infant and mother, effectively encapsulate the psychological underpinnings of CSJ. CSJ group classification is no morally neutral activity. Individuals and groups are either morally condemned or valorised based on *part-object representation*. Race, sex, ability, and identity categories are assigned moral weight, regardless of personal conduct or character. Those with "hated" identity markers are treated as despised entities, while those with "idealised" markers are elevated as inherently good. This fortified defence mechanism, supported by individual and group dynamics, ensures the perpetuation of the ideological Illusion.

To sustain the CSJ Illusion, ambivalence and gratitude are resisted through *destructive envy* and *projective identification*. The ideology resists nuanced, balanced appraisals of the West's history, even though CSJ adherents themselves benefit from Western advancements in civil liberties, science, and governance. Gratitude is perceived as a threat to the unmediated expression of destructive instincts, preventing the utopian dream of an unrepressed CSJ-based society. Primitive envy devalues and spoils what could be valued, and the overwhelming presence of retaliatory aggression renders guilt, the foundation of gratitude, unbearable. Consequently, there is no room for reconciliation, and the moral self-justification of destructive envy keeps the Illusion enviously protected. In CSJ it is prohibited to "develop a positive white identity." In fact, it is deemed "an impossible goal, as white people are considered inherently and irredeemably racist" (DiAngelo, 2018, p. 182).

Those who have internalised the Illusion project their guilt onto condemned identity bearers. Those targeted by this projection often identify with the guilt, manifesting in private confessions or public displays of self-debasement. Following the death of George Floyd and the subsequent Black Lives Matter (BLM) protests, a public ritual gained prominence whereby sports teams, leagues, and public figures were taking the knee as a public protest against a system deemed socially unjust and irreparably racist. This ritualistic display by prominent sports stars, celebrities, and politicians lent moral legitimacy to the resentment narrative. For many black and indigenous demonstrators, this gesture served to proliferate resentment among victim groups, while condemning all white people as responsible for such injustice. The public nature of these displays, the ubiquitous panic around racial threat in America, and the unquestioning endorsement of this narrative by media outlets and commentators created a shared social "reality" that made scrutiny of these messages difficult. White participants identified with the projected guilt and took the knee as an act of self-deprecation and condemnation for their inherent complicity in systemic injustice. Such public rituals of primitive envy and projective identification reinforce the ideological enchantment of ideological Illusion.

In Kleinian terms, the Illusion of CSJ generates a perceptual world of paranoid and projective defences consisting of binary victim and oppressor identities. However, the inclusion of a condemned Other who allies with victim groups against a hostile oppressor, expands this binary into a triadic structure. This subversive collusion between pristine victims and traitorous allies against a demonised oppressor, highlights the anti-Oedipal dynamics of CSJ.

The Anti-Oedipal Illusion of Fatherless Bliss

The Oedipus Complex has been a central theme in psychoanalytic thought, since before it acquired that designation. Freud initially referred to it as the "nuclear complex," considering this developmental process universal, with both individual (ontogenetic) and societal (phylogenetic) outcomes (Freud, 1910).

The Oedipus complex is a crucial phase in psychosexual development, marking the infant's emergence from earlier stages into a relational constellation where a third Other challenges the exclusive, narcissistic world of the mother-infant dyad. This phase coincides with the genital stage, preceded by the oral and anal stages respectively. Later psychoanalysts in the object relations school incorporated pre-Oedipal relational dynamics into the Freudian superstructure, enhancing the understanding of both psychological development and pathogenesis. Early developmental processes serve as a blueprint for the character structures of both individuals and societies. In Freudian psychoanalysis, the Oedipus drama is not restricted to individual psychology, but exists as a supraordinate narrative, "phylogenetically inherited schemata" in the collective psyches of masses (Freud, 1918, p. 119).

In terms of psychological development, the infant emerges from a symbiotic relationship with the Mother, becoming aware of a Paternal rival who threatens the infant's narcissistic Illusion that it is the centre of the Maternal universe, and omnipotent to please Mother entirely on its own terms. The infant now confronts the reality of *difference*: unlike the preceding anal-sadistic phase where he has omnipotent control over the nature of objects, the Oedipal drama introduces differences in sex (material difference) and generations (chronological distinction). The intrusion of the Paternal rival signals a significant moment of disillusionment, or *castration*, as a narcissistic wound in the infant. The perceived betrayal by the Mother and jealousy toward the Father lead to deep, unconscious rage. However, as the Mother lovingly endorses the Father, the infant feels guilt over these hostile wishes on the Father. This guilt he transforms into reparative identification with the Father, giving rise to the Superego. The end of the Oedipus complex entails a paradox: reunification with the Mother is only possible through the endorsement of Paternal prohibitions (Chasseguet-Smirgel, 1986).

Originally formulated in libidinal terms involving the early body ego and primary relationships, Oedipal psychology also reflects the complex interaction between the Pleasure Principle and the Reality Principle. This psychology lies in the staggered relationship individuals (and societies) have with domains of meaning-making, both internally and externally. The internal domain (represented by the Maternal universe and the Pleasure Principle) consists of desires and phantasies driven by instincts; a pristine world of mirroring and fusion, unmediated gratification to maternal bliss (primary narcissism) and certainty, dominated by feelings and emotions, and rewarded for relational closeness (Schwartz, 2016).

In contrast, the external domain (represented by the Paternal universe and the Reality Principle) comprises realities and demands, uncertainties, delayed gratification, prohibitions, governed by thinking and logic, with rewards based on mastery and competence.

> The father makes his appearance as an intrusion into this idyll. He has a relationship with [the mother] that does not revolve around the child and therefore stands as a barrier between the child and mother. He puts an end to the child's primary narcissism. The father's *no* separates the child from this mother and [the sheer enjoyment] of their connection (Schwartz, 2016, p. 35).

Integrating the Paternal enables regulation of both gratification and destruction instincts, leading to psychological disinvestment from the preceding oral and anal-sadistic stages and modulation of the earliest paranoid and depressive anxieties. Failure to integrate these dynamics leaves individuals in an unrepressed state, more inclined toward personality dynamics typical of oral and anal-sadistic stages, managed by primitive defenses. Healthy societies depend on internalised ethical conscience, respect for law, and adherence to cultural norms. The infrastructure of such societies is Oedipal in its individual and collective dynamics and serves as safeguards against unrestrained sexual and aggressive instincts.

The gravest threat to individuals and societies lies in the seductive belief that the Paternal, or Reality, can be disavowed and primary narcissism re-established through unmediated fusion with the Maternal. Perverse anti-Oedipal dynamics are evident in severe cases of addiction, sexual deviance, and anti-social behaviour, and undergird the Illusion in ideological movements.

> An ideology always contains within it a phantasy of narcis-
> sistic assumption linked to a return to a state of primary
> fusion, equally excludes conflict and castration and thus
> operates within the order of Illusion. The leader in these
> ideological groups does not appear… to be a representa-
> tion of the father. These groups aim at an eradication of
> the Oedipus complex and the world of the father. The
> leader is an analogue of the mother of the pervert. Just as
> the latter gives her little impubescent boy to believe that he
> has no need to grow or to mature in order to take his fa-
> ther's place, and thereby spares him having to face up to
> conflict and castration, the leader lulls the group with the
> possibility of being able to achieve total happiness, in a
> rediscovered land of plenty (Chasseguet-Smirgel, 1985, p.
> 193).

The utopian, revolutionary instincts in subversive movements are therefore the illusory manifestation of anti-Oedipal processes. In this anti-Oedipal world, the Father—symbolising reality, duty, and responsibility—is demonised. The anti-Oedipal Mother and Infant collude against the Father seeking to dismantle the Oedipal world. Infatuated with the Illusion, their aim is to re-establish the pristine world of primary narcissism. This illusory world is constructed upon perverse dynamics of reality disavowal, unmediated gratifi-cation, and negation of differentiation. It prohibits maturation, in-sulates the Mother-Infant bond, and viciously retaliates against any threat to it. It is constructed upon perverse compassion in service of the Infant's gratification.

The most obviously anti-Oedipal of CSJ theories, both in its theoretical inspiration and the psychological dynamics it targets, is *Queer Theory*. While assuming the pre-eminence of sex and sexuality as a structuring aspect of social life, Queer Theory goes beyond the sexual and targets the *normative* of society as the primary object of subversion. As an extreme form of standpoint epistemology, Queer Theory idealises subversive hyper-subjectivity, treating cultural, sci-entific, and objective categories with hostile suspicion (Pluckrose &

Lindsay, 2020). "Queer is by definition *whatever* is at odds with the normal, the legitimate, the dominant. *There is nothing in particular to which it necessarily refers.* It is an identity without an essence" (Halperin, 2003, p. 62, *italics original*).

Queer Theory positions itself as anti-normative, anti-essential, anti-stable, and by implication, anti-civilisationist. Freud showed that civilisation is only possible when society is structured according to the neuroticising dynamics of Oedipal psychology. This is achieved by the endorsement of pleasure-depriving consensus reality, cultural and legal norms (identifying with the castrating Father) as a precondition for a peaceful society.

Contrary to renunciation of pleasure in Oedipal psychology, Queer Theory philosophically sophisticates and operationalises anti-Oedipal psychology—and therefore of perversion—in its disavowal of the Paternal. What is objectively and externally structured is experienced as a narcissistic infliction, deemed oppressive, and therefore targeted for destruction. In their quest to bring an "end to the system of renunciation altogether" (Whitebook, 1996, p. 22), queer revolutionaries take delight in vandalising what society holds sacred (Firestone, 1970) and to see it denature into the utopian anal-sadistic universe (Chasseguet-Smirgel, 1984). Their perverse sublimation of extreme desire has given rise to bizarre identities (Ziemna, 2024), thrill-seeking sexual behaviour (Bersani & Philips, 2008), the depathologising of severe psychopathology (Thorneycroft, 2020), the warping of medical ethics (Pfeffer et al., 2022), and the sexualisation of children (Dyer, 2016). By organising and mobilising activist groups based on a shared agenda to subvert normative society, the Illusion of a Queer utopia is invoked. And in the anti-Oedipal world of Queer Illusion, any notion of restraint from unbridled indulgence induces the anti-Oedipal rage against society, seeing it as "some heterosexist plot rather than understanding it as intrinsic to Being" (Weatherill, 2017).

The West's susceptibility to gratification-based ideology can be ascribed to a rise in *common-enemy*-type social religion (Lukianoff & Haidt, 2018) due to the cultural shift in the West from *dignity culture* to *victimhood culture*. Dignity culture is characterised by toleration of minor insults, self-restraint, and reliance on institutional recourse for severe infractions (Campbell & Manning, 2018). Taking the law into one's own hands as a self-justified practice in response to minor slights is uncharacteristic in dignity cultures due to the implicit belief of inherent, universal human dignity—a *common-humanity* social religion.

In a *victimhood culture*, certain identities are sacralised, minor slights and *perceived* offences are amplified, and institutional structures are used to retaliate against offenders. Victimhood culture, with its doctrine of CSJ, has fostered *microaggression* policing, language and belief scrutiny, and cancel culture (Özkırımlı, 2023). Members of victim groups may be protected against traumatic *triggers* as they are treated as wounded infants who are vulnerable to certain language, gestures, or humour. Supportive *allies* from dominant groups often ensure that *safe spaces* and *debriefing sessions* be provided to offended victims. These CSJ rescuer-victim alliances have promoted a culture of *safetyism* where members of dominant groups are reminded to be aware of their *privilege* and the risk of causing *harm*. In addition to creating a therapeutic culture (Aubry & Travis, 2015), these rescuer-victim alliances have resulted in *vindictive protectivism* (Lukianoff & Haidt, 2018) which "involves the tendency to punish offenders in the name of guarding the feelings of those thought to be weak and disadvantaged" (Campbell & Manning, 2018, p. 25). This culture promotes manufactured outrage, online pile-ons, public cancellations, workplace expulsions, and has resulted in a remarkable increase in prejudice (Legault et al., 2011), even tragedy (Sarkonak, 2023).

When Freud wrote *The Future of an Illusion,* he did not consider how the Illusion could comprise of the anti-social instincts he only mentioned in passing. In our age, the inversion (or rather *perversion*) of relational dynamics and moral imperatives by the anti-Oedipal universe have saturated general sensibilities in the West. This sentiment is often seen in responses to anti-social events involving individuals CSJ deems innocent victims: a dangerous gang member of Congolese ancestry who met his fate by police shooting, is not deemed a criminal whose demise means justice for terrorised neighbourhoods; he is seen as an innocent victim (*anti-Oedipal infant*) of a murderous police state and oppressive justice system (*anti-Oedipal Father*). His death and the acquittal of the police officer is therefore protested (*anti-Oedipal maternal compassion*) "for justice, and for real change" (*anti-Oedipal Illusion*) (Reynolds, 2024). Or the Hamas fighters who invaded Israel on 7 October 2023, brutalising, murdering and kidnapping hundreds of innocent partygoers, parents, children, and elderly, are not seen as genocidal terrorists; instead, their terror was pitied as an act of "mourning" (*anti-Oedipal maternal compassion*) committed by "martyrs" (*idealised anti-Oedipal infant*), while the innocent victims are seen as oppressive enemies (*anti-Oedipal Father*) (Nelson, 2023).

The Fatherless world of CSJ and the primacy of standpoint epistemology of the reality-disavowing Infant, inevitably leads to clashes with those who have adequately cathected facts and reality. At an individual level, the Illusory dynamics in CSJ foster *paranoid splitting, primitive envy*, and *guilt intolerance* as well as *perverse dynamics* of *anti-Oedipal* psychology, which collectively may result in *narcissistic large-group regression*.

Entitlement Ideology – Illusory Security in Groups

The psychology of groups or masses has fascinated psychoanalysts from its very inception. Freud was particularly interested in how individuals, through their group identification and participation, could act out of moral character and resort to the kind of unthinkable cruelty reported under Nazi and Soviet regimes. Later, social scientists and psychoanalysts developed models to explain the regressive process involved in mass radicalisation to the point of committing atrocities.

By the time Freud wrote *Group Psychology and the Analysis of the Ego* (1921), he had not distinguished between Ego Ideal and Superego. As the inheritor of the Oedipus and castration complexes, the Superego was regarded as the prohibitory force against incest, or unmediated access to primal bliss. In addition to injunctions of the Ego Ideal, the Superego "also comprises the prohibition: 'You *may not be* like this (like your father)' - that is you may not do all that he does; some things are his prerogative" (Freud, 1923, p. 34). The Ego Ideal aims to recover lost omnipotence and reinstalls Illusion, while the Superego breaks the symbiotic bond and orients toward external reality (Chasseguet-Smirgel, 1985).

To understand individuals' vulnerability to radicalisation, it is essential to examine two aspects of the Superego: its capacity for extreme cruelty and its potential to dissolve under collective dynamics. In group settings, the Superego's restraints disappear as the group's ideals, often personified by a leader, replace the individual's Ego Ideal. Members identify with one another and collectively project idealising defences onto the leader, creating a unifying force that produces a blissful regression to primary narcissism, where Superego scruples vanish. While Freud likens the group ideal to the Primal Father, whose identification anchors the group's endorsement of its ideals, later analysts regarded the group, its leader, and its ideology as representations of the Almighty Mother: "The group becomes, for its members, the substitute of this lost object" (Anzieu, 1984, p. 60). In this regressed state, the Superego's paternal prohibitions are expelled, and the group experiences an illusory omnipotence, intolerant of any delay between desire and fulfilment. "It cannot tolerate any delay between its desire and the fulfilment of what it desires. It has a sense of omnipotence; the notion of impossibility disappears for the individual in a group" (Freud, 1921, p. 15). With the paternal universe removed, the Ego merges with the group and its ideals, approximating illusory primary narcissism. This merger enables individuals to enact unethical policies, impose indiscriminate sanctions, and commit atrocities, driven not by fear of personal Superego retribution but by a dread of losing the group's omnipotent unity or facing punishment for disobedience to its ideals. This process is reinforced through ritualistic homogenisation, manifesting in the use of catchphrases, confessions, chants, jargon, symbols, and insignia, all of which sustain group identification and preserve the Illusion of omnipotence. This large-group regression is ultimately a state of Illusion, which disavows external reality that threatens this state, and which compels regressed group members to enviously and destructively enact revenge upon an identified culprit, ranging from demonising stereotypes to unconscionably violent and genocidal behaviour (Volkan, 2004).

Large-group psychology is ubiquitous in all cultures around the world, and functions as healthy narcissistic investment to offer individuals a sense of self-definition, belonging, transgenerational continuity, and self-esteem. Large-group identity offers its members a sense of sameness across time, and offers its members narcissistic incentive which enables them to individuate and separate as whole persons. It offers them shared prejudice in the form of racial pride, national prestige, religious exceptionalism, and inversely, negative sentiments toward members of other tribes, nations, religions, and ideologies. This large-group distinction between the preferred in-group and ill-favoured out-group, is something Freud called the *narcissism of minor differences* (Freud, 1930, p. 114).

Social fissures already present between large groups, compensated against through friendly relations, generosity, and fair social transactions, which come apart and lead to hostile polarity in *narcissistic large-group regression*. This takes place when an activating event—either through a threatening act, instigation by a bad-faith actor or influential leader, or even a natural disaster—resuscitates a *chosen trauma* and induces the collective narcissistic and envious core of the large-group, resulting in a tribalistic in-group/out-group split (Kleinian *paranoid splitting*). This chosen trauma is "a collective mental representation of an event that has caused a large group to face drastic common losses, to feel helpless and victimised by another group, and to share a humiliating injury . . . [A]lthough each individual has his or her own unique identity and personal ration to the trauma, all (or almost all) group members have developed injured self-images as a result" (Volkan, 2004, p. 48).

During narcissistic large-group regression an illusory process of *time-collapse* takes place when "the chosen trauma is then experienced as if it has happened only yesterday: feelings, perceptions, and expectations associated with a past event and past enemy heavily contaminate those related to current events and current enemies, leading to maladaptive group behaviour, irrational decision-making and resistances to change" (Volkan, 1999, p. 47). In Kleinian terms, *symbolic equivalence* gets enacted, as opposed to *symbolic functioning*. With symbolic functioning, the person appreciates that an external entity *represents* something internal to themselves, and manages to keep the external object separate from the symbolic internal representation. In severe pathology and psychological regression, this distinction is not appreciated. Instead, the external object is experienced as identical to the internal representation, and is engaged with as the thing-in-itself —a process of symbolic equivalence (Bion, 1963). In this state, a *suitable target of externalisation* is identified (Volkan, 2014, p. 53) and perceived as indistinguishable from the historical enemy. What used to be minor differences about which members of large groups would stereotype each other and banter, are suddenly turned into borderlines distinguishing the enemy from the in-group. "The enemy is often thought of as a lower class of human, and, at worst, as actually less than human" (Volkan, 2004, p. 107). The current humiliation is experienced as indistinguishable from historical humiliation; the current activating event equivalent to historical invasions and attacks; the current enemy embodies the historical enemy; and other than what happened in the chosen trauma, the current enemy needs to be defeated and destroyed. Such destruction takes the form of *purification* (Volkan, 2014, p. 100) and ranges from purging language from impure or alien words, to persecuting and murdering those who hold to heretical views or who belong to unwanted subgroups within society.

Volkan accurately captures the blindly envious group-dynamics and the narcissistic group-character during large-group regression. Following an activating event and the regressive large-group split, the in-group is deemed morally idealised, innocent, and unjustly disadvantaged. The sense of shame, humiliation, and worthlessness is psychologically evacuated and projected into the demonised Other. Due to unfair suffering of the in-group and unjustified benefit of the out-group historically, discourses of justified retaliation start to emerge in the form of the *entitlement ideology*. Entitlement ideologies are a shared sense of entitlement to recover what was lost in history, as remembered, modified, and enacted during a state of heightened existential anxiety. Entitlement ideologies are rationalised attempts at recovering primary narcissism captured in the image of historical trauma.

With morally guided and superego scruples dissolved, the individual ego merges with the group ideal of narcissistic bliss, establishing the *modus operandi* to recover lost narcissistic glory: by destroying the cause of humiliation (the Kleinian *devalued other* and the Freudian *Oedipal Father*), the paradisaic state of Maternal comfort can be restored (*Illusion*). While legal structures are still in place, large groups rally around charismatic leaders, adopt jargon, slogans, and songs. During processions they enact rituals of humiliation, struggle, and victory. They design insignia or flags, magically imbued with the substance or spirit of the group. The flag is treated as if it were the victimised group itself. As narcissistic large-group regression intensifies, it usually leads to acts of dehumanisation in the form of discrimination, violence, and even genocide.

Volkan's formulation of narcissistic large-group regression largely focuses on civil conflicts based on natural, religious, and political group identities. He focuses less on the development of narcissistic large-group regression that builds over time without a precipitating event that catalyses time-collapse. His model furthermore lacks examples of voluntary self-deprecation or masochistic large-group regression. Critical Social Justice is an entitlement ideology that catalyses a unique form of narcissistic large-group regression: its tribalism goes beyond strictly natural, religious, and political large-group identities; instead, tribalistic in- and out-group splitting is achieved based on a combination of both natural and social identity markers. The grievance that fuels such regression has built over time excluding an explicit precipitating event. Due to the flux of offense-causing conditions proliferating under CSJ, every "micro-aggressive" linguistic expression, cultural artefact, custom, law, or concept has been used as cause for outrage. This intentional open-loop system of offense generation, even at microscopic level, ensures the proliferation of resentment. This has created the illusory state of paranoid threat in which CSJ adherents have been primed to interpret events like the death of George Floyd—or any other incident—as an attack on a victim group. Finally, CSJ with its guilt and shame induction makes masochistic or suicidal participation in large-group regression possible—or even morally imperative. This explains the online and real-life public displays of self-denigration by CSJ *allies* as if they were themselves guilty of heinous atrocities against the victim group.

It has become standard practice in CSJ-informed discourse to sanctify the grievance of victimised in-group representatives (applied *standpoint epistemology*) by framing these in historical terms. This practice of historical referencing aims to legitimise otherwise bogus complaints, it demoralises attempts at refuting baseless claims, and it achieves the regressed state for the projective enactment of the Illusion: events in the present are experienced in historical terms, resulting in time-collapse to a period of existential threat. CSJ-adherents who have cathected a victimhood identity assume the illusory state of large-group regression, which includes the paranoid split of idealised racial-sexual-gender-ability-based in-groups and hated out-groups. Remembered, imagined, and summoned humiliation is projected into the demonised target group and their token-representatives, which includes the instinct to destroy the enemy.

In the Anglophone West, university and college campuses have become renown for the spread and endorsement of radical CSJ ideologies. It has become a common occurrence to violently protest dissenting voices on campuses, and to subject wrong-thinking fellow-students and lecturers to violent attacks and intimidation. Critical Race Theory and Decolonial Theory have played a central role as *entitlement ideologies*, breeding resentment among students and faculty at universities in South Africa, UK, Ireland, and North America. When George Floyd died in 2020, and Hamas attacked Israel on October 7, 2023, narcissistic large-group regression had been well underway. Students at the most prestigious universities had already lived in the illusory world of unbearable systemic oppression, in which the evil white Westerner was the demonised other. The said events triggered *time-collapse*, and their violent protests and encampments were an enactment of the Illusion in which the evil Other is overthrown to establish antiracist, decolonised utopia. Even though these events took place on college campuses, they reflected the sentiments harboured in other organisations of the educational, corporate, and media world.

Conclusion

The yearning for the restoration of primary narcissism predisposes individuals and masses to succumb to ideologies that promise such restoration. The most effective of these ideologies tend to be those that best align with the most primal of our instincts, perversely masked as somehow dignifying, and during a time when existential anxiety is at its highest (Desmet, 2022). Critical Social Justice theories embody the psychology of the Illusion in its paranoid splits of identity-based idealisations and devaluations; its anti-Oedipal, envious disavowal of what is structuring and pleasure-depriving; and its collective induction of identitarian large-group regression. Perennially, ideological Illusion triumphs over otherwise stable civilisations (Alderman, 2024). Ultimately, those capable of bearing ambivalence, having resolved destructive envy, and having integrated an Oedipal relationship with reality will be better equipped at reckoning with unforgiving reality.

References

Alderman, B. (2024). *Eternal Youth and the Myth of Deconstruction.* Routledge.

Anzieu, D. (1984). *The Group and the Unconscious.* (B. Kilborne, Trans.). Routledge & Kegan Paul. (Original work published 1975).

Aubry, T., & Travis, T. (2015). "What is 'Therapeutic culture,' and Why Do We Need to Rethink It?" In T. Aubry & T. Travis (Eds.). *Rethinking Therapeutic Culture.* University of Chicago Press.

Becker, E. (1973). *The Denial of Death.* The Free Press.

Benjamin, J. (1995). "Sameness and Difference: Toward an "Overinclusive" Model of Gender Development," *Psychoanalytic Inquiry, 15,* 125 – 142.

Bersani, L., & Philips, A. (2008). *Intimacies.* University of Chicago Press.

Bion, W. R. (1962). *Learning from Experience.* Karnac Books.

_____ (1963). *Elements of Psycho-Analysis*. Karnac Books.

Boyers, R. (2019). *The Tyranny of Virtue*. Scribner Book Company.

Campbell, B. & Manning, J. (2018). *The Rise of Victimhood Culture. Microaggressions, Safe Spaces, and the New Culture Wars*. Palgrave Macmillan.

Casey, P. J. (2023). "Lived Experience: Defined and Critiqued," *Critical Horizons, 24*(3). 282 – 297. https://doi.org/10.1080/14409917.2023.2241058.

Chasseguet-Smirgel, J. (1984). *Creativity and Perversion*. Free Association Books.

_____ (1985). *The Ego Ideal. A Psychoanalytic Essay on the Malady of the Ideal*. Free Association Books.

Collins, P. H. (2000). *Black Feminist Thought: Knowledge, Consciousness, and the Politics Of Empowerment* (2nd ed.). Routledge.

DiAngelo, R. (2018). *White Fragility. Why It's So Hard For White People To Talk About Racism*. Penguin Books.

Dyer, H. (2016). "Queer Futurity and Childhood Innocence: Beyond the Injury of Development," *Global Studies of Childhood, 7*(3), 290 – 302. https://doi.org/10.1177/2043610616671056.

Freud, S. (1910). *Five Lectures on Psycho-Analysis. S. E., 11*. 1 – 56. London: Hogart.

_____ (1918). "From the History of an Infantile Neurosis," *The Wolf-Man. S. E., 17*. 5 – 56. London: Hogart.

_____ (1927). *The Future of an Illusion. S. E., 21*. 5 – 56. London: Hogart.

_____ (1930). *Civilisation and its Discontents. S. E., 21. 57 – 145*. London: Hogart.

Fromm, E. (1947). *Man for Himself: An Inquiry into the Psychology of Ethics*. Rinehart.

Garfinkel, H. (1956). "Conditions of Successful Degradation Ceremonies," *American Journal of Sociology, 61*(5), 420 – 424. University of Chicago Press.

Hanania, R. (2023). *The Origins of Woke. Civil Rights Law, Corporate America, and the Triumph of Identity Politics.*

Kaufmann, E. (2018). "Liberal Fundamentalism: A Sociology of Wokeness," *American Affairs, 4*(4), 188–208.

Kendi, I. X. (2023). *How to be an Antiracist.* Vintage.

Klein, M. (1946). "Notes on Some Schizoid Mechanisms," In M. Masud R. Khan (Ed.). *Envy and Gratitude and Other Works 1946 – 1963.* (pp. 1 – 11). The International Psycho-Analytical Library.

____ (1957). "Envy and Gratitude," In M. Masud R. Khan (Ed.). *Envy and Gratitude and Other Works 1946 – 1963.* (pp. 77 – 102). The International Psycho-Analytical Library.

Le Bon, G. (2002). *The Crowd. A Study of the Popular Mind.* Dover Publications.

Legault, L., Gutsell, J. N., & Inzlicht, M. (2011). "Ironic Effects of Antiprejudice Messages: How Motivational Interventions Can Reduce (but Also Increase) Prejudice," *Psychological Science, 22*(12), pp. 1472-1477. https://doi.org/10.1177/0956797611427918.

Lorde, A. (1981). "The Master's Tools Will Never Dismantle the Master's House." In C. Moraga and G. Anzaldua (Eds.). *This Bridge Called my Back: Writings by Radical Women of Color.* Persephone Press.

Lukianoff, G. & Haidt, J. (2018). *The Coddling of the American Mind. How Good Intentions and Bad Ideas are setting up a Generation of Failure.* Penguin Press.

Marcuse, H. (2014). "Re-examination of the Concept of Revolution," In D. Kellner, & C. Pierce (Eds.). *Marxism, Revolution and Utopia.* (pp. 333 – 343). Routledge.

Nelson, C. (2023). "Universities in Crisis | 'We Need to Reckon With How Horrific Liberation Can Be': How Lara Sheehi Rationalised The Hamas Pogrom," *Fathom Journal,* June, 2023.

Özkırımlı, U. (2023). *Cancelled: The Left Way Back from Woke.* Polity Press.

Pfeffer, C. A., Hines, S., Pearce, R., Riggs, D. W., Ruspini, E., & White, F. R. (2023). "Medical Uncertainty and Reproduction of the 'Normal:' Decision-Making Around Testosterone Therapy in Transgender Pregnancy," *SSM – Qualitative Research in Health, 4,* Article 100297. https://doi.org/10.1016/j.ssmqr.2023.100297.

Pluckrose, H., & Lindsay, J. (2020). *Cynical Theories: How Activist Scholarship Made Everything About Race, Gender and Identity - And Why This Harms Everybody.* Pitchstone Publishing.

Reynolds, J. (2024, October 22). "Protesters Gather After Met Police Marksman Cleared of Chris Kaba Murder," *The Standard.* Retrieved November 25, 2024, from https://www.standard.co.uk/news/london/chris-kaba-protests-met-police-marksman-cleared-of-murder-mark-rowley-b1189212.html.

Sarkonak, J. (2023, July 21). "Toronto Principal Bullied Over False Charge of Racism Dies From Suicide," *National Post.* Retrieved November 25, 2024, from https://nationalpost.com/opinion/jamie-sarkonak-toronto-principal-bullied-over-false-charge-of-racism-dies-from-suicide

Schroeder, C. & DiAngelo, R. (2010). "Addressing Whiteness in Nursing Education the Sociopolitical Climate Project at the University of Washington School of Nursing," *Advances in Nursing Science, 33,* 244 – 255, https://journals.lww.com/advancesinnursingscience/fulltext/2010/07000/addressing_whiteness_in_nursing_education__the.7.aspx

Sensoy, Ö., & DiAngelo, R. (2017). *Is Everyone Really Equal? An Introduction to Key Concepts in Social Justice Education* (2nd ed.). Teachers College Press.

Stokes, D. (2023). *Against Decolonisation.* Polity Press.

Thorneycroft, R. (2020). "Crip Theory and Mad Studies: Intersections and Points of Departure," *Canadian Journal of Disability Studies, 9*(1), 91 – 121. https://doi.org/10.15353/cjds.v9i1.597.

Volkan, V. D. (1999). "Psychoanalysis and Diplomacy: Part I. Individual and Large Group Identity," *Journal of Applied Psychoanalytic Studies, 1*(1), pp. 29 – 55.

_____ (2004). *Blind Trust: Large Groups and their leaders in times of crisis and terror.* Pitchstone Publishing.

_____ (2014). *Psychoanalysis, International Relations, and Diplomacy. A Sourcebook on Large-Group Psychology.* Karnac.

Weatherill, R. (2017). "Clinical Encounters: The Queer New Times," In N. Giffney, & E. Watson (Eds.), *Clinical Encounters in Sexuality: Psychoanalytic Practice and Queer Theory* (pp. 329 – 341). Punctum Books.

Whitebook, J. (1995). *Perversion and Utopia.* The MIT Press.

_____ (2023). "Psychoanalysis and the Frankfurt School," In J. Mills, & D. Burston (Eds.), *Critical Theory and Psychoanalysis. From the Frankfurt School to Contemporary Critique* (pp. 1 – 25), Routledge.

Winnicott, D. W. (1963). "The Development of the Capacity for Concern," In *Maturational Processes and the Facilitating Environment* (pp. 73 – 82).

Ziemna, J. (2024). "Self-Creation of Other-Than-Human Identities: A Netnographic Analysis of Identity Labels in the Alterhuman Community on Tumblr," *Avant, 15*(2). https://doi. org/10.26913/ava2202406.

7
Gender Ideology and the Transgender Debate– Cancel Culture, Anthropology and the Evolution of Sex Differences

Gary Clark

Woke policy *is* lunacy.
-*Norman Finkelstein*[1]

Introduction

In this chapter I explore the political phenomenon of cancel culture—a tactic employed by both the right and left side of politics. I then look at one of the most insidious manifestations of left wing cancel culture in recent times, that is, the denial of biological sex in human cultural life, academia, and science. More specifically I look at the recent cancellation of a group

---

1 Finkelstein, N., *I'll Burn That Bridge When I Get to It: Heretical Thoughts on Identity Politics, Cancel Culture and Academic Freedom*. Sublation Media, 2023, p. 59.

of 'gender critical' female anthropologists because it was deemed their views on biological sex would cause "harm" to members of the transgendered community.

I use this incident as an opportunity to explore the importance of evolved biological differences between the sexes for anthropological and evolutionary research. After discussing the evolutionary literature on these issues, I briefly illustrate the utility of the approach I outline with examples from the ethnographic literature. I explore these issues in terms of Carl Jung's concepts of Eros and Logos—concepts which seek to capture the masculine and feminine dimensions of both individual psychology as well as human cultural symbolism. I conclude by emphasising that members of the transgender gender community should have nothing to fear from evidence of evolved biological sex differences. For example, while sex is binary and there are only two human sexes, cross-cultural data suggests that it is common for some individuals to identify with the social roles and behaviours of the opposite sex. This seems to be a part of natural biological variation with such forms of identification having possible evolutionary causes. In this sense I chart a middle path between the Scylla and Charybdis of "gender critical" feminism and transgender rights, emphasising how the arguments about sex-based rights put forward by the former do not necessarily represent a threat to the latter.

Cancel Culture, Faux Leftism, and the Ideological Subversion of Science: From the Cold War to Gender Ideology

In the West 'cancel culture' and the associated suppression a free speech has tended to be a phenomenon associated with the political right. For example, during the Cold War under McCarthyism draconian silencing, blacklisting, persecution, and imprisonment of ideological opponents became a prominent feature of political life.[2] Similar forces have been at work in America and among its allies for decades and up to the present moment, with dissident critics of American foreign policy and military interventions being subject to state-based suppression, manipulated evidence, constant surveillance, defamation, threats, and imprisonment.[3] To achieve these objectives, America has deployed an unconstitutional and complex system of surveillance, in which it illegally spied on the domestic population in service of the elite oligarch class and military industrial complex.[4] Reputational destruction, loss of career opportunities or imprisonment are often the price paid for those whose speech exposes these phenomena to public scrutiny—what the war correspondent Chris Hedges has called the *wages of rebellion.* [5]

The curtailment of free speech in such contexts is a product of intersections between the media, corporations, and the state in which parameters of debate are defined and limited—with social costs imposed upon those who breach these limits.[6] This can have deleterious effects when the public is misinformed about the ramifications of foreign policy and military interventions, with certain facts highlighted while others are emitted in order to promote propaganda favourable to one side in a conflict.[7] One of the obvious examples of this phenomenon is the impact of the pro-Israeli lobby on American, UK, and Western politics more generally, with the censure and cancellation of voices critical of Israel—often by weap-

---

2 Fried, A. et al. *Mccarthyism: The Great American Red Scare : A Documentary History.* Oxford University Press, 1997.

3 Melzer, N., *The Trial of Julian Assange: A Story of Persecution.* Verso Books, 2023.

4 Greenwald, G., *No Place to Hide: Edward Snowden, the NSA, and the U.S. Surveillance State.* Henry Holt and Company, 2014.

5 Hedges, C., "Wages of Rebellion," *Public Affairs*, 2015.

6 Herman, Edward S. and Noam Chomsky, *Manufacturing Consent : The Political Economy of the Mass Media.* 1st ed., Pantheon Books, 1988.

7 McGilvray, James A. Chomsky, *Language, Mind, and Politics.* Polity Press, 1999. Key Contemporary Thinkers, pp. 178-180.

onizing dubious accusations of antisemitism and equating criticism of Israel with antisemitism in order to provide the Israeli state with moral cover for its war crimes.[8]

Following the Hamas attacks on Israel on October 7, 2023, and the consequent ethnic cleansing of Gaza by the Israeli state, this censorious tendency has become increasingly apparent throughout Western institutions, with pro-Palestinian voices in academia, the tech sector, and journalism being subject to draconian suppression, cancellation, police investigation, and arrest.[9] Commentators on this phenomenon have argued we are in danger of sliding into a new McCarthyism.[10] Only time will tell if the West's much vaunted support of free speech can withstand these political pressures, or whether it will succumb to draconian right-wing forces in our culture.

This kind of suppression on the part of the state in relation to geopolitical objectives is nothing new and examples can be found throughout history and across the globe. However, the West has witnessed a new development in recent years with draconian forms

---

8 Mearsheimer, J.J. and S.M. Walt., *The Israel Lobby and US Foreign Policy*. Penguin Books Limited, 2008. viii and 9-10; Finkelstein, Norman G., *The Holocaust Industry : Reflections on the Exploitation of Jewish Suffering*. 2nd ed., Verso, 2003; Finkelstein, N., *I'll Burn That Bridge When I Get to It: Heretical Thoughts on Identity Politics, Cancel Culture and Academic Freedom*. Sublation Media, 2023, pp. 496-511.

9 Phillips, A. "Full List of Journalists Fired over Pro Palestinian Remarks." *Nesweek,* October 25, 2023; Farge, E. "UN Experts Decry Arrest of Pro-Palestinian American Journalist in Switzerland." *Reuters,* January 27, 2024; Quinn, R., "Tenured Jewish Professor Says She's Been Fired for Pro-Palestinian Speech." *Inside Higher Ed.*, September 27, 2024; *International Federation of Journalists*, "Police Used Anti-Terror Legislation to Raid the Electronic Intifada's Journalist Home.", October 22, 2024; Lawrence, C., "MIT Student Effectively Expelled for Opposing Gaza Genocide," *World Socialist Website*, December, 2024. Abunimah, Ali; "UK Police Raid Home, Seize Devices of Ei's Asa Winstanley," *The Electronic Intifada*, October 17, 2024; Snider, M., "Google Fires More Workers over Pro-Palestinian Protests Held at Offices, Cites Disruption," *USA Today*, vol. April 23, 2024.

10 Tamkin, E. "Are We Sliding Toward Mccarthyism," *The New Republic,* January 29, 2024.

of suppression becoming a characteristic of the political left. Traditionally the political left had fought for free speech rights because it was the ability to freely express your mind in face of the draconian forces of the state and the political right that was necessary for effective political activism. The emergence of censoriousness and attempts to suppress free speech on the part of left-wing identity or woke politics reverses this historical trend. Importantly, it betrays the very free speech rights that the political left has fought so hard for.[11]

In reaction to woke identity politics or what we might call social justice ideology, a burgeoning cottage industry has emerged critiquing this phenomenon and seeking to undermine its intellectual foundations.[12] Whilst this literature offers a variety of sustained critiques of woke social justice ideology, the quality of the scholarship is marred by its own reactionary and often implicit conservative ideological biases—or in some cases explicit.[13] I say implicit ideology because the authors of these texts may not admit to or recognise their analysis contains omission of crucial information that effectively constitute implicit ideological biases. For example, while these texts rightly bemoan the suppression of free speech, it tends to be the suppression of free speech by the identitarian left in academia and the media that is of primary concern. They seem to show very little concern with right wing forms of cancel culture of the kind discussed above.

---

11 Chomsky, N., "Free Speech in a Democracy," *Daily Camera*, September, 1985.

12 See for example: Haidt, J. and G. Lukianoff. *The Coddling of the American Mind: How Good Intentions and Bad Ideas Are Setting up a Generation for Failure.* Penguin Books Limited, 2018. Pluckrose, H. and J.A. Lindsay; *Cynical Theories: How Activist Scholarship Made Everything About Race, Gender, and Identity—and Why This Harms Everybody.* Pitchstone Publishing, 2020; Doyle, A. *The New Puritans: How the Religion of Social Justice Captured the Western World.* Little, Brown Book Group, 2022.

13 Lindsay, J.A., *Race Marxism: The Truth About Critical Race Theory and Praxis.* New Discourses, 2022.

An example of this bias in evident in *Unlearning Liberty: Campus Censorship and the End of American Debate*, in which the author Greg Lukianoff details the firing of Professor Thomas Klocek from DePaul University in 2004. Klocek got into an argument about Palestinians, Islam, and terrorism with students and after complaints were filed, he was, it seems, unjustly suspended.[14] As the pro-Palestinian activist and scholar, Norman Finkelstein, points out, Lukianoff did not note Finkelstein's own highly politicized tenure denial at DePaul —a case that garnered national headlines with Harvard Law Professor, Alan Dershowitz, corresponding with California governor Arnold Schwarzenegger, in order to block publication of a University of California Press book by Finkelstein.[15]

The approach to woke identity politics in this essay is not one that overlooks right wing cancellation campaigns but rather sees both forms of suppression as means by which establishment political forces seek to maintain power. In the case of woke identity politics I do not accept the premise of many of the authors cited above that it represents actual left-wing politics. On the contrary, I suggest it is a form of *faux* leftism that uses identity politics as a shroud to veil what are essentially right-wing policies which favour the oligarchic class and which undermine class-based solidarity. And while doing so the establishment elite can cloak their economic interests in a patina of progressive virtue—a phenomenon evident in the weaponisation of identity politics to undermine Berne Sanders' class-based economic populism by the Democrat establishment elite and their supporters.[16] When Jeff Bezos and the billionaire class are supporters of your movement it suggests your movement has gone astray—a movement whose 'hollowness . . . now echoes across

---

14 Lukianoff, G., *Unlearning Liberty: Campus Censorship and the End of American Debate*. Encounter Books, 2014, 117-118.

15 Finkelstein, N., *I'll Burn That Bridge When I Get to It: Heretical Thoughts on Identity Politics, Cancel Culture and Academic Freedom*. Sublation Media, 2023, p. 33.

16 Ibid., pp. 62-68.

a vast political abyss' while offering a 'therapeutic theater to salve the guilty conscience of the guilty-as-sin.'[17]

One of the most egregious of these developments is the obfuscation around issues of sex and gender. Noting the incursion of political ideology into science in recent years, Jerry Coyne and Luana Maroja argue that the discipline of biology is being subverted by a progressive political ideology that forbids the discussion of topics which may be deemed offensive and cause "harm." Of course, people's subjective feeling of being offended is not a criterion by which we should accept or reject scientific findings. Coyne and Maroja argue that such moves have resulted in "ideology . . . poisoning" biology as "social justice" ideology "elbows aside our real job: finding truth." One of the ideas that has come under attack by such ideological forces is the notion that sex in humans is not a discrete and 'binary distribution of males and females but a spectrum.' As Coyne and Maroja aver, denying 'the dichotomy of sex prevents us from understanding one of biology's most fascinating generalizations: the difference between males and females in behavior and appearance.'18 This ideological subversion of biology has made its way into major scientific journals, as well as academia, with researchers and writers who dare to utter the unutterable being cancelled.[19]

Anthropology is particularly vulnerable to this trend given it is a discipline that has been in many ways influenced by post-1968 developments in the academy such as post-structuralism, postmodernism, and social constructionist critiques of putatively oppressive

---

17 Ibid., pp. 63 and 65.

18 Coyne, J. and Maroja, L., "The Ideological Subversion of Biology," *Skeptical Inquirer*, vol. Volume 47, no. No. 4, 2023.

19 Hooven, Carole K., "Academic Freedom Is Social Justice: Sex, Gender, and Cancel Culture on Campus," *Archives of Sexual Behavior,* vol. 52, no. 1, 2023, pp. 35-41; Meigs, J. "Unscientific American: Science Journalism Surrenders to Progressive Ideology," *City Journal,* Spring, 2024.

Western constructs of race, sex and gender.[20] One of the more re-cent manifestations of this approach is evident in gender theory —for example the works of Judith Butler—in which both sex and gender are argued to be not objective realties but constructed by discourses of power and oppression.[21] For Butler, as articulated in her famous theory of performativity, gender "is not a fact" but only emerges socially through "the various acts of gender" that we per-form and which create 'the idea of gender, and without those acts, there would be no gender at all.'[22]

More recently this style of thinking has moved out of the acad-emy, giving rise to a new sociocultural phenomenon predominately in Western countries—one focussed on gender and the putatively oppressive social constructs that give rise to it. This ideological be-lief system involves decoupling of the concepts of male and female from biological sex, with the associated assertion that sex is not binary but a spectrum—a set of beliefs known as "gender identity ideology." [23]

On the 25th of September in 2023 the advocates of gender ide-ology came into conflict with a group of feminists wanting to pres-ent a panel on the importance of biological sex in anthropological research. The panel, which was part of a conference organised by the American Anthropological Association (AAA) and the Canadi-an Anthropology Society (CASCA), was entitled "Let's Talk About

---

20 Fox, R., *The Tribal Imagination: Civilization and the Savage Mind.* Harvard University Press, 2011, pp. 315 and 17; Clark, G., *Carl Jung and the Evolutionary Sciences: A New Vision for Analytical Psychology*, Taylor & Francis, 2025, pp. 58-59.

21 Butler, J., *Gender Trouble: Feminism and the Subversion of Identity.* Taylor & Francis, 2011.

22 "Performative Acts and Gender Constitution: An Essay in Phenomenolo-gy and Feminist Theory," *Theatre Journal*, vol. 40, no. 4, 1988, p. 522.

23 Lawford-Smith, H., *Gender-Critical Feminism.* Oxford University Press, Incorporated, 2022, pp. 92-116; Hilton, E. Wright, C. "Two Sexes." In *Sex and Gender: A Contemporary Reader*, edited by A Todd Sullivan, S., Taylor & Francis, 2023, pp. 16-34.

Sex, Baby: Why Biological Sex Remains a Necessary Analytic Category in Anthropology." It was originally accepted but later cancelled by the conference organisers who argued such a panel of 'gender critical' women would cause "harm" to members of the transgender community.

The feminist researchers sought to discuss various topics such as the importance of sex in biological and cultural anthropology, the importance of sex-based rights for women, and the danger posed to these rights by gender ideology, which doesn't define a woman in terms biological sex but in terms of an internal gender identity that either males or females can be in possession of. Science historian Alice Dreger noted the irony that a group of women wanting to talk about sex-based rights, and the alleged silencing of women's unique experiences and voices by gender identity ideology, had their attempt to discuss such issues silenced. As she avers, if the conference organisers "want to fight against the core claim of gender-critical scholars—that defense of trans rights is accruing harm to women—can't they see they've just *proven* the point?"[24]

The (AAA) and (CASCA) released a letter that elaborated on the reasons for the cancellation. In it the authors wrote:

> Around the world and throughout human history, there have always been people whose gender roles do not align neatly with their reproductive anatomy. There is no single biological standard by which all humans can be reliably sorted into a binary male/female sex classification. On the contrary, anthropologists and others have long shown sex and gender to be historically and geographically contextual, deeply entangled, and dynamically mutable categories.[25]

---

24 Dreger, A. "How a Canceled Panel on Sex Plays into Censorship by the Right: A Guest Post," *Retraction Watch*, vol. October 1, 2023.

25 "No Place for Transphobia in Anthropology: Session Pulled from Annual Meeting Program," *American Anthropological Association*, vol. September 28, 2003.

In a follow up letter in defence of the decision it was argued the panel participants were advocating the notion "that sex is a biological binary; a concept that is rejected by current biological anthropology and human biology, and highly disputed across contemporary biology."[26] In response to the assertions made in these letters, evolutionary biologist Colin Wright wrote the following:

> Each of these assertions is empirically false. An individual's sex can be determined by observing their primary sex organs, or gonads, as these organs determine the type of gamete an individual can or would have the function to produce. The existence of a very rare subset of individuals with developmental conditions that make their sex difficult to assess does not substantiate the existence of a third sex. Sex is binary because there are only two sexes, not because every human in existence is neatly classifiable. Additionally, while some organisms are capable of changing sex, humans are not among them. Therefore, the assertion that human sex is 'dynamically mutable' is false.

Wright concluded that the "cancellation and subsequent response by the two organizations shows the extent to which gender ideology has captured academic anthropology."[27]

The remainder of this chapter will take this incident as an opportunity to discuss the importance of biological sex in anthropological research. I will explore the literature on the biology of sex as a crucial part of evolutionary research and particularly research in human evolutionary studies. I will then move on to discuss several ethnographies from around the globe that demonstrate a cross-cultural concern with biological sex, and that such concern is manifested in multiple domains from subsistence patterns, division of

---

26 Fuentes, Agustin et al. "Letter of Support for AAA's Withdrawal of Session from the Annual Meeting." 2023.

27 Wright, Colin., "Dis-Empaneled; Bowing to Political Pressure, Two Leading Anthropological Associations Cancel a Conference Discussion on the Centrality of Biological Sex," *City Journal*, 2023.

labour, to ritual life and religious symbolism. I will conclude by arguing that the while sex is in all essential respects a binary biological phenomenon, this does not represent a threat to the rights and dignity of the transgender people. In fact, evolutionary and cross-cultural approaches based in the reality of biological sex, which acknowledge variation in personality and gender identity, suggest that identifying with the gender roles and behaviours of the opposite sex is a normal part of human psychological and behavioural variation.

The Evolution of Sex: The Male/Female Binary

The differences between males and females have a deep evolutionary origin, with the main distinguishing feature being males produce small gametes or sperm and females produce large gametes or ova. These differences are seen throughout the animal kingdom, from mice to elephants, from chimpanzees to humans. Downstream effects of the different gametes and associated reproductive strategies of each sex, result in different hormonal profiles, differences in anatomy, muscle mass and bone morphology, as well as average differences in psychology.[28]

One of the most distinguishing features between the sexes is difference in hand grip and upper body strength. This is most likely related to the evolved male social role of hunting and making and using weaponry involving motor behaviours such as throwing.[29] This would have produced evolutionary pressure for greater upper

28 Geary, D.C., *Male, Female: The Evolution of Human Sex Differences.* American Psychological Association, 2010.
29 Hyde, J. S., "The Gender Similarities Hypothesis," *American Psychologist,* vol. 60, no. 6, 2005, pp. 581-92.

body strength in males[30] —evidence for which occurs approximately two million years ago with the emergence of *Homo erectus* where we see not only increased archaeological evidence of hunting and complex tool manufacture, but also of modern shoulder and upper body morphology. [31]

Much of the research into sex-based differences contradicts the fundamental assumptions of gender theory and social constructionism which argue the human mind is a blank slate or *tabular rasa* and that any differences we may see in human psychology result from environmental or sociocultural influences.[32] Evidence of the untenable nature of this conception of human psychology comes from multiple domains from studies of infant, childhood, and adolescent development, to cross-cultural research into sex based social roles, ritual, and symbolism. Significantly, Jung was opposed to the *tabular rasa* view of human psychology, arguing that the infant is born with psychobiological predispositions inherited from our species evolutionary past. Some of the most important aspects of this inheritance are the average differences between female and male psychology—differences Jung sought to capture in his theory of Eros and Logos.[33]

Newborn infants, who have yet to be socialised or influenced by cultural factors, show evidence of this deep evolutionary origin

---

30 Isen, J. et al. "Genetic Influences on the Development of Grip Strength in Adolescence," *American Journal of Physical Anthropology*, vol. 154, no. 2, 2014, pp. 189-200; Young, R. W. "Evolution of the Human Hand: The Role of Throwing and Clubbing," *Journal of Anatomy*, vol. 202, no. 1, 2003, pp. 165-74.

31 Roach, Neil T. et al. "Elastic Energy Storage in the Shoulder and the Evolution of High-Speed Throwing in Homo," *Nature*, vol. 498, no. 7455, 2013, pp. 483-86.

32 Barkow, J.H. et al. *The Adapted Mind: Evolutionary Psychology and the Generation of Culture.* Oxford University Press, 199; Pinker, S. *The Blank Slate: The Modern Denial of Human Nature.* Penguin Books Limited, 2003.

33 Clark, G., *Carl Jung and the Evolutionary Sciences: A New Vision for Analytical Psychology,* Taylor & Francis, 2025, pp. 75-116.

with male newborns showing a stronger interest in physical-mechanical objects while female infants show a stronger interest in faces—which may be an early manifestation of the higher female propensity for empathic ability to read emotions from facial expressions.[34] As young boys grow, cultural and environmental factors interact with these biological predispositions, resulting in different play behaviour than that evident in girls, that is, cultural "variations" on the theme of underlying biological differences in psychology and behaviour.[35] These differences during the early stages of life, later become evident in adulthood where we see population level differences in sex-based psychology, social behaviour, and vocational interests.[36]

Evidence that such sex differences are not socially constructed, but a biologically channelled characteristic of our species, comes from cross-cultural research. For examples such differences, and their psychosocial correlates, are found among the Hadza, a hunter-gatherer people of Tanzania in Africa, with boys being given bows and arrows from as early as two to three years of age, with every male being given them by six years of age, while among Indigenous communities in Brazil young boys engage in mock fighting against one another as well as small animals.[37] These play behaviours seem

---

34 Connellan, J. et al. "Sex Differences in Human Neonatal Social Perception," *Infant Behavior and Development*, vol. 23, no. 1, 2000, pp. 113-18; McClure, Erin B., "A Meta-Analytic Review of Sex Differences in Facial Expression Processing and Their Development in Infants, Children, and Adolescents," *Psychological Bulletin*, vol. 126, no. 3, 2000, p. 424.

35 Fry, Douglas P., "Rough-and-Tumble Social Play in Humans," *The Nature of Play: Great Apes and Humans*. Guilford Press, 2005, p. 55.

36 Stewart-Williams, Steve and Lewis G Halsey., "Men, Women and Stem: Why the Differences and What Should Be Done?" *European Journal of Personality*, vol. 35, no. 1, 2021, pp. 3-39; Gruber, June et al. "The Future of Women in Psychological Science." *Perspectives on Psychological Science*, vol. 16, no. 3, 2021, pp. 483-516.

37 Marlowe, F., *The Hadza: Hunter-Gatherers of Tanzania*. University of California Press, 2010, p. 84; Gosso, Yumi et al. "Play in Hunter-Gatherer Society," *The Nature of Play: Great Apes and Humans*. Guilford Press, 2005, pp. 213-53.

to provide the developmental basis for latter forms adult behaviour. As Joyce Benenson summarises research in this area:

> Puberty causes boys to grow so much heavier, taller, and more muscular than girls that there is almost no overlap between the two sexes in these physical skills. Before adolescence, boys differ little from girls in their height, weight, muscle mass, and physical skills, except of course for throwing. The difference in throwing force and velocity occurs even in the tiniest hunter-gatherer communities.[38]

Benenson has argued that this evolutionary trend results in young boys and men developing different forms of social psychology to girls and women with cooperation between groups of male friends who collectively seek to protect the group from harm being the hallmark of male sociality. As she argues, male morality and psychology is a result of the male evolutionary role as group protectors against abstract enemies, the enemy that "wakes people in the night' and that seeks 'to destroy you and all that you love."[39] In terms of our evolutionary past, such threats would have come primarily from animal predators as our hominin ancestors moved out of ancient forest habitats and into more open ecologies with higher predation risk.[40] These evolutionary pressures most likely gave rise to the forms of upper body and hand strength as well as shoulder morphology noted above in relation to *Homo erectus*.

These sex-based differences manifest themselves in differences in play activity in young girls compared to young boys. While boys demonstrate a preference for activities associated with hunting, mechanical propulsion, and throwing, cross-culturally young girls

---

38 Benenson, J., *Warriors and Worriers: The Survival of the Sexes*. OUP USA, 2014, pp. 28.

39 Ibid., pp. 28, 29.

40 Clark, G. et al. "Hominin Musical Sound Production: Palaeoecological Contexts and Self Domestication," *Anthropological Review*, vol. Vol 87, 2024, pp. 17-61.

show a preference for doll play and learning maternal behaviours from other women of the group.[41] These differences do not seem to be a result of socialisation—although the manner in which such biological predispositions manifest themselves seem to be influenced by cultural factors. Carolyn Edwards, an anthropologist who studies sex segregated social behaviour in hunter-gatherer children, argues that these differences, far from being the products of sociocultural factors, are a result of self-socialisation driven by biological predispositions. As she writes:

> The system of self-socialisation is founded on attraction to like-sex community members followed by identification. Girls are predisposed in their development to maintain proximity to adult females, where they receive maximal opportunity to attend selectively and maintain proximity to infants, with the result that they gain knowledge and practice in nurturing styles of interaction. As they gain knowledge and practice, they become more skilled caregivers, with the result that nurturant interaction becomes differentially rewarding to them.[42]

The above is merely a brief survey of the vast literature on evolved sex-based differences, highlighting some of the main research findings. In my book *Carl Jung and the Evolutionary Sciences: A New Vision for Analytical Psychology*, I provide a much more extensive analysis of this data, arguing that such research provides support for Jung's concept of Eros and Logos—that is, feminine and masculine principles evident in individual psychology as well as cultural symbolism globally.[43]

---

41 de Waal, F., *Different: What Apes Can Teach Us About Gender.* Granta Publications, 2022, pp. 311, 268.

42 Edwards, C.P. "Behavioral Sex Differences in Children of Diverse Cultures," *Juvenile Primates: Life History, Development and Behavior*, edited by M.E. Pereira, University of Chicago Press, 2002, p. 337.

43 Clark, G., *Carl Jung and the Evolutionary Sciences: A New Vision for Analytical Psychology*, Taylor & Francis, 2025, pp. 75-116.

Jung's theory of sex-based differences was not essentialist in orientation, and while acknowledging differences between male and female psychology, he postulated Eros and Logos as tendencies that can exist in both males and females. Nevertheless he argued these concepts are generally applicable, and in the words of Anthony Stevens, 'possesses *statistical validity*.'[44] This accords with modern research into sex-based differences that demonstrates a population level bimodal distribution with a great deal of overlap between males and females. This means that there are some males who exhibit female typical psychological traits and behaviours while some females exhibit male typical traits and behaviours.

Cross-cultural research has demonstrated that there are a small number of people in societies around the world whose gender orientation seems to be different from the majority of individuals of their sex—a phenomenon commonly known in contemporary Western culture as transgenderism. It is important to emphasise that such variation in gender orientation may have a biological and evolutionary origin.[45] Consequently, advocates for the rights of transgender people should not see the concept of evolved sex-based differences or of biological sex as incongruent with the transgender experience. That experience seems to be part of the natural psychobiological variation of human populations, in which there is overlap between the two sexes with some members of each sex having more affinity with the psychosocial orientation of the opposite sex. This does not, it should be emphasised, invalidate the notion that sex is binary. There are only two sexes, and with the exception of extremely rare examples of intersex (approximately 0.018 of the population) where there may be some ambiguity in regard to specific sex traits, the

---

44 Stevens, A., *Archetype Revisited: An Updated Natural History of the Self*. Brunner-Routledge, 2002, p. 228.

45 Vasey, Paul L. et al. "Kin Selection and Male Androphilia in Samoan Fa'afafine," *Evolution and Human Behavior*, vol. 28, no. 3, 2007, pp. 159-67; VanderLaan, D. P. et al. "Male Androphilia in the Ancestral Environment. An Ethnological Analysis," *Human Nature*, vol. 24, no. 4, 2013, pp. 375-401.

vast majority of human beings are unambiguously male or female.[46] However, it is crucial to note that individuals who identify with the social roles and behaviours of the opposite sex do not *become* the opposite sex.

A Brief Survey of Ethnographic Evidence

In *Women Like Meat: The Folklore and Foraging Ideology of the Kalahari Ju/hoan*, Megan Biesele offers an extensive analysis of African forager culture and its basis in what she calls "the basic polarities" of "men, women, and their work." In this culture males and females go through different initiation rites with young girls being initiated into adulthood during their first menstruation, while young men are initiated into adulthood when they become hunters and make their first kill. As Biesele avers, the initiation of "young boys" involving a "ceremony of the first kill" is the "structural equivalent of the menstrual right."[47]

As Biesele eleborates, the "complementary roles of men and women' are manifest in 'the social division of labour into hunting and gathering' —a polarity evident in both ritualised dance and folklore in which attributes "associated with women (such as menstrual blood, breast milk, gathering utensils) are considered antithetical to those connected with men (like semen, arrows, arrow-poison)."[48] In order that men abide by cultural norms and offer sufficient meat to a prospective mate and her kin, women engage in rituals of solidarity often using ochre (symbolic of blood); as Camilla Power avers 'women use idioms of bleeding together to express connection and

---

46 Sax, Leonard, "How Common Is Intersex? A Response to Anne Fausto-Sterling," *The Journal of Sex Research*, vol. 39, no. 3, 2002, pp. 174-78.

47 Biesele, M., *Women Like Meat: The Folklore and Foraging Ideology of the Kalahari Ju/'hoan*. Witwatersrand University Press, 1993, p.138.

48 Ibid, pp. 85, 87.

belonging.'[49] Such solidarity increases the collective power of women in such societies, while mitigating male dominance, encouraging egalitarian behaviour, and sharing the bounty of the hunt with mates and their kin.[50]

Morna Finnegan analyses such coalitionary behaviour in her paper "The Politics of Eros: Ritual Dialogue and Egalitarianism in Three Central African Hunter-Gatherer Societies." Finnegan analyses African female ritual in terms of Eros, and echoing Jung, associates the concept with qualities such as "love, lust, joy . . . intercourse" and "the libidinal, sexual or life instincts." She also contrasts the attitude towards the sexed female body evident in African hunter gatherer cultures with that of Western intellectuals and gender theorists. For example, in discussing Judith Butler's *Gender Trouble*, Finnegan notes the "standard practice within feminist anthropology [is] to repudiate any essential relationship between the biological body and cultural identity" —a perspective in which "the ongoing deconstruction of the body has come to seem the only 'natural' fact." Commenting on this critique, she notes the African "symbolic preoccupation with the very terms recent Western gender theory disposes of at the outset—sex, menstrual blood, gestation, birth, and parturition."[51] As she writes:

> In its creativity and doubling capacity the body, particularly the female body, is a powerful cultural player. In a direct reversal of much Western philosophical and feminist theory, where biology is what diminishes or reduces the social

---

49 Power, C., "Lunarchy: The Original Human Economics of Time," *Solarizing the Moon: Essays in Honour of Lionel Sims*. Archaeopress, 2022, p. 12.

50 Knight, C. and J. Lewis., "Towards a Theory of Everything," *Human Origins: Contributions from Social Anthropology*. Berghahn Books, 2016, p. 95.

51 Finnegan, M., "The Politics of Eros: Ritual Dialogue and Egalitarianism in Three Central African Hunter-Gatherer Societies," *Journal of the Royal Anthropological Institute,* vol. 19, no. 4, 2013, p. 697.

> person, biology here is what enlarges it . . . That the female procreative body could express a collective agency which is both active and political, an agency expressed through public ritual celebrations of reproductive sex, birth, blood, and the female genitals, has rarely been considered . . . [D]uring women's dances there is a recurrent statement about the specifically female power that is birth, and the sexual economy that runs parallel to it. In amplified body-statements, women publicly capitalize on their power as the producers of children.[52]

Denial of the importance of biology, and the associated notion that sex and gender are socially constructed, turns out to be somewhat ironically an idiosyncratically Western conception at odds with the attitude towards the sexed body in non-Western cultures. The irony resides in the fact that gender theorists claim to be overcoming Western ideology and ethnocentrism, when in actual fact they are one of its most recent exponents.

In his book *Amazonian Cosmos: The Sexual and Religious Symbolism of the Tukano Indians*, Gerardo Reichel-Dolmatoff analyses the culture of the Tukano Indians as an elaboration of basic physiological and biological differences between males and females. In Tukano culture, the ecology is divided into masculine and feminine domains, which in broad terms correspond to the different foods hunted by men and those cultivated by women. For example, the domestic sphere and the garden is considered to be feminine as this is where women spend most of their time during the day and where food is prepared, whereas the forest is where men hunt. As Reichel-Dolmatoff writes, "the forest has essentially a masculine character while the produce of the river and of the fields has a feminine character . . . the forest and its animals belong strictly to the sphere of man."[53] Importantly, while the animals of the forest are considered to be

---

52 Ibid, p. 707.

53 Reichel-Dolmatoff, G., *Amazonian Cosmos: The Sexual and Religious Symbolism of the Tukano Indians*. University of Chicago Press, 1974. p. 55.

part of the masculine domain, once the bounty of the hunt crosses the threshold of the maloca or domestic dwelling, it enters the feminine domain. As he continues, the 'threshold or limit between spheres of activities must be strictly observed . . . once this threshold is crossed, the prey enters the feminine sphere where it will be transformed into food.'[54]

Myth, ritual, and various aspects of Tukano culture involve what Reichel-Dolmatoff refers to as "[g]ynaecological symbolism."[55] For example, the Tukano believe the current condition of reality emerged from a primal paradisical condition referred to as *Ahpikondia*. This primal condition is associated with female symbolism, such as milk and uterine imagery, forming the basis of the belief that the cosmos is itself of a uterine nature. Importantly domestic dwellings are thought to be microcosmic manifestations of this macrocosmic phenomenon; that is, symbolically "the hearth represents the uterus" symbolising in the domestic sphere "how humanity was born."[56]

Significantly, when a child is born it is believed to have been severed from the primal paradise of *Ahpikondia*. Consequently, important rituals are performed to reintegrate the child with that primal condition as represented in the domestic domain of the house or maloca. As Reichel-Dolmatoff writes:

> When the umbilical cord is cut, the child is in a very dangerous state; his contact with the maternal uterus and with the cosmic uterus of *Ahpikon-dia* is broken, but he has still not been incorporated into the uterus of the maloca. The circuit is broken . . . [The] women bring the child and enter the moloca with it, safe and sound when they pass through the door, the contact with *Ahpikon-dia* is re-established, the circuit is closed again, and the newly born child affects the passage from one uterine existence to another.[57]

---

54 Ibid, p. 231.

55 Ibid, p. 208.

56 Ibid, p. 108.

57 Ibid, p. 140.

Another important domain where we find symbolic elaborations on female reproductive biology is in the cultivation of altered states of consciousness by ingesting the psychedelic compound Ayahuasca or what is also called yagé. Ayahuasca (Banisteropsis caapi) is a central aspect of Amazonian spiritual life, with the imagery experienced during Ayahuasca visions being an important component of the artistic and religious aspects of the culture. Significantly, by drinking Ayahuasca members of the community are able to re-experience the primal condition out of which humanity is believed to have emerged. As one informant remarks when comparing the world of the everyday with this alternative realm of experience: 'here is a wall, a shell that separates the natural world from *Ahpikondia*. This shell impedes vision; men who live in our world do not see *Ahpikondia*. In order to see it they must drink yage.'[58]

Ayahuasca visions include seeing 'luminous bodies in movement' as well as the experience of dying and entering "another dimension" and establishing contact with the "divine."[59] Significantly, this spiritual domain of experience is conceived in terms of gynaecological symbolism; as Reichel-Dolmatoff avers the "supernatural sphere" experienced during Ayahuasca visions is "conceived in terms of . . . passive sexual contact: the penetration of the cosmic uterus."[60]

Symbolic elaborations of female reproductive biology are also evident in Australia and various other cultures around the globe. For example, to briefly touch on what is a vast literature[61] in Australian initiation rites, young boys are placed in a symbolic uterus from

---

58 Ibid, p. 150.

59 Ibid, p. 174.

60 Ibid, p. 151.

61 For extensive reviews see; Buckley, T., and A. Gottlieb (eds.), *Blood Magic: The Anthropology of Menstruation.* University of California Press, 1988; Knight, C. *Blood Relations: Menstruation and the Origins of Culture.* Yale University Press, 1995.

which they emerge reborn as men.[62] Additionally during ritual, men coat themselves in ochre, a form of blood symbolism that is originally derived from female menstruation and reproductive biology.[63] Significantly, one of the central components in the making of an Aboriginal medicine man—or shaman—is that during visions the 'postulant is swallowed by a mythical snake and reborn as a child.'[64]

Similar phenomena have been noted among the Fang of Gabon in Africa; for example, during the altered states induced by the psychedelic Iboga, participants experience a "return to infancy and to birth—to the life in the womb." Such a return to the 'uterine condition' —which shows striking parallels to the Tukano example noted above—is believed to bring the individual "very close to life in the land of the dead," a sense of closeness which restores 'their own integrity—their pristine condition'[65] In *Carl Jung and the Evolutionary Sciences*, I offer a more detailed analysis of these phenomena from the point of view of evolutionary neuroscience, and the Jungian child and mother archetypes, suggesting such ritual-based transformations of consciousness may represent an ontogenetic regression from adult modes of cortical brain function to more archaic subcortical processes associated with infancy and childhood. Significantly, similar archetypal material is also evident in Western literature—for example, Goethe's *Faust* and Wordsworth's "Immortality Ode."[66]

---

62 Berndt and Berndt, *The World of the First Australians: Aboriginal Traditional Life : Past and Present*. Aboriginal Studies Press, 1988, pp. 252-56 and 76-87.

63 Berndt, R.M. and C.H. Berndt, *Sexual Behavior in Western Arnhem Land*. University of California, 1951. vol. nos. 16-17, p. 55; Warner, W.L., *A Black Civilization: A Social Study of an Australian Tribe*. P. Smith, 1969, p. 268.

64 Elkin, A.P., *Aboriginal Men of High Degree: Initiation and Sorcery in the World's Oldest Tradition*. Inner Traditions/Bear, 1993, 107.

65 Fernandez, J.W. Bwiti, *An Ethnography of the Religious Imagination in Africa*. Princeton University Press, 1982, p. 491.

66 Clark, G., *Carl Jung and the Evolutionary Sciences: A New Vision for Analytical Psychology*. Taylor & Francis, 2025, pp. 144, 158, 175, 180.

Concluding Thoughts

In this essay I presented a brief overview of the evolutionary literature on sex-based differences and discussed the manner in which such differences illuminate cross-cultural social roles, as well as aspects of cultural and religious symbolism. I have also illustrated the utility of Jungian approaches for the interpretation of the ethnographic record. It is hoped this analysis will contribute to a growing body of literature that highlights the importance of biological sex in anthropological and scientific research. Importantly, the approach I've outlined here is one that acknowledges the cross-cultural existence of cross-sex identification. Consequently, biological sex should not be seen as invalidating the transgender experience, which seems to be a natural manifestation of human psychobiological variation.

8

ON BIAS AND CENSORSHIP IN ACADEMIA

NATHAN HONEYCUTT & LEE JUSSIM[*]

Bias and censorship are often treated as entirely different phenomena, and there are good reasons for doing so. The term "bias," alone, has so many different meanings that each, by itself, can and has constituted entire subfields of research (consider bias as "prejudice" and bias as "heuristics"). Censorship, too, has many different aspects, including legal issues, moral issues, political issues, and self-censorship. Further, censorship requires power over others, which means the ability to reward, withhold reward, or punish.

Nonetheless, in this chapter, we will draw on concepts and findings from across the social sciences that converge on the conclusion that bias and censorship intersect in socially, politically, and psychologically important and mutually reinforcing ways that damage academic discourse generally and scholarship in particular. To this end, we will first define terms and then review varieties of censorship in academia. We then briefly review the psychological research on bias, with specific application to biases in academia. We then argue that academia is a social-reputational system thereby ren-

---

[*] Order of authorship is alphabetical; both authors contributed equally.

dering academics particularly vulnerable to social pressures, and this provides the means by which censorship can operate. When fields in the academy have become ideologically (or theoretically) homogenous, the risk of suppressing contrarian or dissident views rises.

And, as we discuss in a subsequent section on political bias, academia has become a club not merely for liberals, but for the most extreme woke identitarian progressives. The core and most toxic component of identitarian progressives is *equalitarianism*. Elsewhere, we have defined equalitarianism as having three central components (Jussim et al., 2023): 1. Discrimination in the present is the predominant reason for inequality; 2. Support for coercive punishment of those who violate progressive/woke/identitarian sacred beliefs, and imposition of equalitarian beliefs and values on others through capturing and pressuring organizations, such as academic bureaucracies and corporate board rooms; and 3. "Equality" means neither equality of opportunity nor even equal outcomes among groups; instead, it means equal *or better* outcomes for groups the woke consider *marginalized, underrepresented, or "minoritized."* As we discussed in Jussim et al., 2023, pp. 231-232, equalitarianism often manifests as:

1. Greater willingness to demonize people for real or imagined prejudice against identity groups deemed deserving of special protections by the progressive left (Jagdeep et al., 2024).

2. Heightened sensitivity to "detecting" racism, sexism, oppression, and other bigotries. This includes seeing more "isms" (racism, sexism, etc.) and "phobias" (transphobia, Islamophobia, etc.) than seen by others (Jagdeep et al., 2024), and greater willingness to conclude many social phenomena reflect "isms" (Jussim, 2022a), especially among one's opponents (Bernstein, Zambrotta, Martin & Micalizzi, 2023).

3. Overestimation of manifestations of discrimination (McCaffree & Saide, 2021).

4. A greater willingness to engage in censorship of speech and science that is perceived as violating equalitarian norms on grounds that it is somehow "harmful" to marginalized groups, typically without feeling any onus for presenting evidence of such harms (Carlos, Sheagley & Taylor, 2023; Kaufmann, 2021; Rausch, Redden & Geher, 2023).

5. Greater social vigilantism: willingness to publicly shame and ostracize those who engage in expression seen as violating equalitarian values (Proulx, Costin, Magazin, Zarzeczna & Haddock, 2022).

6. Willingness to violate basic and universal human rights, such as due process, for those accused of wrongdoing, if the wrongdoing includes allegations of expressions of prejudice or discrimination against some marginalized group.

Our chapter ends with several examples of woke equalitarians attempting to censor research. Because our focus is on academia, this chapter puts aside the variety of other contexts in which these issues may arise, including but not restricted to governments and corporations.

Definitions

Censorship

We define censorship in academia as actions aimed at obstructing particular ideas from reaching an audience for reasons other than low scholarly quality (see also Clark et al., 2023). In this context, it is perhaps also worth quoting from the AAUP (1940/1970) statement on academic freedom: "Controversy is at the heart of the free academic inquiry which the entire statement is designed to foster." This is nicely captured by Rutgers University's policy (from which the first author received his Ph.D. and the second author's home institution policy governing academic freedom (1951/2015, p. 1-2)):

> Since the very nature of a university and its value to society depend upon the free pursuit and dissemination of knowledge…all members of the faculty are expected, whenever and wherever they engage in teaching, research, service, professional practice or clinical practice, as well as in their research and professional publication, freely to discuss subjects with which they are competent to deal, to pursue inquiry therein, and to present and endeavor to maintain their opinions and conclusions relevant thereto. In expressing those ideas which seem to them justified by the facts, they are expected to maintain standards of sound scholarship and competent teaching. Professors, guided by a deep conviction of the worth and dignity of the advancement of knowledge, recognize the special responsibilities placed upon them. Their primary responsibility to their subject is to seek and to state the truth as they see it.

Our point is not that others share the principles described in Rutgers' policy; it is, instead, that it clearly articulates the principle of academic freedom. Censorship, then, is work that is blocked from dissemination. It is important in this context to understand that something can be both censored and available. If a book is banned in Kansas, it may be available in Nebraska. If an article is retracted because it is "objectionable or dangerous" it is censored by the authorities (usually the editor or editorial board) of a journal, even if it gets published somewhere else.

Rejection is Not Inherently Censorship

Importantly, though, there is a difference between censorship and rejection. In science, rejection occurs when an idea *has been explored* and the available evidence has been found wanting. The history of science is replete with rejected ideas, such as a geocentric solar system, flat earth, spontaneous generation of life, and the phlogiston theory of air. These ideas were thoroughly explored and rejected because the evidence available overwhelmingly disconfirmed them.

In normal academic processes, scholars draft papers, submit them for publication (to either books or journals), that work is reviewed by peers in one's fields ("peer review"), and sometimes it is accepted for publication and other times it is rejected. For example, scientific papers that are rejected for failing to meet the conventional standards in a field -- the methods are weak, the statistics are inappropriate, the findings are not viewed as particularly interesting or important. This is not censorship. The paper is not published because it is deemed of insufficient quality, not because (as per our working definition of censorship) it is deemed objectionable or dangerous.

Bias

In the context of deciding which papers to publish or retract, which grants to fund, which speakers to invite or deplatform, or who to hire and/or promote, bias refers to favoring some claims, conclusions, or individuals over others. By "favoring" we do not mean simply "liking" –people can like or prefer certain types of studies, papers, or findings without being biased. Instead, bias means showing favoritism; all things equal (especially the quality of the methods and analyses), if certain findings are deemed more publication-worthy than others, or more deserving of funding, or of being cited, this is bias (for examples, see de Vries et al., 2018; Honeycutt & Jussim, 2020). Before discussing how biases can manifest as censorship, we review three issues: 1. Varieties of censorship; 2. Motivated reasoning as a source of bias in general; and 3. Manifestations of motivated reasoning in academia.

Varieties of Censorship

Scholarship is censored when it is blocked from academic discourse (publications, conferences, colloquia, teaching, etc.) for reasons other than its quality. Although what makes for a quality article is beyond the scope of this chapter,

1. What constitutes "quality" varies from field to field and can itself be disputed and contested;
2. It typically involves aspects such as logic, originality, insightfulness;
3. For empirical sciences, it also typically involves the quality of the methods, appropriateness of statistics, and importance of the findings.

In scientific fields, then, how can one determine if some work or idea has been censored? Work that is blocked from publication, or retracted, without being shown to be wrong, produced by flawed methods, or of trivial value will usually be strong contenders for having been censored.

For example, over the last several years, there has been a disturbing trend in which published scientific papers have been retracted, not because they have been shown to be fraudulent or even riddled with errors, but because academic outrage mobs have accused them of being offensive in some way or causing unspecified "harms" (Jussim et al., 2023). The Committee on Publication Ethics (COPE; n.d.) identifies grounds for retraction as including plagiarism, repeat publication of the same data and: "clear evidence that the findings are unreliable, either as a result of major error (e.g., miscalculation or experimental error), or as a result of fabrication (e.g., of data) or falsification (e.g., image manipulation)." Note that "offensiveness," "someone accuses it of bigotry," and "undocumented allegations of harm" do not appear. Nor do "open letters denouncing it," "thousands of academics on social media are screaming about it," or "essays and blogs have been written about how bad the paper is and why it should never have been published." Thus, the COPE guidelines for retraction constitute a good set of a priori criteria against which to evaluate whether something has been censored versus rejected: If a retraction occurs for reasons outside the COPE guidelines, it is probably censorship, not rejection.

Academic censorship can stem from two different sources. External refers to censorship coming from outside of academia; internal refers to censorship from within academia. Stevens et al. (2020) also argued that internal suppression is the most severe and toxic form, at least in academia in the United States. Academic success hinges on the views of other academics, whereas external efforts to suppress are unusual events and can thus be considered outliers. Scholarship in the U.S. literally hinges to no extent whatsoever on the opinions of non-academic activists, whether on the right or left; it hinges a great deal on what other academics think. Therefore, academics have far more power to censor one another than do outsiders.

Now that we have distinguished between bias, rejection, and censorship, we can turn our attention to an analysis of how biases can lead to censorship. We begin by providing an overview of psychological research on the types of biases that can influence evaluations of the quality of scholarship.

Common Psychological Biases

In this section, we discuss a slew of psychological biases, including those associated with ideological extremism, confirmation bias, misanthropic bias, myside and preference biases, and motivated reasoning. Across these biases, research that conflicts with preexisting beliefs, or that is conducted by ideological opponents, may face more resistance and obstacles in the review and publication process, be harder to obtain funding for, or simply be ignored and overlooked if published.

Ideological Extremism

Ideological extremists routinely view their opponents as holding more extreme views than they really do (Wilson, Parker, & Feinberg, 2020; Westfall, Van Boven, Chambers, & Judd, 2015), and grossly overestimate the levels of prejudice and dehumanization exhibited by ideological opponents (Moore-Berg, Ankori-Karlinsky, Hameiri, & Bruneau, 2020). When fields become ideologically homogeneous, it becomes far easier to sneer at one's ideological opponents, and to express shared values that are only shared by one's comrades-in-arms.

Confirmation Bias

Confirmation bias refers to our tendency to seek, interpret, and create information that verifies our preexisting beliefs (e.g., see Nickerson, 1998). Information that is consistent with our beliefs gets attention, information that is inconsistent gets ignored. This bias, then, can lead information that verifies existing beliefs to be preferred over information that contests those beliefs, potentially creating obstacles to the acceptance and dissemination of information with which one disagrees.

Misanthropic Bias

A more nefarious bias, misanthropic bias refers to our tendency to see another person in a negative light. Negative acts that can be blamed on the other person are emphasized; and people give them less credit for positive acts (Ybarra, Stephan, & Schaberg, 2000). Misanthropic bias can lead people to see their opponents as evil and immoral—as agents with wrongheaded views and motives that must be stopped or shut out.

Myside and Preference Bias

Myside or preference bias (sometimes referred to as desirability bias) occurs when a person evaluates information in ways that are biased toward validating their own attitudes (Stanovich, West, & Toplak, 2013; Tappin, van der Leer, & McKay, 2017). This bias can lead people to hold essentially tribalistic views (Clark and Winegard, 2020), where claims from your side are acceptable, but if the same claim is made by someone of the opposing side, it is dismissed, rejected and even sneered at.

Motivated Reasoning

Similar to, but distinct from confirmation bias, motivated reasoning refers to a desire to seek out, interpret, and *evaluate* information in ways that verifies our preexisting beliefs (Kunda, 1990). People who are highly motivated to reach a particular conclusion may exert a great deal of effort to justify doing so, uncritically accept flawed arguments or evidence that comports well with their preferences, but also work quite hard to discredit arguments or evidence that opposes their preferences.

Academic Biases

There is no reason to believe that academics are any less subject to the common psychological biases described above than are anyone else (see, e.g., Duarte et al., 2015; Honeycutt & Jussim, 2020 for reviews). Nonetheless, the specific ways in which such biases manifest in academia can be quite unique. Some of these are discussed next.

Theoretical

Sometimes a theory or perspective gains such dominance that it becomes difficult for alternative views or findings inconsistent with the theory to gain a foothold in an academic area. In scientific psychology, this has been true with respect to behaviorism in the early 20th century, and with claims emphasizing the power of stereotypes, implicit and explicit biases, situations, expectancy effects, and self-fulfilling prophecies in the latter part of the 20th century (see reviews by Jussim, 2012; Stevens, Jussim, and Honeycutt, 2020). In medicine, a classic example involves the cause of ulcers--which was erroneously yet so confidently believed to be stress that the discovery that it was actually bacteria was not accepted by the medical establishment for decades (Stevens, Jussim, & Honeycutt, 2020). In astronomy, Loeb (2014) provided a slew of cases in which astronomers were wrong yet certain so that progress in the field was often set back for many years when they refused to accept or publish findings providing contrary evidence. For example, at the beginning of the 20th century, there was a consensus among astronomers that the sun was composed of the same materials as the Earth. It took many years to publish the evidence that, in fact, it is made mostly of hydrogen and helium. Such dominance of certain theories or perspectives can lead to substantial gaps in the scientific literature in the form of unasked and unanswered questions (e.g., related to stereotype accuracy, see Jussim, Stevens, & Honeycutt, 2018).

Political

Certain fields in academia can and have become ideological echo chambers. Of course, this is mostly relevant only to scholarship and scholars who work on politicized topics. Nonetheless, many of the topics in the social sciences have been politicized (e.g., oppression, discrimination, various isms, understanding gaps between demographic groups) as have some in the natural sciences (e.g., climate change) and the biomedical sciences (e.g., the efficacy of Covid-19 lockdowns, vaccines, and medical care for people experiencing gender dysphoria). For these types of topics, echo chambers are corrosive to science (Honeycutt & Jussim, 2020) and, most relevant to the present chapter, can inspire censorship.

Data collected in the last 15 years has definitively pointed to a consistent state of ideological homogeneity in the academy, composed of growing majorities of left-leaning faculty, particularly within the social sciences. Depending on the study, the sample (faculty in specific fields; faculty at elite institutions; national sample of all tenured/tenure track faculty), and the measure of ideological or partisan identity (self-report political identification, self-reported voting choices, political party membership, campaign contributions), estimates of faculty on the left range from about 65%-100%, and of faculty on the right from 0-20% (Adekoya, Kaufmann, & Simpson, 2020; Cardiff & Klein, 2005; Carl, 2017; Gross & Simmons, 2007; Honeycutt, 2024a; Honeycutt, 2024b; Honeycutt & Freberg, 2017; Inbar & Lammers, 2012, Rothman, Lichter, & Nevitte, 2005).

Furthermore, it is reasonable to describe the left skew of the academy as "extreme" in two related but different senses. First, the distribution is extreme when compared to the American population, of which, according to Gallup is about 25% liberal, 34% moderate, and 37% conservative (Brenan, 2025). As such, liberals are massively overrepresented among faculty, and conservatives massively underrepresented relative to their baselines among U.S. adults (Honeycutt, 2024b). Not only is the skew extreme, but it is also extreme in these sense that there are vastly more academics (about 40%) who identify as being on the far left, e.g., Marxists, socialists, radicals or activists (Honeycutt, 2024b) than there are Americans who identify as being on the far left—most surveys indicate that 4-15% of Americans are on the far left (Hawkins, Yudkin, Juan-Torres & Dixon, 2018; Pew, 2014; Twenge et al., 2016).

Affective polarization refers to growing partisan animosity toward the other side (Iyengar & Westwood, 2015, who titled their article "Fear and Loathing Across Party Lines"). This state of the affairs is captured by this meme that was regularly tweeted out by academics and others during the Presidential election of 2020:

Figure 1

This sort of fear and loathing is not unique to those on the left—"owning the libs" has been a thing on the right for a long time. But because there are so few on the right in academia, nearly all the fear and loathing *within academia* emanates from those on the left, directed toward those on the right. Emblematic of how this phenomenon manifests in the academy, as we were preparing this chapter, the second author received an email from the Rutgers AAUP, (the faculty union) that included this statement:

> We formalized those efforts in a committee after Trump's election to prepare for the new wave of attacks we know are on the way from a fascist, racist, xenophobic administration.

Further, notable percentages of faculty indicate an explicit willingness to discriminate against those in ideological out-groups (Adekova et al., 2020; Honeycutt & Freberg, 2017; Peters et al., 2020). In turn, many conservative students and faculty generally try to hide their political beliefs (Honeycutt, Jussim, & Freberg, 2019; Honeycutt, 2024a). It should not be surprising, then, that both conservative students and faculty report greater experiences of hostility and discrimination than their liberal and moderate peers (Adekova et al., 2020; Honeycutt, 2022; Honeycutt & Freberg, 2017; Honeycutt, Jussim, & Freberg, 2019; Peters et al., 2020).

When the political identities of those making up particular fields become heavily skewed, there is little to prevent or limit punishment (e.g., censorship) of those one sees as enemies. In fact, such hostility may become normalized (Prentice, 2012). Even if academics may generally espouse high levels of tolerance (e.g., Gross & Fosse, 2012), they generally have no issue expressing political or ideological intolerance (Honeycutt & Freberg, 2017).

According to some scholars, left-leaning norms are so entrenched that discrimination against non-liberals isn't even needed to sustain them (e.g., Prentice, 2012). And the implications are far reaching. Just by sheer numbers, the ideas and theorizing of left-leaning individuals leads to scientific knowledge disproportionally informed by topics and explanations that are interesting and appealing to those who are left-leaning (Jussim, Crawford, Stevens, & Anglin, 2016). So, in essence, the weight of the canon, without active targeted effort against ideological outsiders, may be sufficient to perpetuate censorship. As articulated by Prentice (2012), p. 516-517:

> Ideological homogeneity alone is enough to produce strong liberal norms, which in turn give[s] rise to . . . pressures to conform to liberal views (Festinger, Schachter, & Back, 1950); a reluctance to express nonliberal views (Miller & Morrison, 2009); . . . an inclination to derogate and punish PSPs [personality and social psychologists] who express conservative views (Schachter, 1951).

Thus, scientific conclusions may seem to validate left-leaning perspectives, not because they always provide the best account, but because these narratives are readily accessible, entrenched, and defended, and because alternative explanations face considerable resistance (Jussim, Crawford, Anglin, & Stevens, 2015).

This, in some cases, even moves beyond the research enterprise and might involve blatant activism, such that activist goals trump science. For example, some intellectuals may view climate change as such an important and pressing issue that those who present evidence that contests any aspect of global warming arguments may be at heightened risk of being denounced and ostracized—even when they have strong data on their side (e.g., Pielke, 2016).

Equalitarian

Related, but separate and distinct from political biases, academics may also be subject to equalitarian biases, which some argue are even more powerful than political biases (Clark & Winegard, 2020). Equalitarianism is generally considered to consist of ideas or beliefs that argue that society is morally obligated to pursue equality of outcome on outcomes that are socially valuable, and that if group differences exist, they only exist because of prejudice and discrimination. Consider, for example, Amy Wax who argued that differences in the adoption of "bourgeois values" explains many of the differences in outcomes between whites and blacks in the United States (Wax & Alexander, 2017). Outrage in response to her argument was immediate and forceful (Haidt, 2017). Our point is not whether Wax's argument was correct, but that work inconsistent with equalitarian views was swiftly and almost uniformly condemned by academics.

How Biases Become Censorious: Academia as a Social-Reputational System

Academia is a social-reputational system. This is the central insight necessary for understanding how bias evolves into censorship. That is, one's success as an academic is determined most directly by the subjective evaluations of colleagues, and only indirectly by objective individual performance. Admission to graduate school, peer review of academic publications, obtaining grants, obtaining your first job, tenure/promotion: in each of these areas, other's evaluations constitute the entire proximal influence on receiving (or not receiving) a sought-after reward (or punishment to be avoided). As a consequence, academics are rendered highly vulnerable to social approval because these evaluations are so critical to success.

Such vulnerabilities are a double-edged sword. On the one hand, this reputational system can mete out punishment, so that academics may self-censor in order to avoid the risk of being punished for expressing ideas of which their colleagues disapprove. Recent data confirms this; notable percentages of faculty report engaging in self-censorship (Honeycutt, 2024a). But, critical to the impact of the reputational system, nearly 40% of faculty surveyed (52% among conservative faculty) reported that they were worried about damaging their reputation because someone misunderstands something they have said or done, and nearly a quarter were worried about losing their job because someone misunderstands something they have said or done (Honeycutt, 2024a).

On the other hand, and possibly even more important, the reputational system also offers rewards for expressing ideas of which others approve. Thus, if academics seek the rewards that come with social approval, they may only or primarily express those ideas.

Figure 2 presents the Pyramid of Academic Censorship, a way to understand the processes by which censorship emerges in academia. Censorship is built on phenomena that becomes more common as one goes down the pyramid. Censorship by authorities usually occurs in response to denunciations; not all denunciations are successful (there are more denunciations than, for example, article retractions). Denunciation is a behavioral manifestation of intolerance, but not all intolerance manifests as denunciation. Biases can (but do not necessarily) produce intolerance because they lead to distorted views about the claims and harms caused by views one opposes. And biases are more likely to emerge in the published literature among fields that are ideologically or theoretically homogenous because there are fewer people willing and able to skeptically or critically evaluate or seriously and scientifically contest common claims.

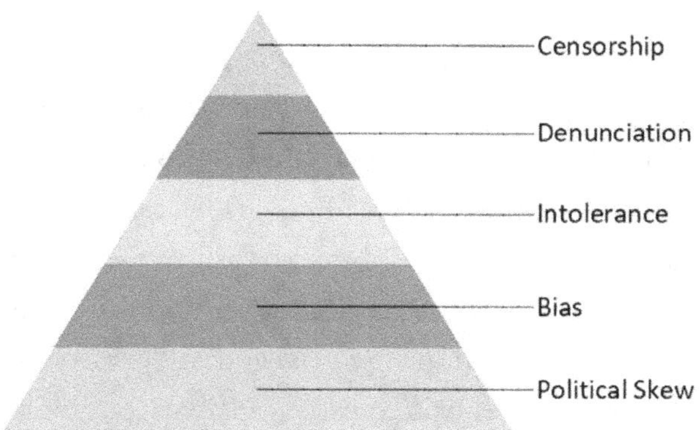

Figure 2

Biases can become censorious in direct and indirect ways (Stevens, Jussim, & Honeycutt, 2020). Direct censorship and suppression may be brought about in this system of reward and punishment via gatekeepers. Eminent, prestigious, or even just more advanced colleagues operating in high-status positions as editors, society officers, department chairs, or administrative officials yield outsized influence over which ideas are encouraged, promoted, ignored, or outright blocked—as gatekeepers over what gets through and what doesn't. Biases can:

- lead to illusions of bad science

- lead to selective calls for rigor

- stem from claims of harm and danger (often unidentified)

- lead to self-censorship

- stem from outrage mobs

We discuss each of these next.

Illusions of Bad Science

Bias tints the way we see the world; it is both possible and plausible for a person to be honest and sincere in their criticism while still reaching unjustified conclusions. Extreme partisans misconstrue and exaggerate positions held by the other side (Westfall, Van Boven, Chambers, & Judd, 2015). There is no reason to believe that academics are immune to this. Most work in the social sciences suffers *some* level of imperfection or limitation, and those can always be jumped on or exaggerated into *fatal flaws* that "justify" rejecting the work. We discuss several examples of this sort of thing at the end of this chapter (see also Jussim, 2020; Jussim et al., 2023, Stevens et al., 2020 for examples).

Selective Calls for Rigor

Selective calls for rigor involve rejecting work one does not like on ostensibly scientific grounds that one does not apply to work one likes. One of our favorites was an article that extolled the rigor of a study finding gender biases favoring men over another showing gender biases favoring women—even though by most conventional criteria for rigor (replication, sample size, use of multiple methods) the study accused of lacking rigor was more rigorous (see Jussim, 2019). It has also been demonstrated to occur in work on race and criminal justice (Savolainen, 2024). There is no reason to believe it has not affected other areas, and many reasons described here suspect it has.

Unidentified Harms and Dangers

Whether it is evolution, profanity, pornography, or bigotry, one of the go-to moves in seeking to censor something is that it is "dangerous" or, in modern parlance, "causes harm." Typically, not a shred of evidence of such harms is actually presented, and one needs to ascribe to the values or worldview of the person leveling the accusation of "harm!" in order to know what they are.

Now, in fairness to this view, we suspect that most people would agree that if there really was a sufficiently extreme bona fide "harm" that could be produced by an article, book, or idea, censoring it could be justified. Consider this purely hypothetical and unrealistic thought experiment. If some article is published, life on Earth will be wiped out. We suspect most would agree that censoring that article is probably a good idea. If one agrees that the idea should be censored, one has to acknowledge that we are now negotiating terms: how much bona fide "harm" must an idea create before it is censored?

Of course, in the real world, ideas do not *directly* cause any harm whatsoever. Nonetheless, they may indirectly cause harm by influencing people's behavior. Consider another thought experiment: A powerful political leader declared the Covid-19 pandemic a hoax. Followers abandoned all precautions, and a massive spike in infections and deaths occurred. The declaration caused harm. Whether such an utterance should be *censored* (say, by media outlets refusing to publish it) is debatable and we take no position on it here. Our only point is that the "harm" claim is not necessarily completely wrong.

Nonetheless, our view is that allegations of "harm" need to meet a high standard to be taken seriously. Clear direct lines to actual harms need to be identified, preferably with evidence or unusually compelling logic, rather than merely declared. Sometimes evidence of harm is abundant and obvious (such as the link between cigarettes and lung cancer). Other times, common sense and a modicum of logic are sufficient to render a harm obvious (no one needs five experiments to know that jumping out of an airplane flying at 20,000 feet without a parachute is a bad idea). In the absence of such a compelling argument (or strong evidence), allegations of harm may or may not be true, but are not credible and need not be taken seriously. In practice, those alleging harm almost never provide either evidence or an argument that approaches the credibility of the argument that jumping out of a plane at 20,000 feet without a parachute is a bad idea (Jussim, 2020). In such cases, the inherent harms caused by censorship (producing a distorted informational ecosystem by permitting some but not other ideas; erosion of academic freedom and free inquiry; limiting the ability of people to access information to make their own decisions) almost surely exceed any "harms" whose existence cannot be empirically or logically verified.

Self-censorship

Fear of social sanctions and anticipation of others' biases provides fertile ground for self-censorship. Researchers may avoid exploring or publishing certain ideas or topics because of fear of social sanctions. Notably, these ideas might not necessarily be factually or scientifically incorrect, but still be anathema to one's colleagues. Self-censorship may also be motivated or driven by the lopsided ideological nature of academia. For example, conservative or non-leftist academics are often advised that they should hide their true beliefs, or avoid studying certain topics, till after attaining tenure (e.g., Stevens et al., 2017; Wood, 2016).

Self-censorship, and the internal conflict it may create for individual academics, was captured well in a podcast by social psychologists Michael Inzlicht and Yoel Inbar (2018). Inzlicht, at about 25 minutes in, stated:

> What if I felt that overemphasis on oppression is a terrible
> idea, hurts alleged victims of oppression, and is bad for

everyone? What if I was outspoken about this? I suspect I would face a lot more opposition. Even though not much could happen to my job security, I'd have a lot of people screaming at me, making my life uncomfortable. And, truly, I wouldn't do it, because I'd be scared. I wouldn't do it because I'm a coward.

To this end, many college and university faculty report engaging in self-censorship, and at higher rates than decades past. For example, Honeycutt (2024a) found that one-in-five faculty reported self-censoring in research topics investigated, and one-in-four in academic publications. Additionally, 27% of faculty (47% of conservative faculty) reported they can't express their opinion on a subject because of how other faculty, students, or the administration would respond. Honeycutt (2024a) also found that one-in-three faculty surveyed reported toning down their writing for fear of causing controversy. For comparison, during the McCarthy Era, 9% of social scientists answered this question in the same way (Lazarsfeld & Thielens, 1958).

Outrage Mobs

So far, we have mostly discussed the psychological connections of bias to censorship for individuals. However, academic censorship often can have a major social component. Bias can also manifest in outrage mobs, particularly in the form of a social media mob uniting and piling-on in denouncing papers or ideas without critical or constructive review. In these situations, editors are pressured to retract articles, funding agencies are pressured to pull funding or support, and/or department heads or university administrators are pressured to terminate faculty contracts, remove faculty from teaching courses, or coerce resignations. In these cases, the mob itself does not directly hold the power to censor, but instead seeks to pressure authorities to do so.

And of course, who in academia, given the extent to which it is a social-reputational system, relishes being the target of a mob of one's colleagues? Even in the absence of a mob, the mere (reasonable) *fear of the mob* may instigate self-censorship.

Examples of Academic Censorship

In this final section, we summarize several real-world examples in which it is easy to see the direct connection of bias to censorship. Each of these cases are clear-cut because they culminated in an article being retracted not because it manifested errors, but because it was denounced as offensive or ostensibly causing harm that were never specifically identified. Additional examples can be found in other recent articles, though some involved failed attempts at censorship or forms of censorship other than retraction (including de-platforming, firings, etc., e.g., see Clark et al., 2023; Jussim et al., 2023; Savolainen, 2024). Even failed attempts, however, reveal the connection between bias and censorship because *attempts* to censor ideas invariably result from allegations of some sort of moral transgression (see Jussim, 2020 for details).

Affirmative Action Cannot be Criticized — The Case of JAHA

Dr. Norman Wang published an article in the Journal of the American Heart Association (hence JAHA; AHA is the association) critical of AHA's affirmative action programs and policies. The paper compiled a wealth of data (including four figures, four tables, and over 100 references) to support the author's conclusion (p. 14) that "Recent affirmative action efforts through diversity, inclusion, and equity programs recognize neither changes in legal limitations, nor data indicating harm to underrepresented minorities. Long-term academic solutions and excellence should not be sacrificed for short-term demographic optics." The article first evoked a social media outrage mob.

Figure 3: Examples of the social media dogpile.

Dr. Qazi was at the time an MD at Stanford University.

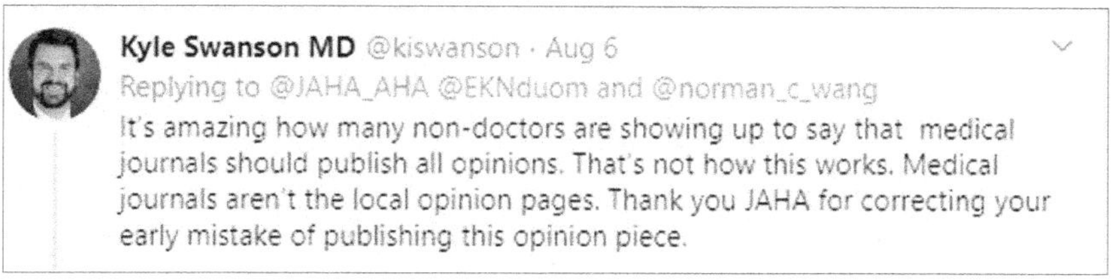

Dr. Swanson is a neurosurgeon in Milwaukee.

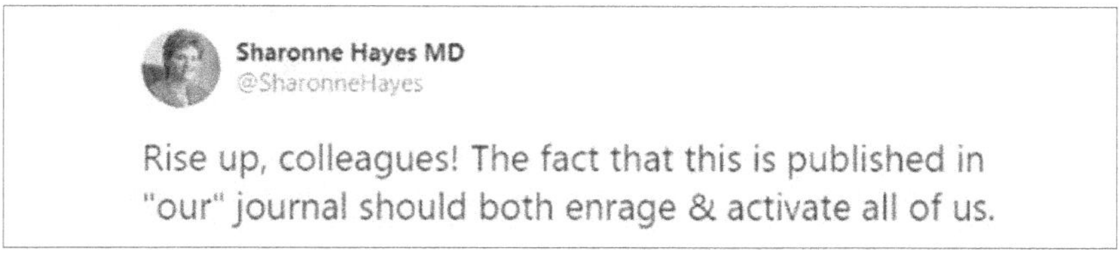

Dr. Hayes was Director of Diversity and Inclusion at the Mayo Clinic.

Although the denunciations were far more extensive than shown, Figure 3 presents instructive examples from the outrage mob displaying the censorious mindset. Dr. Qazi accuses the paper of being "absurd" without refuting anything, and then labels it "racist." Such an accusation expresses moral outrage, but academic freedom protects both expressions of outrage and the "outrageous" ideas about which outrage is expressed. Dr. Swanson commits an ironic logical error of an "argument from authority" —the educational status of critics of the retraction cannot possibly constitute a basis for believing or disbelieving their criticisms (which, instead, need to be evaluated on their merits). It is ironic because the article was on *the ineffectiveness of affirmative action*, and if we are going to play the authority card, then it is social scientists, not MDs, who have the relevant expertise here. Dr. Hayes's comment is little more than "I'm mad and you should be too." This is quintessential moral grandstanding (Tosi & Warmke, 2016).

The editor of JAHA issued several statements surrounding and attempting to justify the retraction (London, 2020). At least one manifests exactly the processes we have described in this paper: Bias produces censoriousness:

> Much more needs to be done to increase diversity, equity and inclusiveness in medicine and cardiology. In my opinion, the article by Dr. Wang does nothing to get us towards that goal . . . In fact, its central purpose was to argue against affirmative action, noting that Black and Hispanic trainees in medicine are less qualified than White and Asian trainees. These opinions do not reflect in any way my views, the views of the JAHA Editorial Board, or the views of the American Heart Association. We condemn discrimination and racism in all forms.

Presented as justification for retraction, this is logically equivalent to: 1. All papers we accept must support affirmative action (the topic of Wang's paper) because affirmative action inherently supports diversity, equity, and inclusion, and reviewing published articles that say otherwise is unacceptable (bias); 2. Wang's article was critical of affirmative action; 3. Therefore, it is racist and should never have been accepted and is now retracted (censorship).

The Case of Angewandte Chemie

Hudlicky (2020) published an article in *Angewandte Chemie* (that is the name of a German chemistry journal that was mostly in honor of one of his colleague's works on organic synthesis). He criticized diversity efforts as a form of discrimination and as a rejection of merit-based hiring, called for a "masters and apprentice" model of training, and characterized Chinese academics as disproportionately publishing papers characterized by "fraud and improper publication" practices (Hudlicky, 2020, p. 5). An outrage mob ensued, and the paper was retracted.

The German Chemical Society, which publishes *Angewandte Chemie*, issued a statement (Herrmann, 2020) explaining and "justifying" their retraction that leads off with this:

> On 4 June, an opinion piece was published in *Angewandte Chemie* that contained offensive and inflammatory language aimed toward people of different genders, races, and nationalities. We apologize that this offensive and misguided essay was published in our journal, and we are deeply sorry for failing the community that puts their trust in us. The views expressed in the essay do not reflect the values of the journal in any way. That this article was published at all has demonstrated a breakdown in editorial decision-making.

Again, the connection of bias to censorship is on full display. Apparently, this editorial board has a consensus on "values" other than getting at truth, and if one does not conform to them, one cannot publish there. And, if somehow one does publish there, and they discover a "values violation," the paper can be retracted.

Censorship of Research on Transgender Issues

The neuroscience journal *Eneuro* published a paper describing a new theory of gender dysphoria (Gliske, 2019) that speculatively linked brain structures to the psychology of experiences of gender dysphoria (strong, persistent feelings of identifying with a different gender and discomfort with one's gender assigned at birth). Once again, the "justifications" for retraction include some manifestly bizarre statements (Society for Neuroscience, 2020). It leads off with this (p. 1):

Flaws regarding the construction of the theory

A theory is proposed that chronic distress, gender nonconformity and incongruence, and body ownership networks would be related. In order to build the theory, the following logic is used:

1. The author hypothesizes that chronic distress, gender nonconformity and incongruence, and body ownership networks would be related.

2. The author looks for information in the literature about the implication of brain regions and networks in relation to the hypothesis to obtain evidence.

3. Thinking to have obtained evidence, the author confirms the hypothesis and then jumps to propose a theory.

This is not the formal way to build up a theory or to verify hypotheses.

The final statement is silly. The paper never claimed to provide empirical *tests* of the theory. Theoretical papers routinely appear in psychology and other disciplines that are based on existing literatures. This is not just our opinion. Retraction Watch (Marcus, 2020) posted a scathing criticism of *ENeuro's* decision, that, among other things, says this: "the journal appears to have badly botched this case" and "it can't fairly hide behind the claim—which it now seems to be making—that it had inadvertently accepted a poorly-done study." This justification for retraction—treating Gliske's paper as an empirical rather than theoretical one—beggars belief because it is so transparently absurd to evaluate a theoretical paper as if it reports new studies. Retraction Watch also made this simple statement, which probably captures the core reasons the paper ran afoul of an academic outrage mob: "A journal has retracted a controversial paper that questioned what it called the 'existing dogma' about gender."

Colonialism Can Only Be Condemned

A political scientist published a paper titled "The Case for Colonialism," (Gilley, 2018), which argued that several countries plausibly described as failed states or close would benefit from a return of colonial practices. The paper was promptly denounced in a petition led by a professor of English that garnered more than 16,000 signatures (Heijun Wills, 2017). Gilley and the journal's editorial board were subject to what they described as credible death threats, and, as a result, the article was retracted.

In classic style, the retraction petition starts off with its version of "we are offended" combined with a manifestly false claim:

> The sentiments expressed in this article reek of colonial disdain for Indigenous peoples and ignore ongoing colonialism in white settler nations. The author ponders "what would likely have happened in a given place absent colonial rule?" (2) with the predictably racist conclusion that peoples and cultures would have remained "primitive," relying upon an obscene, reductive colonial epithet.

The term "primitive," in the petition as if it quoted the article, appears nowhere in the article. Although it is fair to interpret the article as implying that life might have been better in some areas because of colonialism (an argument which we do not evaluate here), there is nothing in it to even imply a view of other peoples as "primitive." The reference to the article as "obscene" highlights the censorious nature of the denunciation.

Conclusion

The main contribution of this chapter has been to identify connections between bias and academic censorship. Although biases have received considerable attention in the burgeoning literature on reforming practices to improve scientific validity and credibility (see de Vries et al., 2018), and although censorship has a long and venerable history of scholarship (Coetzee, 1996), we know of no prior scholarship drawing a straight line connecting the two. There are many reasons for censorship outside of academia that is beyond the scope of the present contribution. Our review, however, indicates that within academia, censoriousness often reflects the political or moral biases of those seeking to censor.

The fundamental argument here is not that biases *inevitably* lead to censoriousness. However, when academic fields become as heavily politically skewed as are the social sciences and humanities, two things happen: 1. There are a far higher proportion of extremists than in the population, so that extreme views are normalized; and 2. There are few, if any, scholars with countervailing biases (or perhaps even scholars willing to question prevailing wisdom) to constitute a check on the type of runaway biases that can and do lead extremists to very distorted views of the world. In this paper, we argued that one manifestation of such distortions is to seek to preclude ideas and even data that offends such a worldview.

References

Adekoya, R., Kaufmann, E., & Simpson, T. (2020). *Academic freedom in the UK: Protecting Viewpoint Diversity*. Policy Exchange. https://policyexchange.org.uk/publication/academic-freedom-in-the-uk-2/.

American Association of University Professors (1940/1970). "1940 Statement of Principles on Academic Freedom and Tenure, With 1970 Interpretive Comment." Retrieved from: https://www.aaup.org/reports-publications/aaup-policies-reports/policy-statements/1940-statement-principles-academic.

Bernstein, M., Zambrotta, N. S., Martin, S. D., & Micalizzi, L. (2023). "Tribalism in American Politics: Are Partisans Guilty of Double Standards?" *Journal of Open Inquiry in the Behavioral Sciences.* Retrieved from: https://researchers.one/articles/23.02.00006v3.

Brenan, M. (2025). *U.S. Political Parties Historically Polarized Ideologically.* Gallup. Retrieved from: https://news.gallup.com/poll/655190/political-parties-historically-polarized-ideologically.aspx.

Cardiff, C. F., & Klein, D. B. (2005). "Faculty Partisan Affiliations in All Disciplines: A Voter-Registration Study," *Critical Review,17*(3/4), 237–255.

Carl, N. (2017). "Lackademia: Why Do Academics Lean Left?" *The Adam Smith Institute.*

Carlos, R. F., Sheagley, G., & Taylor, K. L. (2023). "Tolerance for the Free Speech of Outgroup Partisans," *PS: Political Science & Politics, 56*(2), 240-244.

Clark, C. J., Jussim, L., Frey, K., Stevens, S. T., al-Gharbi, M., Aquino, K., Bailey, J. M., Barbaro, N., Baumeister, R. F., Bleske-Rechek, A., Buss, D., Ceci, S., Del Giudice, M., Ditto, P. H., Forgas, J. P., Geary, D. C., Geher, G., Haider, S., Honeycutt, N., . . . von Hippel, W. (2023). "Prosocial Motives Underlie Scientific Censorship By Scientists: A Perspective and Research Agenda," *Proceedings of the National Academy of Sciences,* 120(48), e2301642120. https://doi.org/10.1073/pnas.2301642120.

Clark, C. J., & Winegard, B. M. (2020). "Tribalism In War and Peace: The Nature and Evolution of Ideological Epistemology and Its Significance For Modern Social Science," *Psychological Inquiry, 31*(1), 1-22. https://doi.org/10.1080/1047840X.2020.1721233

Coetzee, J. M. (1996). *Giving offense: Essays on censorship*. Chicago: University of Chicago Press.

Committee on Publication Ethics (n.d.). "Retraction Guidelines," Retrieved from https://publicationethics.org/retraction-guidelines. DOI: https://doi.org/10.24318/cope.2019.1.4.

de Vries, Y. A., Roest, A. M., de Jonge, P., Cuijpers, P., Munafò, M. R., & Bastiaansen, J. A. (2018). "The Cumulative Effect of Reporting and Citation Biases on the Apparent Efficacy of Treatments: The Case of Depression," *Psychological Medicine*, *48*(15), 2453–2455. https://doi.org/10.1017/S0033291718001873.

Duarte, J. L., Crawford, J. T., Stern, C., Haidt, J., Jussim, L., & Tetlock, P. E. (2015). "Political Diversity Will Improve Social Psychological Science," *Behavioral and Brain Sciences*, *38*. https://doi.org/10.1017/S0140525X14000430.

Gilley, B. (2018). "The Case for Colonialism," *Academic Questions*, *31*(2), 167–185. https://www.nas.org/academic-questions/31/2/the_case_for_colonialism.

Gliske, S. V. (2019). "A New Theory of Gender Dysphoria Incorporating the Distress, Social Behavioral, and Body-Ownership Networks," *ENeuro*, *6*(6). https://doi.org/10.1523/ENEURO.0183-19.2019.

Gross, N., & Fosse, E. (2012). "Why are Professors liberal?" *Theory and Society*, *41*(2), 127-168.

Gross, N., & Simmons, S. (2007). "The Social and Political Views of American Professors," *Working Paper Presented at a Harvard University Symposium on Professors and Their Politics*.

Haidt, J. (2017). "In defense of Amy Wax's defense of Bourgeois Values," Retrieved from: https://heterodoxaca- demy.org/in-defense-of-amy-waxs-defense-of-bourgeois-values/.

Hawkins, S., Yudkin, D., Juan-Torres, M., & Dixon, T. (2018). *Hidden Tribes: A Study of America's Polarized Landscape. New York:* More in Common.

Heijun Wills, J. (2017). *Petition · Call for Apology and Retraction from Third World Quarterly.* Retrieved from: https://www.change. org/p/third-world-quarterly-call-for-apology-and-retraction- from-third-world-quarterly.

Herrmann, G. (2020). "An Open Letter to Our Community," Retrieved from: https://onlinelibrary.wiley.com/page/journal/ 15213773/homepage/archive.

Honeycutt, N. (2022). "Manifestations of Political Bias in the Academy," Dissertation, Rutgers University. https://doi. org/10.7282/t3-2y4z-7009.

_____ (2024a). *Silence in the Classroom: The 2024 FIRE Faculty Survey Report.* The Foundation for Individual Rights and Expression. https://www.thefire.org/research-learn/silence-class- room-2024-fire-faculty-survey-report.

_____ (2024b). "The Politics Of University Faculty," https://doi. org/10.31234/osf.io/dnxqh.

Honeycutt, N. & Freberg, L. (2017). "The Liberal And Conservative Experience Across Academic Disciplines: An Extension of Inbar And Lammers," *Social Psychological and Personality Science, 8*(2), 115–123. https://doi.org/10.1177/1948550616667617.

Honeycutt, N., & Jussim, L. (2020). "A Model of Political Bias in Social Science Research," *Psychological Inquiry,* 31(1), 73–85. https://doi.org/10.1080/1047840X.2020.1722600.

Honeycutt, N., Jussim, L., & Freberg, L. (2019). "University students' perceptions of the classroom political climate," *Rutgers University, School of Graduate Studies Electronic Theses and Dissertations,* https://doi.org/doi:10.7282/t3-4v05-ht26/.

Hudlicky, T. (2020). "'Organic synthesis-Where now?' Is Thirty Years Old. A Reflection on the Current State of Affairs," *Angewandte Chemie (International Ed. in English)*. https://doi.org/10.1002/anie.202006167.

Inbar, Y., & Lammers, J. (2012). "Political Diversity in Social and Personality Psychology," *Perspectives on Psychological Science*,7(5), 496–503.

Inzlicht, M. & Inbar, Y. (2018). "WTF is the IDW?" Retrieved from: https://www.fourbeers.com/3.

Iyengar, S., & Westwood, S. J. (2015)." Fear and Loathing Across Party Lines: New Evidence on Group Polarization," *American journal of political science*, *59*(3), 690-707.

Jagdeep, A., Jagdeep, A., Lazarus, S., Fedida, O., Fihrer, G., Vasko, C., … , Viswanathan, I. (2024). "Instructing Animosity: How De Pedagogy Produces the Hostile Attribution Bias," *Network Contagion Research Institute*. Retrieved on 2/21/25 from: https://networkcontagion.us/reports/instructing-animosi-ty-how-dei-pedagogy-produces-the-hostile-attribution-bias/.

Jussim, L. (2012). *Social Perception and Social Reality: Why Accuracy Dominates Bias and Self-Fulfilling Prophecy*. Oxford University Press, USA.

_____ (2019). "Confirmation Bias: Real Bias or Delegitimization Rhetoric?" *Psychology Today*. Retrieved from: https://www.psychologytoday.com/us/blog/rabble-rouser/201908/confirmation-bias-real-bias-or-delegitimization-rhetoric.

_____ (2020). "The Threat to Academic Freedom . . . From Academics," Retrieved from: https://medium.com/@leej12255/the-threat-to-academic-freedom-from-academ-ics-4685b1705794.

_____ (2022a). "Is Everything 'Problematic?' *Unsafe Science*, Retrieved from https://unsafescience.substack.com/p/is-everything-problematic.

Jussim, L., Crawford, J. T., Anglin, S., & Stevens, S. (2015). "Ideological Bias in Social Psychological Research," In J. Forgas, K. Fiedler, & W. Crano (Eds.), *Sydney Symposium on Social Psychology and Politics.*(pp. 91–109). Taylor & Francis.

Jussim, L., Crawford, J. T., Stevens, S. T., & Anglin, S. (2016). "The Politics of Social Psychological Science: Distortions in The Social Psychology of Intergroup Relations," In P. Valdesolo & J. Graham (Eds.), *Claremont Symposium on Social Psychology and Politics.* Routledge.

Jussim, L., Honeycutt, N., Careem, A., Bork, N., Finkelstein, D., Yanovsky, S., & Finkelstein, J. (2023). "The New Book Burners: Academic Tribalism," In J. Forgas (ed.), *The Tribal Mind and the Psychology of Collectivism* (pp. 227-246). Routledge.

Jussim, L., Stevens, S. T., & Honeycutt, N. (2018). "Unasked Questions About Stereotype Accuracy," *Archives of Scientific Psychology, 6*(1), 214–229. http://dx.doi.org/10.1037/arc0000055.

Kaufmann, E. (2021). "Academic Freedom in Crisis: Punishment, Political Discrimination, and Self-Censorship," *Center for the Study of Partisanship and Ideology, 2,* 1-195.

Kunda, Z. (1990). "The Case For Motivated Reasoning," *Psychological Bulletin,* 108, 480–498.

Lazarsfeld, P. F., & Thielens, W. (1958). *The Academic Mind: Social Scientists in a Time of Crisis* (1st US-2nd Printing edition). Free Press.

Loeb, A. (2014). "Benefits of Diversity," *Nature Physics, 10,*616-617.

London, B. (2020). "Diversity, Equity, and Inclusiveness in Medicine and Cardiology," *Journal of the American Heart Association*, 9(17), e014592. https://doi.org/10.1161/JAHA.119.014592.

Marcus, A. (2020, April 30). "Journal Retracts Paper on Gender Dysphoria After 900 Critics Petition," *Retraction Watch*. https://retractionwatch.com/2020/04/30/journal-retracts-paper-on-gender-dysphoria-after-900-critics-petition/.

McCaffree, K. & Saide, A. (2021). "How Informed Are Americans About Race and Policing?" *Skeptic Research Center, CUPES-007*.

Moore-Berg, S. L., Ankori-Karlinsky, L.-O., Hameiri, B., & Bruneau, E. (2020). "Exaggerated Meta-Perceptions Predict Intergroup Hostility Between American Political Partisans," *Proceedings of the National Academy of Sciences*, *117*(26), 14864–14872. https://doi.org/10.1073/pnas.2001263117.

Nickerson, R. S. (1998). "Confirmation Bias: A Ubiquitous Phenomenon in Many Guises," *Review of General Psychology*, 2, 175–220.

Peters, U., Honeycutt, N., Block, A. D., & Jussim, L. (2020). "Ideological Diversity, Hostility, and Discrimination in Philosophy," *Philosophical Psychology*, 1–38. https://doi.org/10.1080/09515089.2020.1743257.

Pew Research Center (2014). "Political Polarization in the American Public," Retrieved from: https://www.pewresearch.org/politics/2014/06/12/political-polarization-in-the-american-public/.

Pielke Jr., R. (2016). "My Unhappy Life as a Climate Heretic," *Wall Street Journal*. Retrieved from: https://www.wsj.com/amp/articles/my-unhappy-life-as-a-climate-heretic-1480723518.

Prentice, D. A. (2012). "Liberal norms and their discontents," *Perspectives on Psychological Science*,7(5), 516–518. https://doi.org/10.1177/1745691612454142

Proulx, T., Costin, V., Magazin, E., Zarzeczna, N., & Haddock, G. (2022). "The Progressive Values Scale: Assessing the Ideological Schism on the Left," *Personality and Social Psychology Bulletin*, 01461672221097529.

Rausch, Z., Redden, C., & Geher, G. (2023). "The Value Gap: How Gender, Generation, Personality and Politics Shape the Values of American University Students," *Journal of Open Inquiry in the Behavioral Sciences*.

Rothman, S., Lichter, S. R., & Nevitte, N. (2005). "Politics and Professional Advancement Among College Faculty," *The Forum*, 3(1). https://doi.org/10.2202/1540-8884.1067.

Rutgers University (1951/2015). "Policy on Academic Freedom (Includes Statement on Professional Ethics)," Retrieved from: https://policies.rutgers.edu/B.aspx?BookId=12137&PageId=459505

Savolainen, J. (2024). "Unequal Treatment Under the Flaw: Race, Crime & Retractionsm," *Current Psychology*, *43*(17), 16002-16014.

Society for Neuroscience (2020). "Synthesis Statement on 'A New Theory of Gender Dysphoria Incorporating the Distress, Social Behavioral, and Body-Ownership Networks'," [Contributors included reviewing editor: Julie Bakker; Contributing editors: Rae Silver, Margaret McCarthy, and Christophe Bernnard; Reviewers: Ute Habel, Sven Muller, and Anntonio Guillamon Fernandez]. *ENeuro*, *7*(2). https://doi.org/10.1523/ENEURO.0149-20.2020.

Stanovich, K. E., West, R. F., & Toplak, M. E. (2013). "Myside Bias, Rational Thinking, and Intelligence," *Current Directions in Psychological Science*, 22, 259–264.

Stevens, S., Jussim, L., Anglin, S. M., Contrada, R., Welch, C. A., Labrecque, J. S., Motyl, M., Duarte, J. L., Terbeck, S., Sowden, W., Edlund, J., & Campbell, W. K. (2017). "Political Exclusion and Discrimination in Social Psychology: Lived Experiences and Solutions," In J. T. Crawford & Jussim, L. (Eds.), *The politics of social psychology* (pp. 220–254). New York, NY: Routledge.

Stevens, S., Jussim, L., & Honeycutt, N. (2020). "Scholarship Suppression: Theoretical Perspectives and Emerging Trends.," https://doi.org/10.20944/preprints202009.0197.v1.

Tappin, B. M., van der Leer, L., & McKay, R. T. (2017). "The Heart Trumps The Head: Desirability Bias in Political Belief Revision," *Journal of Experimental Psychology: General*, *146*(8), 1143–1149. https://doi.org/10.1037/xge0000298.

Tosi, J., & Warmke, B. (2016). "Moral Grandstanding," *Philosophy & Public Affairs*, *44*(3), 197–217. https://doi.org/10.1111/papa.12075.

Twenge, J. M., Honeycutt, N., Prislin, R., & Sherman, R. A. (2016). "More Polarized but More Independent: Political Party Identification and Ideological Self-Categorization Among U.S. Adults, College Students, and Late Adolescents, 1970-2015," *Personality and Social Psychology Bulletin, 42*, 1364–1383. https://doi.org/10.1177/0146167216660058.

Wax, A., & Alexander, L. (2017). "Paying the Price for Breakdown of the Country's Bourgeois Culture," Retrieved from *The Philadelphia Inquirer*. https://www.inquirer.com/philly/opinion/commentary/paying-the-price-for-breakdown-of-the-countrys-bourgeois-culture-20170809.html.

Westfall, J., Van Boven, L., Chambers, J. R., & Judd, C. M. (2015). "Perceiving Political Polarization in the United States Party Identity Strength and Attitude Extremity Exacerbate the Perceived Partisan Divide," *Perspectives on Psychological Science*, *10*(2), 145–158.

Wilson, A. E., Parker, V., & Feinberg, M. (2020). "Polarization in the Contemporary Political and Media Landscape," *Current Opinion in Behavioral Sciences*, *34*, 223–228. https://doi.org/10.1016/j.cobeha.2020.07.005.

Wood, P. (2016). *Should Conservatives Lead Secret Lives?* Retrieved from: https://www.nas.org/blogs/article/should_conservatives_lead_secret_lives.

Ybarra, O., Stephan, W. G., & Schaberg, L. (2000). "Misanthropic Memory for the Behavior of Group Members," *Personality and Social Psychology Bulletin*, *26*(12), 1515–1525. https://doi.org/10.1177/01461672002612006.

9

ANTISEMITIC ANTIZIONISM ON CAMPUS

CARY NELSON

In the spring of 2024, half a year after the Hamas massacres were carried out along Israel's border with Gaza, academic communities worldwide experienced the most pervasive politicization of higher education we have seen in our lifetimes. It included the erection of "Gaza Solidarity Encampments" across major countries not only in North America and Europe but also in the Middle and Far East. Noisy demonstrations were accompanied by overnight tent installations on hundreds of campuses. The movement spread with unprecedented rapidity. It began in the U.S. in mid-to late April, but by early May it had gone global, facilitated by calls for action and protest guidelines distributed on social media. Large anti-Israel demonstrations took place in major cities at the same time. They were followed by anti-Israel initiatives in many communities through 2024 and beyond.

In addition to more than 150 tented, overnight encampments on U.S. campuses, a total of 36 were established across England, Wales, and Scotland. The U.K. had them at Bristol, Cambridge, Leeds, Liverpool, Manchester, Newcastle, Oxford, Sheffield, SOAS (The School of Oriental and African Studies), University College London, and Warwick. In keeping with Ireland's recent history of antizionism there were also encampments at University College Dublin, Trinity College Dublin, and University College Cork. Ireland has since joined South Africa's genocide case against Israel at the International Court of Justice. Japan had seven campus encampments: Hiroshima, International Christian, Kyoto, Sophia, Tama Art, Tokyo, and Waseda. Australia had encampments at eleven institutions, with the most influential in Sydney and the longest at the Australian National University, running from April 29 to August 17. France had them at Sciences Po Paris (The Paris Institute of Political Studies), the Sorbonne, and the École normale supérieure. Spain had an encampment at the University of Valencia, and the movement then spread to Barcelona University, then Madrid, the Basque Country in the north, and Alicante in the east. Some countries had only one: Kuwait at Kuwait University, Jordan at the University of Jordan, Lebanon at Beirut Arab University, Mexico at the National Autonomous University, South Africa at the University of Cape Town, Turkey at Istanbul Teknik University, Yemen at Thamar University, Brazil at the University of Sao Paulo. Some campuses had building occupations in addition to the encampments, among them Newcastle University in Britain, Columbia University in the U.S., Sciences Po in Paris, Ghent University in Belgium, and Gronigen University in the Netherlands. Other campuses, like McGill University in Canada, saw building blockades instead. Even when only a single university in a country experienced one of these events it generated a great deal of national publicity for the movement.

Absent from the encampments and the demonstrators' menu of demands were all the longstanding scenarios for political resolutions of the Israeli-Palestinian conflict. Demands for the creation of a Palestinian state alongside the Jewish one were nowhere to be heard. The replacement scenario, a single state in which Jews and Palestinians would live together happily thereafter, was missing as well. Instead, the demonstrators opted for a fiercely eliminationist agenda. There could be no accommodation with a state waging a purportedly genocidal military campaign against Palestinian civilians in Gaza. Israel would have to be eliminated. As the chants declared in a series of local languages, Palestine must be freed of a Jewish presence from the river to the sea.

This was put forward as a nonnegotiable demand, a declaration, a moral imperative. No one asked for a debate or conversation about whether Israel was an apartheid state, whether the war in Gaza was in fact genocidal in intent, or whether Israel's seven million Jewish and two million Arab citizens had their own rights to political self-determination. The movement believes itself to be in possession of the truth about these matters, affirmative on the first two, implicitly negative on the third. The issues were resolved. It was time to act.

Demonization of Israel was categorical, unqualified. There was nothing good to be said about the country. It was an oppressor state dedicated to destroying an oppressed people, the Palestinians. Reliance on this simplistic dichotomy integrated demonization of Israel with other woke convictions. People who defined themselves as warriors in a series of social justice causes naturally added antizionism to the list. It seemed to demonstrators a clear portrait of good versus evil. The Palestinians are consequently pure victims, lacking any agency that could be marshalled for destructive ends. Given those assumptions it was easy to set aside the appalling reality of the Hamas assault. The accounts were exaggerated, falsified, expressions of Islamophobia. Even prestige feminists like Judith Butler could cast doubt on reports of mass rape, a stand that continues a long tradition of faculty sacrificing their most basic principles in the service of antizionism.

This international consensus among many on the international left meant that a longtime minority position calling for the elimination of Israel had become dominant. It drowned out alternative views on campus and in some local communities. The high degree of consensus provided the psychological satisfaction of group conviction, solidarity, and personal reinforcement for those active in the eliminationist cause. And it replaced university debate with something wholly different: mass endorsement of political certainty.

Unqualified hostility to Israel has a distinct impact on all Jewish campus community members, students, faculty, and staff. Pew statistics show that 80% of American Jews identify with Israel and consider that identification a central part of their identity. In England the percentage is nearly as high, about 75%, whereas in France it is about 70%. That means that Diaspora Jews experience relentless demonization of Israel as a personal assault, not simply as criticism of a distant country.

College students, who are at a critical period of adult identity consolidation, are particularly vulnerable to such assaults. It is often their first time away from home; they are separated from family and community sources of resilience; and they are in a period of experimentation and testing, making important decisions about their future. A deeply felt Jewish identity is both a source of strength and a point of vulnerability.[1]

Antizionists recognize that vulnerability instinctively. Thus, campus conflict over Israel has increasingly shifted away from debates about Israeli conduct to flat condemnations of Israel accompanied by accusations of moral failings on the part of campus Zionists. In tandem with such accusations, members of the antizionist group Jewish Voice for Peace are celebrated as the only true Jews, those who have seen the light and divested themselves of the morally corrupting commitment to the Jewish state.

The mass demonstrations of 2023-2024 presented a new organized challenge to Jews identified with Israel, a challenge that fused local with national and international effects. No longer just sporadic

---

1 See Cary Nelson, Lilli Friedland, and Leslie O'Connell, "The Impact of Antisemitism on Emerging Adults' Jewish Identity—Part I: Defining the Problem," *Journal of Contemporary Antisemitism*, 7:1 (Spring 2024), pp. 35-52.

expressions of an antizionist ideology, local antizionist events were part of a widespread organized international movement. The local events consequently channeled threats and convictions from elsewhere. If you were at a British campus, you wondered whether you would experience the violence that overwhelmed UCLA. Images, demands, and strategies were being copied from country to country; violence could well be imitated as well. And the resulting psychological pressures were being funneled through threatening mobs chanting "Death to Jews" and "From the river to the sea, Palestine will be free."

In a particularly unsettling fashion, Jewish community members' long nurtured and deeply felt Zionist identities were placed in conflict with recently adopted antizionist identities on the part of students at all levels. Commitments to the Jewish state had often formed gradually since childhood, whereas antizionist passions for young undergraduates were often very recent acquisitions. Protestors donned keffiyehs to symbolize their new identification. The result was an unequal battle in which only Jews were at risk of serious psychological harm. But the conflict nonetheless played out as a conflict of identities as much as one of opposing political positions.

The dominant theoretical model among encampment advocates—if it can be thus dignified—is a simple dichotomy opposing victims and victimizers. The binary permits a series of interchangeable terms to be substituted, but the message remains the same. While the lack of nuance or complication suits the simplicity of group chants and posters, it also facilitates a governing form of self-deception among encampment participants: vicarious victimhood. A shared sense of victimhood unites privileged wealthy undergraduates, at least temporarily, with less privileged undergraduates, including students of color, who imagine themselves to have experienced the same history of discrimination as Palestinians. Multiple real historical differences are overridden in the process, and serious political analysis becomes impossible.

But then traditional political analysis has had no place in the 2023-2025 campus political movement. It is an exclusively performative and symbolic form of political activism. As I argue at length in a March 2025 book, *Mindless: What Happened to the University?*, published by *The Jewish Quarterly*, the logic of the encampments functioned not only as a protest against Zionism but also as a rejection of the very idea of a university. Debate, discussion, and analysis were disparaged and discarded. Higher education as a whole was reconceived as indoctrination, the imposition of preexisting political beliefs on student audiences. As endorsement of jettisoning discussion and debate from universities, the implications extend well beyond views of the war in Gaza. It turns antizionism into a force that undermines the principles that have governed higher education for more than a century. It seems highly unlikely that the war in Gaza will be the last issue treated as an exception to those principles.

There is an argument to be made that antizionism is now at the forefront of an anti-intellectual woke agenda being promoted at universities in the U.S. and elsewhere. With the 2023-24 academic year, we saw antizionism's unreflective, programmed, mass character vastly reinforced. It became an article of faith for campus activists. Those who joined the movement were expected to have the conviction of religious converts. It thus melded with other woke agendas that treat different opinions as heresy. But antizionism is taking the lead in persuading people they do not have to analyze political beliefs before adopting them. And once adopted, woke convictions should not be undermined by doubts.

DEI bureaucracies and their influential ideology, which have all the worst characteristic of woke politics, have substantially reinforced that trend. The oppressor/oppressed binary is deeply ingrained in their belief system, and it biases them toward antizionism and against seeing Jews as a minority suffering discrimination. DEI staff frequently see the world in terms of race and insist on applying a racialized perspective to much social interaction. Although I agree that racism is a structural feature of American culture, I do not believe it dominates all social relationships. Propagandizing students to see the world primarily in terms of race has a destructive impact on campus relations and can do long-term damage to students. It actually encourages, rather than discourages, increasing racial segregation.

Instead of resisting these trends, faculty either facilitated or hid from it. Faculty members have always had a central role in defining and reinforcing the traditional educational principles guiding colleges and universities, both through the multidisciplinary American Association of University Professors and through their individual writings and pedagogies. In the current assault on the idea of a university faculty are also playing a key role. Immediately after 10/7, a number of faculty defied expectations by going well beyond justifying the assault as a response to long-term Israeli policies and actually expressed their joy at Hamas's orgy of murder and rape.

Columbia's Joseph Massad made the most headlines because he managed to produce a detailed celebratory essay and get it published in the antizionist online publication *The Electronic Intifada* the very next day, October 8. Perhaps he was following the Hamas Telegram channel and received some of the live streamed videos of the massacre filmed by the terrorists themselves. The views expressed in Massad's 2023 piece clearly did not coalesce recently. In his 2006 "Pinochet in Palestine" he embraces Hamas as the true voice of the Palestinian people and describes it as the one group equipped to "defend the rights of the Palestinians to resist the Israeli occupation."[2] But now he can celebrate Hamas's actual accomplishments on 10/7: "The stunning victory of the Palestinian resistance over the Israeli military on the first day of fighting is a historic event both for Israel, as Netanyahu admitted, and for the Palestinians"; "No less striking was the capture of some of Israel's colonial soldiers and

---

2 Joseph Massad, "Pinochet in Palestine," *The Electronic Intifada,* (November 11, 2006), https://electronicintifada.net/content/pinochet-palestine/6525.

officers in their underwear."[3] He continued in this style, adding to his celebratory rhetoric under the heading "Jubilation and Awe." He soon became a lightning rod for outrage at faculty members endorsing a murder spree. Two members of Columbia's board of trustees declared under oath in the U.S. Congress that they would not award him tenure were he up for consideration now.[4] Nonetheless, he was permitted to teach a course on Zionism in 2025.

Like Massad and many other 10/7 Hamas enthusiasts, Lara Sheehi, then an assistant professor of psychology at George Washington University, had a history. On May 22, 2021, she tweeted: "If you see this and STILL entertain for even a split second that Hamas is a terrorist entity, there is literally zero hope for you, your soul, or your general existence as an ethical human being in this world." Then, in an October 27, 2023, video interview hosted by Jared Ware, Sheehi reacted to Hamas's October 7 pogrom by declaring that "We have to rid ourselves of the romantic notions of what uprisings look like."[5] By 2021 she had already excluded critics of Hamas from the human community. But in 2023 she went much further, endorsing murder, rape, and kidnapping, disparaging the foolish romanticism of those who were a little squeamish about Hamas's actions on Israel's Black Sabbath. At that point, unbeknownst to members of the American Psychological Association, she was actually on leave in Qatar. So most remained supportive of her and her role as 2023-2024 president of APA's Division 39. But in January 2024, when

---

3   Joseph Massad, "Just another battle or the Palestinian war of liberation?", *The Electronic Intifada,* (October 8, 2023), https://electronicintifada.net/content/just-another-battle-or-palestinian-war-liberation/38661.

4   For a transcript of the testimony, see "Columbia in Crisis: Columbia University's Response to Antisemitism," https://www.congress.gov/118/meeting/house/116973/documents/HHRG-118-ED00-Transcript-20240417.pdf.

5   Lara Sheehi, "Against Alienation — Lara Sheehi and Stephen Sheehi on their book Psychoanalysis Under Occupation: Practicing Resistance in Palestine," *Millennials Are Killing Capitalism* (October 27, 2023), https://youtu.be/1imBbXP9EBA?si=aliQyEOWF-TYSgUK.

she announced she had left GWU for a position at Qatar's Doha University, now overtly sharing exile with Hamas leaders, APA was unmoved. Late that year she relocated to South Africa, where she identifies herself as a research fellow at the University of South Africa's Institute for Social and Health Sciences.

Another rapid celebrant was Professor Gilbert Achcar of SOAS, London's School of Oriental and African Studies. In an October 8 essay on his blog, he declared that the "amazing and highly daring" "counter-offensive" carried out by Hamas was "a much more spectacular feat" than the October 1973 war. Using an analogy designed to rattle Jewish readers, he said it "evokes the boldness of the biblical David in his fight against the giant Goliath," that Hamas "fighters" "executed an amazing and highly daring offensive." He proceeded to add new posts until gathering them into a short book, *Israel's War on Gaza,* which reprints all of his blog posts on the Gaza War.[6]

Cornell's Professor Russel Rickford waited a full week before declaring himself exhilarated by the Hamas attack.[7] Canada's Tamari Kitossa of Brock University withheld his intervention until December, when he extolled "the miraculous Hamas attack on Be'eri kibbutz on October7, 2023," where 132 Israelis were slaughtered and 32 taken hostage.[8]

These and other faculty pogrom endorsements circulated on social media and created what amounted to a collective effusion about the events of 10/7. It served as a permission structure for

---

6   Gilbert Achcar, *Israel's War on Gaza.* (London: Resistance Books, 2023).

7   See Ryan Quinn, "Cornell Leaders Condemn Prof. 'Exhilarated' by Hamas Attack," *Inside Higher Education* (October 18, 2023), https://www.insidehighered.com/news/quick-takes/2023/10/18/cornell-leaders-condemn-prof-exhilarated-hamas-attack.

8   Tamari Kitossa, "Zionism and the 'Destruction of Palestinians': Apartheid or Nazism? – Conclusion" (December 14, 2023), https://professorscorner.ca/zionism-and-the-destruction-of-palestinians-apartheid-or-nazism-updated/.

others on campus to follow their lead in public or private conversations. While it was especially encouraging to have a faculty member on your own campus behave that way, it wasn't necessary. Like everything else about the encampment spring, every contribution, every action, occurred everywhere else as well.

Celebrating murder, rape, and kidnapping could hardly count as political advocacy. Although some, including Judith Butler, try to rationalize extreme political violence, to incorporate it within rational argument, others prefer simply to embrace it. Butler is jaded enough and sufficiently hostile to Israel to describe Hamas butchering children, burning families alive, and decapitating corpses as "tactics." She recommends a discussion about whether or not these are the right tactics, good ones, although she sheepishly declares she doesn't *like* them, like a child saying she doesn't like lollipops or spinach.[9] Despite reeking of self-satisfaction in her argument, what Butler actually displays is not the triumph of reason but complete moral abnegation. She has willfully emptied herself of any morality informed by empathy. She is, as she always has been, something of an outlier among high profile antizionists. Rather than joyously discard enlightenment rationality, as Massad and others did, she burlesques it. She leaves us with the grotesque task of working through each of Hamas's crimes to decide whether they merit acceptance as an anti-colonial strategy.

Taken together, the 10/7 responses from Massad, Butler, Achcar, and others set the stage for what we get in spring 2024—the mass disparaging of enlightenment reason. Student/faculty mobs chanting in praise of their death cult. Treating campus Zionists as complicit in Israel's purported genocide. Forcefully blocking Jewish access to libraries, central squares, or other campus facilities in

---

9 See https://x.com/MaxAbrahms/status/1766292754961695218 and https://x.com/MaxAbrahms/status/1766292754961695218 for Butler's Paris performance.

a discriminatory disavowal of educational rights. Contemptuously rejecting debate and dialogue as routes to increasing understanding and resolving disputes. Disguising their identities with masks. Demanding that Jewish cultural or religious institutions be barred from campus. Shunning and exiling those with whom they disagree. Demanding that Zionists be excluded from campus. Working to instill psychological stress and fear of physical harm in their opponents.

But above all it is the categorical opposition to a Jewish state, indeed the manifest hatred it draws, that marks a major change in campus and community politics by disallowing the personal identities of Jewish students, staff, and faculty. Each of the elements listed in the previous paragraph feeds into and enhances the antisemitic character of post 10/7 antizionism, but the non-negotiable demand for Israel's elimination is the core watershed feature. Moreover, it is not a temporary condition. It is the new normal for campus antizionism, defining the baseline condition for the reception of the majority of Jewish community members and the group politics they confront.

These are the features of our newest antisemitism. While many prefer to pretend otherwise, this newest antisemitism makes one of the main debates of recent decades obsolete. That debate took the form of several interchangeable questions: What is the line dividing antisemitism from antizionism? Has a given behavior crossed the line from antizionism to antisemitism? As Brendan O'Neill observes in *After the Pogrom,* in the shadow of the campus encampments and the mass demonstrations against Israel from New York to London, "the thinness of the line between so-called anti-Zionism and anti-Semitism had never been more apparent."[10] But what O'Neill describes as "the hysteria and the boiling animus" of anti-Israel hate quite erases that dividing line. Those passions do "not belong to the realm of political criticism or political protest, but rather to that

---

10 Brendan O'Neill, *After the Pogrom: 7 October, Israel and the Crisis of Civilisation.* (London: Spiked Ltd., 2024), p. 120.

ancient universe of fear and loathing for one people and one people only," namely antisemitism.[11] We have spent years discussing their relationship, with antizionists typically insisting that antizionism and antisemitism are separate in theory and practice. The result, argues Tal Fortgang in *Mosaic*, is "endless, pedantic, circular discussions about where exactly to draw the line between anti-Semitism and anti-Zionism."[12] Hamas's conduct on 10/7 itself made unbridled hate the basis of its murderous hostility to the Jewish state. When students and faculty celebrate the Hamas assault, they embrace the same passions.

A strict distinction between antizionism and antisemitism requires thinking of antizionism as a narrowly political position. But the longing for Zion has been embedded in Judaism itself and in Jewish culture for centuries. As Alyza Lewin points out, the "yearning for Zion—the emotional tie with Israel—is a deep, spiritual, integral part of Jewish identity."[13] As Zionism is fundamental to Jewish peoplehood, antizionism cannot be limited to political effects. Prior to the creation of a Jewish state, a purely theoretical antizionism could be confined to disagreements about whether a Jewish state was politically advisable.

But with the founding of Israel in 1948, the spiritual longing for Zion attached itself to a political entity. Antisemitism focused on Israel immediately became a major feature of Arab culture and gradually spread to the West over decades. But in the West the deeper implications of antizionism could be suppressed or deflected by focusing on criticism of Israeli government policies. It was a radical-

---

11   Ibid., p. 151.

12   Tal Fortgang, "How the Incoming Administration Can Restore Jewish Civil Rights," *Mosaic,* (December 2, 2024), https://mosaicmagazine.com/essay/politics-current-affairs/2024/12/how-the-incoming-administration-can-restore-jewish-civil-rights/.

13   Alyza D. Lewin, "Recognizing Anti-Zionism as an Attack on Jewish Identity," *Catholic University Law Review,* 68:4 (Fall) 2019), https://scholarship.law.edu/lawreview/vol68/iss4/8/.

ly new form of antizionism, with antisemitic implications, especially in the light of Israel's post-Holocaust founding, but not decisive or inescapable ones. Israel could be reformed. But then in the wake of 10/7, antizionism became relentlessly eliminationist. Israeli policy reform no longer sufficed. Jewish identity therefore was invested in a state that demonstrators were demanding be erased from the earth.

By 2024, several events had the combined result of turning Israel into the pariah of nations on the international left:

1. In 2021, reports from Amnesty International and Human Rights Watch underwrite the accusation that Israel is an apartheid state. The reports meet with elaborate analyses disputing their arguments, but that has no effect on those operating with confirmation bias.

2. In 2021, over 100 academic departments for the first time issue formal commitments to the BDS agenda.

3. In July 2023, the American Anthropology Association becomes the academy's first major disciplinary group to endorse a boycott of Israeli universities. Small faculty associations had begun doing so in 2013.

4. In 2023, in response to the new war in Gaza, the number of academic departments denouncing Israel substantially increases, with several new academic disciplines represented.

5. Worldwide anti-Israel demonstrations in 2023-2024 lend collective force to antizionism.

6. The false accusations that Israel is committing genocide and enforcing a starvation regime in Gaza gain momentum in 2023-2024. Amnesty International predictably supports the accusation. South Africa presents a comparable case before the International Criminal Court (ICC) in December 2023. In November 2024

      the ICC issues arrest warrants for Israeli prime minister Netanyahu and defense minister Gallant.

7. The April-May 2024 Gaza Solidarity Encampments on university campuses worldwide make antizionism the public face of a mass movement in higher education. A minority of students are able to take over campuses. These mass demonstrations produce an unprecedented level of anti-Jewish intimidation.

8. In August 2024, the American Association of University Professors reverses its 20-year policy opposing academic boycotts in an effort to encourage boycotts of Israeli universities. The following year the AAUP abandoned all pretense of political neutrality and declared that the US should no longer supply Israel with either offensive or defensive weapons.

Even though these claims are fanciful and wholly unsupported by evidence, this entire sequence of events has made it possible for some antizionists to insist Israel is the lynchpin of the social justice movement worldwide. The encampments repeatedly declared that people of color in their own country and worldwide would never be free until Israel was defeated. That kind of hollow generalization is hugely destructive to the real liberation struggles that must be focused on local conditions, be informed by local and national history, and be fought against real opponents. The claim is also tailor made for the suspicion that it is Jews worldwide, not just Israelis, who are keeping people in bondage. The resulting conspiracy theory then draws on centuries of antisemitic conspiricism for its evidence, its paranoia, its passion, its imagery, and its fatal delusions.

The combined effect of the developments above has also made it much easier to suggest that personal Zionism represents something more fundamentally wrong and less readily correctible than an error in political judgment. For the antizionist cohort, personal devotion to Israel presents as a serious character flaw or a defining psychological disorder. In one of their several joint interviews, Lara Sheehi's husband and collaborator Stephen discounts thousands of years of Jewish history in Israel, declaring in their interview with *Rendering Unconscious* that the Jewish Israelis have "a psychotic relationship to the land." He underlines the claim with a hostile psychoanalytic formula for which he offers no evidence and no explanation: "The connection to Palestine is one built on psychosis."[14] It is a vicious slander that his partner endorses. Unsurprisingly, *The Diagnostic and Statistical Manual of Mental Illnesses*, the American Psychiatric Association's professional reference book on mental health issues, does not list Zionism as a form of mental illness. It is unethical and professionally disqualifying for a clinician to claim it is one. Nonetheless, those who insist otherwise believe it is reasonable to exclude Zionists from progressive organizations on the grounds that they are dangerously ill. They are fundamentally unfit. Jews can heal themselves by disavowing Zionism, but they cannot simply live in peace thereafter. They must testify to their antizionism repeatedly, again and again whenever required.

The eight events enumerated above intersected with the variety of anti-Israel and antisemitic tactics deployed over 2023-2025. Their cumulative impact partly overwhelmed the direct effects of local actions. While I raised this point earlier, it is now possible to press the resulting conclusions still further. The Anti-defamation League's compilation of 2023-24 antisemitic incidents on U.S. campuses includes 57 incidents of fliers drawing attention to Israeli hostages abducted to Gaza being torn down or defaced. But there were numerous other hostage poster desecrations worldwide. As Brendan O'Neilll reports, "Supporters of Israel put up 'KIDNAPPED' posters in cities across Europe and the US. And almost everywhere

---

14 "Lara & Stephen Sheehi on Palestine: Psychoanalysis Under Occupation," *Rendering Unconscious*, Episode 185 (February 6, 2022), https://www.youtube.com/watch?v=3A7k6UXw1i8.

they were attacked, ripped, graffitied, stomped, binned. Everywhere you looked in London you'd see remnants of the posters, scarred with the jagged claw marks of those who had tried to destroy them. These flapping shreds of paper, with just the eye or mouth of the kidnapped Jew still visible, were a testament to the anti-civilizational delirium that blew up in the West after Hamas' pogrom."[15] Once a particular tactic becomes a vehicle for a worldwide flood of resentment and hate, the consequences are everywhere, whether or not posters were defaced in a given locale. The college president who proudly announces that posters were not damaged on his or her campus offers a remark that has only limited bearing on the local threat environment. Ditto with divestment resolutions, 80 of which were debated and voted on in the US, with seventy-one passed and only nine defeated. Over 360 U.S. campuses across 46 states suffered anti-Israel incidents. ADL's count of the total number of U.S. rallies, demonstrations, and encampments in 23/24 was 1,418,326.[16]

The warranted conclusion is clear: higher education in much of the world became a hostile, antisemitic environment in the wake of the Hamas murders. We are not on our way to colleges and universities once again becoming a welcoming environment for Jews. A radically antizionist woke consensus now defines the international left, and higher education is its leading edge. A newer antisemitism mired in hate has become a reliable feature of postsecondary education.

Throughout the English-speaking world, which is the environment I know best, the response of higher education administrators was similar: avoid action that would anger either antizionist or Zionist campus constituencies. In other words, college presidents in particular made the most self-protective choice: do nothing. Some

---

15 O'Neill, op. cit., p. 19.

16 "Anti-Israel Activism on U.S. Campuses, 2023-2024," *Anti-Defamation League*, (September 16, 2024), https://www.adl.org/resources/report/anti-israel-activism-us-campuses-2023-2024.

risked making pronouncements but avoided action. Many chose silence and passivity. They were quite right that no action would please both factions on a polarized campus. Finding the courage to act decisively against antisemitism could come with a price: the antizionist cohort would call for your resignation, and the press would dutifully report that as evidence of major discontent. Complaints from the Jewish community could be met with grand, empty promises. Opportunistic cynicism was the best survival strategy.

Some administrators, however, acted to further empower antisemitism. The "U.S. House of Representatives Staff Report on Antisemitism" describes several examples, one of which details administrative actions at Northwestern University:

> Northwestern reached a shameful agreement appeasing its encampment after President Michael Schill chose radical anti-Israel faculty members Jessica Winegar and Nour Kteily to negotiate on the school's behalf with the antisemitic encampment. The negotiators abused their positions to support encampment organizers, with Kteily writing that he aimed to "get some amazing wins" for them. Northwestern's Provost Kathleen Hagerty endorsed this approach, affirming Kteily after he advised students on how to pressure trustees on advancing divestment. Hagerty also supported Kteily's recommendation that Northwestern boycott Sabra hummus due to it being perceived as an Israeli product. The final agreement contains an apparent mechanism for implementing such a boycott through a provision for students to provide input on dining services and vendors.[17]

The report faults a number of campus administrators for their failure to be honest about their negotiations with anti-Israel demonstrators.

---

17 "U.S. House of Representatives Staff Report on Antisemitism," (December 18, 2024), pp. 8-9, https://www.speaker.gov/wp-content/uploads/2024/12/House-Antisemitism-Report.pdf.

It is very difficult to be confident that anything short of severe financial penalties will bring real reform to universities. Both public institutions and those receiving government funds in many countries are vulnerable to such consequences. While I am immensely wary of government oversight, I no longer see much choice. Faced with documented public complaints, my own campus, the University of Illinois Champaign Urbana issued a "Joint Statement on Anti-Semitism" in 2020 promising corrective action. The administration mixed committed and resistant appointees to an advisory committee, which helped produce stasis. Then it did nothing for four years. A new 2024 agreement issued in response to a pending report from the Office of Civil Rights promises more substantive action. None occurred through the end of 2025, despite extensive written advice from a bi-campus group I co-chair, Faculty for Academic Freedom and Against Antisemitism.[18] We shall see.

It is not as if corrective action is unimaginable. Many campuses have adopted policies prohibiting overnight encampments, demonstrations blocking access to campus facilities, disruptive chanting after dark, and other activities. One hopes enforcement will follow. After reviewing impressive faculty task force reports from Columbia, UCLA, Stanford, and the University of Washington, I would urge US campuses to adopt a firm policy prohibiting the use of classrooms for political indoctrination as a particularly important step. Enforcement should concentrate on graduate student employees who teach many of the courses that undergraduates take at large universities. The problem courses are concentrated in the very humanities and social sciences departments that are most committed to antizionism. TAs combine the less restrained passion of undergraduates with the classroom authority of faculty, but they do not have the academic freedoms that faculty possess, nor the job security that tenure provides. Graduate employees should be given a clear

---

18 All our recommendations are under "Chapter News" on our website, Fafaa.net.

warning. Repeat offenders should get a hearing and then be fired.

Whether universities have the internal resolve to carry out even that achievable reform is far from clear. As several reports have documented, antizionist faculty successfully lobbied to eliminate or reduce penalties for students who violated regulations and committed crimes on a number of campuses. They urged on demonstrators who destroyed property, blocked access to campus facilities, and terrorized the community. Then those same faculty, among them some who celebrated Hamas's inhumanity, demanded forgiveness for the students who had nothing but hatred in their hearts for their Jewish peers. On many major US campuses, antizionists have won seats on the faculty senate and on union executive committees. They now have an organization, Faculty for Justice in Palestine, to press them to maintain their radicalism. And some faculty under the sway of DEI ideology will join the resistance to curtailing antisemitism. Can university administrators find the courage to act against antisemitism when those faculty will call for their heads for doing so? The answer is: not on their own.

While it might seem desirable to build a working long-term coalition between NGOs fighting antisemitism, sympathetic government committees, and the emerging faculty groups dedicated to reform, that is unlikely. The Jewish NGOs, all competing for the same donor dollars, have never even been willing to embrace transparent collaboration among themselves. But temporary collaboration on specific projects is possible.

We do, moreover, know what these different groups can contribute. Faculty members, using their research and argumentative skills, can document antisemitic patterns on a campus thoroughly and in several cases have done so. NGOs have financial resources, administrative skills, and substantial community and government contacts which they have sometimes been willing to use in the past. Government committees have subpoena powers to uncover truths hidden from the faculty and can draft significant legislation, both of which powers they have begun to exercise dramatically. All this will be necessary to effect change even if it cannot be fully coordinated.

The groups aligned with antizionism, however, have a singleness of focus and purpose that Zionism cannot match. Part of that is due to the fact that antizionists display no need to adopt realistic or achievable goals. Despite claims to represent Palestinian interests, their movement actually does not do so. That is now supremely evident in its support for Hamas, which sees great political advantage in mass Palestinian deaths. The 2023-24 academic year saw antizionists once again insisting that the Israeli-Palestinian conflict is not complex, that the important issues at stake are straightforward, even simple. Israel is bad, Palestinians are good. Furthermore, if you are not aiming to configure a path toward a consensual solution to the conflict, but rather just dedicated to extinguishing one of the two contending parties, the solution does seem simple: get rid of Israel and condemn all its supporters worldwide.

The absurd character of this formulation is glaringly evident in its chanted motto: Palestine will be free from the river to the sea. Ever since Hamas promoted the declaration, it has meant embracing a *Judenrein* dystopia. But no one is free living under the yoke of an Islamist dictatorship. No one is free when Hamas is in power. Hamas has never offered Gaza a viable future guaranteeing freedom of speech, freedom of religion, freedom of sexual orientation, freedom of political choice, or freedom of association. The encampment students like to insist that no one is free until everyone is free. But Gazans will not be free until they are free of Hamas. The blissful woke consensus about the conflict pretends none of this is true.

Israelis, moreover, cannot be free living beside a paramilitary force poised to kill Jewish men, women, and children at will. A force, indeed, dedicated to doing so as long as there are still Jewish targets alive. Deciding how to neutralize that hostile force, however, is very complicated, given that it is embedded among nearly two million noncombatants. There are no laudable solutions. You cannot very well compromise with a murderer determined to keep on killing. Yet as we have seen as Israel's ground operations in Gaza have unfolded since October 27, 2023, there are no clean, wholly commendable military options.

I remain persuaded that the practical details required for a viable 2-state solution are achievable. Finding the political will on both sides is a challenge of quite a different magnitude. The practicalities have long included the expectation that a Palestinian state would be demilitarized, retaining a police force but not a standing army or offensive weapons. That requirement is if anything more essential since 10/7. I have met Palestinians who insist that a state must have the right to an army. I always reply that means there will never be a Palestinian state. I compiled a list of requirements in my book *Israel Denial*, but I would add some additional security guarantees now, such as that Israel must have the ability to monitor Gaza's border with Egypt and the authority to interdict smuggling.[19] By the time this essay is published I would hope Hamas has been completely eliminated as a military and political force because neither peace nor a productive Gazan economy are possible otherwise. Eliminating Hamas as an idea will take perhaps two generations living in peace under a "separate but cooperate" motto. I list some key areas of cooperation in previous publications as well. Energy and agriculture are two.

In the woke version of a resolution, students worldwide wave their magic wands and Israelis board boats and planes to vacate their country and head anywhere where they are wanted, which means nowhere on earth. Those with dual citizenship have an option, but not the others. Does anyone think Britain, Canada, France, Germany, and the U.S. will each accept a million Jews? There is no "return" for the half of Israelis descended from those who fled Arab re-

---

19 Cary Nelson, *Israel Denial: Anti-Zionism, Anti-Semitism, & the Faculty Campaign Against the Jewish State*. (Bloomington: Academic Engagement Network & Indiana University Press, 219), pp.46-66.

gimes. There is no "return" for those who survived the death camps in Poland or those who finally were able to leave the Soviet Union.

As she suggested in her 2012 *Parting Ways: Jewishness and the Critique of Zionism*, Judith Butler will reassure them their beautiful spiritual fate must be to wander the earth ever thereafter. No, she will not be joining them. I wish that I could merely feel contempt for the pied piper theorist of tomorrow's wandering Jew. But there are flesh and blood families involved. If Joseph Massad is antizionism's patron saint of hatred among the faculty, Judith Butler is its premier useful idiot, balancing Massad's malice with an otherworldly fantasy of redemption.

Even if these faculty members, among antizionism's premier academic advocates, discount evidence, disparage morality, and pursue illusions, their claims are conceptually vulnerable to thorough analysis and the application of reason. The campus movements of 2023-2025 may have rejected enlightenment values, but the enlightenment values that justify academic freedom, the collective search for the truth most of all, give us principles to employ in contesting dominance by the campus left. The key is to organize and build alliances among those opposed to antisemitism. The woke edifice upholding the authority of antisemitic antizionism is fundamentally irrational. In that, at least, it is vulnerable for those willing to listen.

But the practical task of making that vulnerability decisive in campus politics remains daunting. There are, however, at least two struggles we must win. The first is to establish rules that, when violated by any constituency, meet with fair punishments for those responsible. Protestors who break into and occupy buildings, and damage property should be expelled from campus and prosecuted. For the most part that did not happen in 2024. Time, place, and manner restrictions should be applied to all and enforced. Students, faculty, and staff who persistently disseminate hate speech on social media should be disciplined, with penalties increasing for repeat violations. Departments should be strictly prohibited from issuing statements on controversial political matters. The second priority is to institute mandatory antisemitism training for all students and all staff with student-facing responsibilities. Established Jewish organizations should be involved in designing or approving that training. Demands for it were not widespread before the 2023-24 academic year, but they are now. They should include adoption of the full IHRA Definition. Its eleven examples should not be used as a disciplinary code but rather as an educational tool. It provides for structured discussion about whether statements are antisemitic.

That leaves unaddressed what is overall the most intractable source of campus antisemitism—entire academic departments ruled by radical antizionism, namely antizionism devoted to the eradication of the Jewish state. Those departments often receive ideological support from academic disciplines officially committed to radical antizionism. They disseminate hate, indoctrinate students, and poison the campus environment. They cannot be reformed. Nonetheless, I cannot support the demand that they be closed down and their faculty terminated. They can be placed into receivership, meaning that a head or director and a majority of the executive committee be appointed from outside the department. The woke antizionist faculty cohort would then no longer control personnel decisions or recruitment. All these steps are necessary if sanity is to be restored to the campuses of the West.

About the Contributors

Bret Alderman received his PhD in Depth Psychology in 2013 from the Pacifica Graduate Institute in Carpinteria, California. His publications include the books *Symptom, Symbol, and the Other of Language: A Jungian Interpretation of the Linguistic Turn* (2016) and *Eternal Youth and the Myth of Deconstruction: An Archetypal Reading of Jacques Derrida and Judith Butler* (2024). His recent interests include ideological possession, deconstruction, gender, and the interface between psychology and philosophy, as well as the encroachment of political ideologies into therapeutic settings.

Jonathan Church is an economist with two decades of experience working in the private and public sectors. His professional background is in energy, antitrust, intellectual property, valuation, forecasting, inflation, index number theory, statistics, and finance. In 2016, he began writing a weekly column for *The Good Men Project*, with a focus on current affairs, social justice, and masculinity. He currently serves as a contributing editor for *Merion West* and hosts the "Escaping Ideology" podcast series. He has been published in *Quillette*, *Areo Magazine*, *Arc Digital*, *The Agonist Journal*, *Merion West*, *The Good Men Project*, *Culturico*, *New Discourses*, *The Washington Examiner*, *The Daily Stoic*, *Voegelin View*, and *The Federalist*. He has also published poetry in *Lummox*, *Big Hammer*, and *Street Value*, as well as short stories in Vending Machine Press and *The Agonist Journal*. He has authored two books, *Reinventing Racism: Why 'White Fragility' Is the Wrong Way to Think about Racial Inequality*, and *Virtue in an Age of Identity Politics: A Stoic Approach to Social Justice*. He graduated from the University of Pennsylvania with a B.A. in economics and philosophy, and from Cornell University with an M.A in economics. He is also a CFA charter holder.

Gary Clark
PhD is currently a Visiting Research Fellow in the School of Biomedicine at the University of Adelaide in Australia. Since 2012, he has been a member of the School's Biological Anthropology and Comparative Anatomy Unit. His research focus includes the evolution of music, palaeoanthropology, and evolutionary approaches to analytical psychology. He is the author of numerous academic articles and the book, *Carl Jung and the Evolutionary Sciences*.

Nathan Honeycutt
PhD is a visiting scientist at Rutgers University, and a research fellow at the Foundation for Individual Rights and Expression (FIRE). His research has primarily investigated political diversity and discrimination among university faculty and students. He has published articles on political bias, political polarization, scientific integrity, and censorship in higher education. He is also a founder of, and active participant in, the Society for Open Inquiry in Behavioral Science, and is adjunct professor of psychology at the University of Arkansas.

Lee Jussim is Distinguished Professor of Psychology at Rutgers University, where he has chaired the Psychology Department, the Anthropology Department, and the Program in Criminal Justice. He has published over 140 articles and chapters and seven books. His scholarship addresses stereotypes, prejudice, expectancy effects and accuracy; how dysfunctional academic norms in everything from peer review to methods to political biases threaten the validity of much work produced by the social sciences; and, more recently, radicalization in academia and the wider society. His book, *Social Perception and Social Reality*, contested the psychological canon that social perception was mostly biased, and received the American Publishers Award for best book in Psychology in 2012. He is a founding member of the Academic Freedom Alliance and the Society for Open Inquiry in the Behavioral Sciences, which aspires to be an antidote to the denunciatory, censorious turn in academia. He also writes essays on social science and academia at *Unsafe Science*, on Substack.

Jon Mills PsyD, PhD, ABPP, is a Canadian philosopher, psychoanalyst, and clinical psychologist. He is Honorary Professor, Department of Psychosocial & Psychoanalytic Studies, University of Essex, UK, on faculty in the Postgraduate Programs in Psychoanalysis & Psychotherapy, Gordon F. Derner School of Psychology, Adelphi University, USA, and on faculty and a Supervising Analyst at the New School for Existential Psychoanalysis, USA. Recipient of numerous awards for his scholarship including 5 Gradiva Awards, he is the author and/or editor of over 35 books in psychoanalysis, philosophy, psychology, and cultural studies including most recently *End of the World: Civilization and Its Fate*. In 2015 he was given the Otto Weininger Memorial Award for Lifetime Achievement by the Canadian Psychological Association.

Cary Nelson

is Jubilee Professor of Liberal Arts & Sciences and Professor of English Emeritus at the University of Illinois Champaign-Urbana, and an affiliated professor at the University of Haifa. He is currently chair of the national Alliance for Academic Freedom and co-chair of the multicampus Illinois group Faculty for Academic Freedom and Against Antisemitism. He is a former president and was national resident of the American Association of University Professors from 2006-2012. His 37 authored and edited books include *Israel Denial: Anti-Zionism, Anti-Semitism, & the Faculty Campaign Against the Jewish State* (2019), *Hate Speech and Academic Freedom: The Antisemitic Assault on Basic Principles* (2024), which received a Bernard Lewis Prize, and most recently, *Mindless: What Happened to Universities?* (2025). He was awarded an honorary doctorate from Ben Gurion University of the Negev.

David Pilgrim

PhD is Honorary Professor of Health and Social Policy at the University of Liverpool and Visiting Professor of Clinical Psychology at the University of Southampton. He trained and worked in the NHS as a clinical psychologist before completing a PhD in psychology and then a Masters in sociology. With his mixed background, his career was split between clinical work, teaching, and mental health policy research. He remains active in the Division of Clinical Psychology and the History and Philosophy Section of the British Psychological Society, and was Chair of the latter between 2015 and 2018. His publications include *Understanding Mental Health: A Critical Realist Exploration* (Routledge, 2015) and *Key Concepts in Mental Health, 5th Edition* (Sage, 2019). Others include *A Sociology of Mental Health and Illness* (Open University Press, 2005)—winner of the 2006 BMA Medical Book of the Year Award, *Mental Health Policy in Britain* (Palgrave, 2002), *Mental Health and Inequality* (Palgrave,

2003) and *Living with Health Inequalities* (Routledge, 2023) (all with Anne Rogers). His recent books are *Child Sexual Abuse: Moral Panic or State of Denial?* (Routledge, 2018), *Critical Realism for Psychologists* (Routledge, 2020) and *Identity Politics: Where Did It All Go Wrong?* (Phoenix Books, 2023).

Michael Shermer, PhD is the publisher of *Skeptic*

magazine, host of The Michael Shermer Show podcast, and the author of *Why People Believe Weird Things, The Science of Good and Evil, Why Darwin Matters, The Believing Brain, The Moral Arc, Conspiracy: Why the Rational Believe the Irrational,* and *Truth: What it is, How to Find it, Why it Matters* (forthcoming). For 18 years he was a monthly columnist for *Scientific American,* and for 12 years he taught "Skepticism 101: How to Think Like a Scientist" at Chapman University.

Jaco van Zyl is a South Africa-trained clinical psychologist and psychoanalytic

psychotherapist in Ireland. He has a special interest in trauma-spectrum disorders, personality and mood disorders, and somatoform disorders. Informed by the historical and contemporary political challenges of his home country, Jaco uses a psychoanalytic lens to explore the psychology of groups, the function of ideology, and of adopted narratives and rituals within political and ideological movements. He is a co-director of Critical Therapy Antidote, a co-host of the CTA podcast, and has written articles for *Merion West, Critical Therapy Antidote, Genspect,* and the *Journal for Psychodynamic Psychotherapy.*

www.ingramcontent.com/pod-product-compliance
Lightning Source LLC
Chambersburg PA
CBHW071209240726
48654CB00009B/706